T0301772

COMPARATIVE
COMPETITION
LAW

COMPARATIVE
COMPETITION
LAW

Thomas Weck
Monopolies Commission, Germany
University of Bonn, Germany

Masako Wakui
Kyoto University, Japan

World Scientific

NEW JERSEY · LONDON · SINGAPORE · BEIJING · SHANGHAI · HONG KONG · TAIPEI · CHENNAI · TOKYO

Published by

World Scientific Publishing Co. Pte. Ltd.

5 Toh Tuck Link, Singapore 596224

USA office: 27 Warren Street, Suite 401-402, Hackensack, NJ 07601

UK office: 57 Shelton Street, Covent Garden, London WC2H 9HE

Library of Congress Cataloging-in-Publication Data
Names: Weck, Thomas, 1978–   author. | Wakui, Masako, 1969–   author.
Title: Comparative competition law / Thomas Weck, Monopolies Commission, Germany,
    University of Bonn, Germany, Masako Wakui, Kyoto University, Japan.
Description: New Jersey : World scientific, 2024. | Includes bibliographical references and index.
Identifiers: LCCN 2023032351 | ISBN 9789811279256 (hardcover) |
    ISBN 9789811279263 (ebook) | ISBN 9789811279270 (ebook other)
Subjects: LCSH: Antitrust law--European Union countries. | Antitrust law--United States. |
    Antitrust law--Japan. | Restraint of trade--European Union countries. |
    Restraint of trade--United States. | Restraint of trade--Japan. | Comparative law.
Classification: LCC K3850 .W43 2024 | DDC 343.07/21--dc23/eng/20230929
LC record available at https://lccn.loc.gov/2023032351

British Library Cataloguing-in-Publication Data
A catalogue record for this book is available from the British Library.

For any available supplementary material, please visit
https://www.worldscientific.com/worldscibooks/10.1142/13496#t=suppl

Desk Editors: Nimal Koliyat/Sandhya Venkatesh

Typeset by Stallion Press
Email: enquiries@stallionpress.com

Printed in Singapore

Preface

The rules to protect competition in relevant markets converge in the globalized economy. Nevertheless, differences remain. For practitioners, it is necessary to take these differences into account when doing business across borders or when advising clients on cross-border business. Regulators and scholars, on the other hand, may be interested in examining how other countries deal with problems similar to their own. However, the literature comparing the competition rules of different jurisdictions is scarce. This is even more true if one considers that relevant developments in competition law nowadays take place in Europe and the U.S. as well as in Asia. With this book, we aim to take a step toward filling this gap. We provide a systematic comparative overview of the rules in the EU, the U.S. and Japan, covering both substance and procedure. Interesting developments in other jurisdictions are examined in text boxes. We hope that readers will find this book useful.

The idea of this book was born at the symposium organized at National University of Singapore (NUS), and a lecture on comparative competition law by Thomas Weck. Masako Wakui has been lecturing on / Japanese competition law, which was originally based on U.S. law but went through substantial amendments reflecting Japan's own needs. The authors would like to thank Professor Thomas Fetzer, University of Mannheim, Germany, and Associate Professor Burton Ong (NUS) for providing the initial fora for the reflection and discussion that triggered the idea of this book project.

We would further like to thank Professor Kawahama (Kyoto University) for providing his support to this book project, as well as Shin-Ru Cheng, Assistant Professor of Kyoto University and Adjunct Professor of the National Yang Ming Chiao Tung University, Taiwan, and doctoral candidate Sangyun Lee (Korea University) for taking the time and effort to review the manuscript and to all of them for their extremely valuable comments.

Thomas Weck
Masako Wakui

About the Authors

Thomas Weck is Associate Professor of Public Law, Regulatory Law and Comparative Law at Frankfurt School of Finance and Management. He previously was Lead Analyst at the Monopolies Commission in Bonn (2012–2022), after having worked at a British and an American law firm in Brussels (from 2007 to the end of 2012). His work focuses on competition and financial market regulation. He is a Member of the Academic Society for Competition Law.

Masako Wakui is a Professor at the Graduate School of Law, Kyoto University and a Visiting Scholar at Newcastle University, UK. She has previously taught at Osaka City University and Rikkyo University and served as a Chief Researcher for the Japan Fair Trade Commission (JFTC) Competition Policy Research Centre, as a Commissioner at the Osaka Prefecture Labour Relations Commission and as a Member of the Interconnection Policy Committee, the Information and Communications Council, the Ministry of Internal Affairs and Communication and various other advisory and study groups at the JFTC and other administrative bodies. Currently, Dr. Wakui is a Board Member of the Japan Association of Economic Law and the Co-Head of the Asian Chapter of the Academic Society for Competition Law.

Contents

Chapter 1

Introduction

This book provides an overview of the rules on competition and compares the law in the European Union (EU), the United States of America (U.S.) and Japan. It is meant for practitioners working in a cross-jurisdictional context, as well as for scholars and students interested specifically in the parallels and differences of the jurisdictions covered. To keep things simple, it focuses on the **rules and the leading cases**. However, new approaches are currently being developed for competition in the digital sphere. In that regard, this book lays particular stress on the recent developments regarding digital markets.

In this introductory chapter, readers first find some basic information on the objectives of competition/antitrust law and on the legal systems covered in this book **(Sections I–II)**. The following section gives an overview of the historical development of the antitrust rules, which is closely linked with problems of market power identified in the course of history **(Section II)**. A third section explains that the enforcement regimes in the U.S., the EU and Japan certainly feature different characteristics today but that also notable similarities exist when it comes to court review **(Section III)**.

I. The objectives of competition law

The protection of competition has become a cornerstone of today's market economies. However, whereas all competition lawyers may agree on that finding, the question of what makes competition an objective of legal protection gives rise to controversies as well as misunderstandings across jurisdictions internationally.

Agreement at least exists that the objective of competition rules is not to protect individual market participants. Rather, **competition is protected as a process**. Moreover, the objective is only to protect **functioning (efficient) markets** against interference by individual market participants. It is not to provide protection against any disadvantages for market participants that may arise in malfunctioning markets, e.g., disadvantages due to limited production capacities or missing information.

However, beyond that, the legal systems diverge. In the **U.S.**, for instance, economic thinking plays a major role in the understanding of the legal objectives of antitrust law. It is hotly debated currently whether the "consumer welfare standard" continues to be the benchmark under which interference with the market is to be considered anticompetitive only if it raises the prices of goods above competitive levels or diminishes their quality.[1] A counter position is taken by the proponents of the "New Brandeis" movement, who argue that any trend toward monopolization may harm consumers due to the diminished competition.[2]

In the **EU**, the European Court of Justice (ECJ) limits itself to interpreting the EU Treaties and does not take a side in economic controversies. On the basis of the Treaties, the Court has held that the EU establishes an internal (or "common") market, which is one of the fundamental objectives now set out in Article 3(3) Treaty on European Union (TEU) and a legal proxy for uniform market conditions across EU Member States.[3] According to the ECJ, the EU competition rules protect the internal market against distortions of competition and against the erection of barriers between Member States.[4] However, up to now, the Court has refused to define competition. It has only defined when competition is "undistorted", and that is if all market participants enjoy "equal chances"

---

[1] *Reiter v. Sonotone Corp.*, 442 U.S. 330, 343 (1979); *Rebel Oil Co. v. Atlantic Richfield Co.*, 51 F.3d 1421, 1433 (9th Cir. 1995).

[2] Wu, The Curse of Bigness: Antitrust in the New Gilded Age, 2018; Khan, The New Brandeis Movement: America's Antimonopoly Debate, 9 Jeclap 131 (2018); critically: D. Daniel Sokol, Antitrust's "Curse of Bigness" Problem, 118 Mich. L. Rev. 1259 (2020).

[3] See ECJ, Judgment of 13 July 1966, *Italy/Council of the EEC and Commission of the EEC* (32/65, ECR 1966, p. 389), ECLI:EU:C:1966:42, at pp. 404–406.

[4] Protocol 27 to the Treaties expressly confirms that the internal market *includes a system ensuring that competition is not distorted*.

(i.e., suppliers and consumers alike).[5] However, similar to the courts in the U.S., the ECJ also recognizes that suppliers' interferences with the competition may only be permitted if they are outweighed by consumer benefits on balance.[6]

In **Japanese** law, the answer to what competition law is all about is nuanced. AMA Article 1(1) provides that *[t]he purpose of this Act is to promote fair and free competition.* AMA Article 2(4) spells this out further by reference to activities of supplying or receiving supplies. However, in the application of the law, the relevance of competition objectives may differ depending on which statutory provision is being used. For instance, Article 3 prohibits private unreasonable restraints of trade, which is understood to cover hard-core cartels but which does not require a finding of such effects. Then again, unfair trade practices within the meaning of Article 19 may fall into three different categories which require a lessening of free competition, the use of unfair methods in competition or the abuse of a superior bargaining position in which the anti-competitive effect is not necessarily clear.

In any event, the fact that all legal systems mentioned above recognize competition as an objective of legal protection does not bar policy makers from also pursuing **other legal objectives**. In this case, policy makers may find it necessary to find compromises. An objective that is particularly likely to conflict with the protection of competition is **industrial policy**, that is, the protection of suppliers who are in the political interest. In this context, it should be noted that the industrial policy competence in Article 173(3) of the Treaty on the Functioning of the European Union (TFEU) expressly does "not provide a basis for the introduction by the Union of any measure which could lead to a distortion of competition". This is because industrial policy bears the risk of contributing to a fragmentation of the EU internal market.

Finally, the protection of competition can only be limited to the relevant jurisdiction, e.g., the U.S., the EU or Japan. In contrast, the relations of each jurisdiction to other jurisdictions are governed by the law of nations, i.e., **international law**. In international law, distortions of

---

[5] Cf. ECJ, Judgment of 13 December 1991, *RTT/GB-Inno-BM* (18/88, ECR 1991 p. I-5941) ECLI:EU:C:1991:474, §25: Undistorted competition can "be guaranteed only if equality of opportunity is secured as between the various economic operators".

[6] See Article 101(3) TFEU, which is interpreted as containing a general principle to that effect.

competition are not relevant. What is relevant instead is the **principle of reciprocity**. That implies that also industrial policy measures distorting competition may be legitimate if they are adopted to counter similar measures by another state in international business relations.

II. Civil law and common law

The concepts underlying the competition rules apply not only in various market situations but also in different legal contexts. The differences relate to the substance of the law (e.g., what are the legal requirements to form an agreement or a contract?), the legal procedure (e.g., how can harmful agreements be neutralized?) and also the methodology for interpreting the legal rules. Since the **methodology** is key to understanding how the rules work in practice, one should recall the following important differences between the legal systems covered in this book:

- The **U.S.** follows a "**common law**" **tradition**. This means that the primary source of law is the case law. Although the legislature can also prescribe rules, fundamentally, it is the courts that make "law" through their decisions where no legislative statute exists. While the statutes bind the courts, the courts interpret them, which then also become part of the law.
- The **EU** is a non-homogeneous jurisdiction that is autonomous of the EU Member States but built upon their legal traditions. The majority of the EU Member States are **civil law** jurisdictions and based on Roman traditions. This means that it is principally the legislature which prescribes new rules of law in legal codes. The codes may take account of overarching principles that usually are not directly enforceable. However, the law is typically only found in written legislation or in regulations and guidelines based on that legislation. That said, a peculiarity of the EU system is that the ECJ has the power to interpret EU law in a binding fashion.[7]
- **Japan** is likewise a "civil law" country where the legislature prescribes new laws in the form of statutes. Although court judgments (particularly the ones from the Supreme Court and other upper courts) often inform subsequent case law, they are not formally binding.

---

[7] See Section IV.2 in this chapter.

This approach actually came from continental EU Member States, notably Germany and France.

To be sure, both "civil law" and "common law" systems have **gradually aligned** with one another in recent decades. This is true particularly regarding the rules on competition. When it comes to prohibiting (potentially) anticompetitive behavior, the current U.S. competition law is built upon several statutes such as the Sherman Act. Meanwhile, both the EU and Japan use general statutory provisions in their supreme competition laws, which are complemented by detailed subordinate rules. In all jurisdictions, the principal courts and agencies add to the interpretation through case law, decision practice and guidelines. As a general matter, statutory rules — be it the Sherman Act, Articles 101 & 102 TFEU or the Antimonopoly Act — can be interpreted in terms of their wording; the systematic structure of individual provisions, entire statutes and the legal system as such; the intentions of Legislature and the history of individual provisions; and the objective targets pursued with the provisions.

Because the competition law statutes tend to use very general and abstract wording, there is ample **scope for interpretation**. The dynamic nature of the economic activities also implies that the gap is inevitable. In common law jurisdictions, a statute is usually applied in strict compliance with the limits of the wording of that statute. In case of perceived legal gaps, common law lawyers prefer an inversion of the legal argument over an analogy. In civil law jurisdictions, in contrast, courts use the treatment of statutory gaps to instill flexibility into the legal system. Thus, when courts identify a gap, they need to analyze the legislature's intentions behind it. One option is that the legislature deliberately refrained from framing the rules differently: What is not in the law is not intended to be in the law. This, just like in common law, calls for the inversion of the legal argument. However, another option is that regulatory loopholes are unplanned. In this case, civil courts apply the relevant rule by analogy.

III. Some remarks on the history of competition/ antitrust law

The 19th century was marked by the rapid **industrialization** of the United States and Europe, followed by other parts of the world including Japan. The industrialization process quickly revealed the importance of economies of scale and scope. Whereas manual production requires a substantial investment of resources in each item produced, the main cost of factory production is the "fixed cost" of building the factory. In contrast, the cost of producing additional goods ("marginal cost") by a factory is much lower than the cost of manual production. Consequently, industrial production enjoys a **competitive advantage** over manual production. However, **industrialization** revealed that this advantage comes **along with negative side effects** — not on the factory owner but on society. One of the social effects of industrial production was that production became increasingly carried out by big companies in which certain stakeholders (i.e., the owners/investors and management) exercised full control over the production process and gained the largest shares of the profits. Those who had been running independent businesses in the past lost their independence and were increasingly integrated into the company production process. Thus, they turned into workers who only possessed their labor. This comes along with less equality of wealth: the factory owner usually becomes rich while the workers remain poor.[8]

The development of industrialization was not homogeneous everywhere and also gave rise to different policy reactions. However, in the end, the views adopted in the U.S. prevailed everywhere. This led to the modern rules for the protection of competition, which place great weight on efficient market operations and the interests of consumers. The following sections provide an overview of the developments in the U.S., in Europe and in Japan.

1. United States

During the industrialization of its economy, the U.S. experienced a **rapid development of production and supply**. This development was free from constraints existing in Europe and other parts of the world where monopolies had been created through sovereign grants of trade privileges. Over time, technological advancements such as steamship and railway networks connected the regions, and the whole country formed a large single market and industrialized its economy. Hence, industrialization offered many opportunities to start and build up a business. However, the success of industrialists raised concerns over time that large enterprises

---

[8]See Pashley, Pauperism and Poor Laws, 1852, republished: Cambridge 2011, on the development of "pauperism" in Britain in the 19th century.

would be able to amass economic power, allowing them to raise prices without the need to take competitors into consideration. In the absence of competitive pressures, they would also not be forced to pass on efficiency gains to consumers (e.g., by lowering their prices). This **market power** was understood as undermining economic welfare by reducing output. Such power was also considered problematic due to the possibility of harming consumers, farmers and small businesses.

The concerns about market power did not come from nowhere. **Markets in the U.S. were increasingly dominated** by only a few companies in the second half of the 19th century. The 1860s witnessed the rise of Western Union, which obtained a market share in telegraph communications of roughly 90%. Around 1880, Standard Oil obtained a market share in the petroleum-refining capacity of likewise about 90%. In 1890, American Tobacco Co. obtained a similar market share in cigarettes.

The increased concentration in the U.S. spurred public policy efforts for a pushback. This led to new rules which (more or less) took account of the economic principles contributing to market power or the harm associated with its exercise by dominant companies. Sectorial regulation came first. Regarding electricity, gas, water, telecommunications, railways and postal services (network industries), federal **public utility regulations** were introduced, which would allow for public intervention in terms of price/quality setting. The Supreme Court confirmed that this type of regulation was legally admissible, despite various challenges between 1875 and 1945.[9] In fact, the network industries have remained subject to varying levels of regulation in many jurisdictions to this day. This is due to economic features which they have in common: Those industries enjoy a **natural monopoly** due to the following factors:

- The full scope of services can be provided by one company alone.
- Building up the network comes along with substantial irreversible costs, which means that the supply of networks (upstream) and potentially also the provision of network services (downstream) are not contestable by others.
- The network operator is consequently able to build up market power and the market does not operate efficiently (market failure) as the network operator can restrict access to the network and charge excessive fees for using it.

---

[9]See *Munn v. Illinois*, 94 U.S. 113 (1876); *Smyth v. Ames*, 169 US 466 (1898); *FPC v. Hope Nat. Gas Co.*, 320 U.S. 591 (1944).

In contrast, company behavior resulting in market power and even monopolies was more difficult to capture as a general matter. In the first attempt, U.S. state corporation laws were introduced to prohibit companies from growing beyond "state size". However, in order to circumvent these laws, so-called **trusts** emerged that operated across state borders. Certainly, some limited protection was also available also under the common law of trade restraints originally developed in Britain. However, under these rules, only the parties to a contract were entitled to sue. This limited entitlement barred outside parties (e.g., consumers) from suing for harm incurred, e.g., in a cartel or exclusive contract. Common law of trade restraints was also limited as it did not capture pure unilateral behavior, e.g., predatory pricing.

Therefore, the U.S. Congress ultimately passed so-called **anti-trust laws** to address the economic and legal issues mentioned before. The most fundamental provisions were included in the **Sherman Act** (1890), which prohibits collusion and unilateral behavior to exclude other firms from the market.[10] In its early days, the Sherman Act may appear to have been sufficient. In 1911, the U.S. Department of Justice succeeded in court and managed to break up Standard Oil and American Tobacco. However, the action to also break up U.S. Steel failed.[11] An important reason was that the company had never succeeded in effectively integrating the acquired enterprises, was inefficient and lost market shares. The Supreme Court consequently held that it was not a true monopolist that merited divestment.[12] Furthermore, the Supreme Court's interpretation in *Standard Oil* that only unreasonable restraints of trade are prohibited by the Sherman Act prompted the legislator to introduce the **Clayton Act** (1914) and the **FTC Act** (1914) to rebuild the competition law regime. Under the FTC Act, an administrative agency whose independence is guaranteed by statute was established and was given the power to regulate unfair methods of competition.

However, in the 1930s, economists began to stress the importance and advantages of **product differentiation**, which reflects consumer preferences (and willingness to pay) within the market. The new discussion raised awareness of an issue that (potentially) had not been addressed

---

[10] 15 U.S.C. §§1 ff.

[11] *Standard Oil Co. of New Jersey v. United States*, 221 U.S. 1 (1911); *United States v. American Tobacco Company*, 221 U.S. 106 (1911).

[12] *United States v. United States Steel Corp.*, 251 U.S. 417 (1920).

sufficiently in the existing antitrust legislation. This was discrimination in pricing favoring big retailers over smaller ones and the exclusion of wholesalers from the supply chain. To close the (perceived) gap, Congress amended the Clayton Act (1934) and passed the Robinson-Patman Act (1936). The latter Act was to protect small businesses and intermediaries from large chain stores by prohibiting suppliers (producers and wholesalers) to engage in certain types of discriminatory pricing toward resellers.[13] It has remained in place to this day, although it has proved difficult to enforce in a way that is consistent with broader antitrust policies.[14]

The 1930s also witnessed a growing understanding of markets. Chamberlain's theory on monopolistic competition gave the economists new insights into how competition dynamics could work taking into account product differentiation. A more dynamic view then gained ground with the reception of *Schumpeter's* works, an Austrian who argued that competition exists not only around products but also around technologies.[15] **Technological competition** means that new technologies obliterate older ones. In any event, both the interest of suppliers in differentiated products and technological innovation means that freedom of market entry must be protected.

Good to know: The definition of relevant markets

The concept of defining "relevant markets" in antitrust law is a consequence of the interest in products and markets. Relevant markets are delineated based on the substitutability (or homogeneousness) of products (product market), the geographic area (geographic market) and, occasionally, the time frame of their supply, which is relevant, e.g., for cultural or

(Continued)

---

[13]Pub. L. No. 74–692, 49 Stat. 1526 (codified at 15 U.S.C. §13).
[14]The Supreme Court has held that the Robinson-Patman Act should be construed consistent with such policies; see *Brooke Grp. Ltd. v. Brown & Williamson Tobacco Corp.*, 509 U.S. 209, 220 (1993). Regarding a possible revival in the context of enforcing antitrust law in digital markets, see Kim, Amazon-Induced Price Discrimination Under the Robinson–Patman Act, 121 Columbia L. Rev. 160 (2021).
[15]Schumpeter, *The Theory of Economic Development.* Harvard University Press, Cambridge 1911; *Theorie der wirtschaftlichen Entwicklung*, 2nd Ed., 1926.

> *(Continued)*
>
> sports events, or trade fairs.[16] Having a market definition has been considered a legal requirement for a long time in order to establish a "dominant" (EU) or "monopoly" (U.S.) position. However, establishing such a position requires an analysis of the economic facts, and economists increasingly question the relevance of (defined) relevant markets when it comes, e.g., to proving a foreclosure/exclusionary strategy. The courts have shown a certain willingness to accept claims of dominance or monopolization also in cases where markets are two-sided or multi-sided, i.e., where a platform supplier provides services in parallel to different user groups. However, whether it is possible to completely dispense with the market definition requirement is unclear to date.

After World War II, the so-called **Chicago School** of economists gradually gained followers with the idea that government intervention does not tend to be more efficient than the market and that free markets best allocate resources in an economy.[17] In the sphere of competition law and policy, the Chicago School emphasized the rational interactions between businesses and consumers. Most practices which had been seen as anticompetitive before, or on the notion that small businesses need protection, were now explained as efficient practices. The Chicago School successfully insisted on the need to analyze the market participants' interactions rather than to decide cases merely on structural factors, such as market share and entry barriers. By refusing to show hostility against bigness, it also fostered flexibility in the assessment of antitrust cases: The legal tradition was that courts would use rigid *per se* rules in their assessment of market behavior restraining trade. The Chicago School's reasoning led to the substitution of *per se* rules by a "rule-of-reason" standard, particularly for restraints affecting the relationship between suppliers and resellers (vertical restraints).[18]

---

[16]See, e.g., European Commission Notice on the definition of the relevant market for the purposes of Community competition law, O.J. C 372, 9 December 1997, pp. 5–13.

[17]With that approach, the Chicago School distinguished itself from the earlier Harvard School; see Piraino, Reconciling the Harvard and Chicago Schools: A New Antitrust Approach for the 21st Century, 82 Indiana L.J. 345 (2007) for details.

[18]See, e.g., *Leegin Creative Leather Products, Inc. v. PSKS, Inc.*, 551 U.S. 877 (2007), and Chapter 3, Section V.3(c)(2).

The most influential development based on the Chicago School was certainly the **consumer welfare standard**. Under this standard, intervention is only warranted for transactions that harm allocative efficiency and at the same time raise the prices of goods above competitive levels or diminish their quality.

However, many assumptions adopted by the Chicago School were **not well founded**. For instance, strictly favoring the lowest price would mean that large companies are allowed to use their size (or economies of scale) in competition and to drive competitors out of the market. However, whereas large companies may focus their research and development on improving the quality of existing products, small competitors may have incentives to focus on new products allowing them to improve their market position more substantially.

As noted before, the Chicago School has come under attack in recent years. Based on a perceived lack of enforcement *vis-à-vis* large digital platform operators, the so-called **Neo-Brandeisians** (labeled as such after an ephemeral earlier school of thought) argue that the focus of U.S. antitrust law on consumer welfare is too narrow and that antitrust policy should focus on broader competition interests, including also protection of other stakeholder interests (e.g., investors and workers). At the time of writing, this new perspective has led to revived FTC enforcement policies and proposals of new legislation in the U.S.[19]

2. Europe

In Europe, competition law developed out of a **legal transplant**. When the European Treaties were ratified in the middle of the 20th century, only Germany, out of the seven original EU Member States, had a competition regime in place, whereas no competition regulation existed in Italy, Belgium and Luxembourg and only limited rules in the Netherlands and France. However, also the German competition rules had not developed in a legal system that valued competition or the protection of consumers. Instead, the rules had been imposed on a country that had traditionally cultivated state interests and vendor-friendly industrial policies. This state-oriented legacy continues to weigh on the EU today, as there are still strong interests in pushing back on competition protection whenever Europe's economic well-being is under threat.

---

[19]See notably Khan, Amazon's Antitrust Paradox, 126 Yale L.J. 564 (2017).

The differences in the development between Europe and the U.S. had existed from the very beginning: For example, the evolution of industrialization had had a different **starting point** in Europe. The European economy had been more fragmented (no single market) and marked by a long history of power struggles between the sovereigns and the people, and also the European sovereigns (and people), among each other.

In Germany, the Prussian reform movement (inspired by *Adam Smith*) abolished the monopolies of manufacturer gilds (*Zünfte/Gilden*) and introduced the principle of **economic freedom (*Gewerbefreiheit*)** in 1810. This allowed entrepreneurs to develop their businesses and to engage in free market activity. The state furthered its success actively with industrial policy measures which also included heavy economic espionage in rival nations, particularly the United Kingdom. The market activities of entrepreneurs were fueled further by the capital inflow following the wars of 1864, 1866 and 1870/1871. However, around 1873, speculation led to a financial crisis (*Gründerkrach*) and depression (*Gründerkrise*). Considering the advantages of market power, company owners quickly resorted to cartelization in order to save their businesses. Cartels remained accepted throughout the era of imperialism in Germany. Admittedly, after World War I, the abuse of economic power became controversial temporarily.[20] However, the economic structure of the country did not fundamentally change in the coming years. In the years after 1933, the national-socialist state even orchestrated cartelization and actively furthered monopoly capitalism.

After their victory in World War II, the allied forces considered the amalgamation of state and economic power in Germany to be one of the root causes of Nazism. In the protocol of the Potsdam Conference, they concluded that the German economy must be **decentralized** as the market power of German enterprises was one of the elements posing a threat to democracy and peace.[21] Thus, in the late 1940s, the Western allies forced the decartelization as well as deconcentration of I.G. Farben and other large German corporate groups. That being said, German economists continued to see a role for the state in the economy, also in Germany as a democratic country. The **ordoliberal** school argued that the state should protect competition and control private economic power as a fundamental requirement for social justice (beyond consumer welfare) and

---

[20] See Regulation against the abuse of economic power (2-Nov-1923, [1923] RGB I, 1067).
[21] Protocol of the Potsdam conference, 17 August 1945.

democracy. The German Competition Act (*Gesetz gegen Wettbewerbsbe-schränkungen*) of 1957 was influenced by ordoliberal thinking to a substantial extent.

In parallel, post-war European countries began to embrace the idea of market integration as a tool to ensure the non-recurrence of war in Europe, while facilitating economic growth. The large U.S. internal market and U.S. antitrust law influenced this discussion in Europe, as did German ordoliberalism. The Spaak Report (1956), which set out political ideas for a European Economic Community, described the prevailing European view on competition and the role of regulation at the time:

> The establishment of normal conditions of competition and the harmonious development of the whole of the economies concerned make it possible to envisage arriving by successive stages at the suppression of <u>all protective measures which currently form an obstacle to trade and which are responsible for the fragmentation of the European economy. These normal conditions of competition demand rules and procedures with a view to counteracting the effect of State interventions **or monopoly situations**</u>, and they call for common action to eliminate the balance of payments difficulties which threaten to stand in the way of expansion...
> (Emphasis added.)

The founding Treaties of the European Communities (1951/1957) in fact all included certain rules related to competition. The **Treaty on the European Coal and Steel Community** (ECSC, 1951–2002) prohibited price, unfair competitive practices and discriminatory practices. Additionally, it empowered a High Authority competent to fix maximum or minimum prices within the ECSC or in relation to export markets. ECSC members were required to inform the High Authority of actions liable to endanger competition. Further provisions dealt with distortive agreements, concentrations and abuse of dominant positions, customs duties and dumping. The **Treaty on the European Economic Community** (EEC, 1957; later, EU) provided for the creation of an internal market as a system with undistorted competition (today, Article 3(3) TEU, <u>Prot. 27</u>). It included Articles to protect the fundamental freedoms of market participants against the erection of barriers between Member States (today, Article 34 ff. TFEU).[22] In addition, it included competition rules

---

[22]This protection was complemented by fundamental rights in the Lisbon Treaty of 2009.

resembling §1 and §2 of the U.S. Sherman Act, which prohibited anti-competitive collusion (today, Article 101 TFEU) and unilateral abuse of dominance (today, Article 102 TFEU). Other rules dealt with state-owned enterprises (SOEs) and services of general economic interest (today, Article 106 TFEU). As another particularity of EU law, the Treaty prohibited measures of economic aid granted by the Member States, in order to prevent "subsidy races" between those states (today, Article 107 ff. TFEU). Further rules dealt with industrial policy, trade and development aid (today, Article 173, 205 ff. TFEU). The **Treaty on the European Atomic Energy Community** (EAEC, 1957), which entered into force in parallel to the EEC Treaty, includes limited provisions on competition as well.[23]

3. Japan

The **Japanese economy** was marked by small enterprises and a very limited number of large corporate groups called *zaibatsu* **until World War II**. These industrial and financial vertically integrated business conglomerates formed the backbone of the heavy industry and financial power of the Japanese war economy. Following the lost war, Japan came under U.S. occupation and had to accept measures to restructure the economy.

These measures included the **Antimonopoly Act** (AMA), which was passed in 1947. Based on the AMA, the *zaibatsu* were broken up and less powerful groups of banks, manufacturers, suppliers and distributors were formed (*keiretsu*). The AMA also submitted the economy to new rules on private monopolization, unreasonable restraints of trade (cartels), unfair trade practices (boycott, RPM, etc.) and merger control.

Starting in the 1950s and up to the early 1970s, Japan experienced a **resurgence of industrial policy**, which was enforced by the Ministry of International Trade and Industry (MITI), the predecessor of today's Ministry of Economy, Trade and Industry (METI). Industrial policy increasingly dominated competition policy (enforced by the Japan Fair Trade Commission (JFTC)), which led to the legalization of cartels and of government support of large-scale mergers. However, over time, the cost of industrial policy became apparent: In the 1960s, consumer prices started showing an upward trend, and after 1972, Japan was hit severely

---

[23] Article 3(2), 60 ff. Euratom Treaty.

by the oil crisis, which gave rise to exceptional and unabsorbable price shocks. At the same time, the JFTC uncovered a number of hidden cartels. In reaction, the AMA was amended to empower the authority to impose administrative penalties for competition infringements (1977).

The AMA remained largely unchanged until 2005 when it was further amended to strengthen and modernize administrative enforcement. Other amendments followed, most recently an amendment in 2019 to strengthen the cartel leniency system.

Good to know: Korea

In Korea, the market shows some structural similarities as compared to the pre-war Japanese market: It is marked, on the one hand, by a small number of powerful and vertically connected groups of large companies (*chaebol*), which bear some resemblance to the former Japanese *zaibatsu*. On the other hand, a great number of Small and Medium Enterprises (SMEs) exist, which form the backbone of the Korean internal market. The national economy was almost shattered after the Korean War (1950–1953) but started to develop more rapidly in the 1970s and 1980s.[24]

The development of Korean competition law (essentially) started with the Monopoly Regulation and Fair Trade Act, which came into effect in 1981. However, this act has not been the only statute dealing with issues of market regulation. Other relevant statutes include the Fair Transactions in Subcontracting Act, Act on Fair Transactions in Large Retail Business, Fair Transactions in Franchise Business Act and Fair Agency Transactions Act. The awareness of the importance of protecting fair trade received a boost after the Korean Financial Crisis of 1997, following which the Korea Fair Trade Commission (KFTC) began to enforce the Korean competition rules increasingly vigorously. The Financial Crisis of 2008 then contributed to an exacerbated "bipolarization" between chaebol and SMEs, the reduction of which has become an important competition policy objective for the KFTC besides market efficiency. In 2022, the Korean legislature also passed a new act concerning the digital economy (see Chapter 5, Section IV.1).

---

[24]Seth, South Korea's Economic Development, 1948–1996.

IV. The legal systems of today compared: Different enforcement regimes but notable similarities in court review

After having provided some background on the economic and historical background of antitrust and competition regulations in the U.S., the EU and Japan, this section sets out some important characteristics of the current regimes for the enforcement of the relevant rules and for court review.

1. U.S.

In the U.S., two federal agencies are mainly entrusted with the enforcement of the federal antitrust rules. One is the **Antitrust Division of the Department of Justice** (DOJ), which enforces the Sherman Act in civil and criminal actions before the U.S. District Court in Washington, D.C., and may also recover damages suffered by the United States in this context. In addition, the DOJ can bring actions under the Clayton Act in order to obtain civil injunctions and, again, to recover damages suffered by the United States. The second federal agency is the **Federal Trade Commission** (FTC), which is responsible for the administrative enforcement of the FTC Act. The FTC also has competences under the Clayton Act regarding mergers and additional competences under the U.S. labeling, consumer credit and warranties statutes, among others. The FTC and DOJ have published Joint Guidelines, e.g., on collaboration among competitors and mergers.[25] In addition, several sector regulators exist at U.S. federal level, which have competences in competition-related matters. This includes the federal banking regulators, the Federal Communications Commission, International Trade Commission and the Federal Energy Regulatory Commission.

At the U.S. **state level**, additional antitrust laws exist. These statutes are enforced by the state attorneys general. In addition, private parties can

---

[25] FTC/DOJ, Antitrust Guidelines for Collaborations Among Competitors, April 2000; Vertical Merger Guidelines, 30 June 2020; Horizontal Merger Guidelines, 19 August 2010; Antitrust Guidelines for the Licensing of Intellectual Property, 12 January 2017; Antitrust Guidelines for the Licensing of Intellectual Property, 13 January 2017. Regarding mergers, the FTC published new draft guidelines in summer 2023.

bring claims under both the federal and the state antitrust rules. In private litigation, the states can likewise be private parties for purposes of enforcing the federal rules.

The structure of the U.S. enforcement system could, in principle, lead to widely divergent enforcement policies, but this is actually not the case. Just the contrary: The system is **largely homogeneous**, and the divergence is limited. That is mainly for two reasons:

(1) One is that U.S. federal laws trump state laws due to the U.S. Supreme Court's wide application of the **interstate commerce clause** in the U.S. Constitution.[26] States can only provide for broader antitrust protection if U.S. federal law allows such. This is the case, e.g., when it comes to actions for indirect cartel damages (the so-called "*Illinois Brick* repealer" statutes).[27]

(2) Another reason is the **system of court precedents** in U.S. law. As a feature of common law, court decisions by higher courts are binding on lower courts and may overrule lower court decisions and older case law. In the federal court system, precedent can develop rather quickly as court review is centralized and streamlined, starting at the U.S. District Court, then going to the D.C. Court of Appeals (D.C. Cir.) and ultimately to the Supreme Court (U.S.). The states certainly have their own court review systems, but state courts take into account decisions rendered in other jurisdictions, including at the federal level, as so-called persuasive authority.

2. EU

In the EU, the **main enforcer** of the EU competition rules is the **European Commission**. The European Commission is not only an administrative agency, but it is also responsible for submitting legal proposals to the Council and the European Parliament (as the EU's legislative institutions). This responsibility provides substantial power to the European Commission. By way of example, one may refer to Articles 1–3 of Regulation 1/2003, which interpret the rules on exceptions from the EU cartel prohibitions (as not requiring a formal exception letter), allocate the burden of proof regarding anticompetitive behavior and regulate the

---

[26] Article I §8 Cl. 3 of the U.S. Constitution; *Summit Health v. Pinhas*, 500 US 322.
[27] See Chapter 6, Section IV.2(b).

power of the EU Member States to set their own competition rules. In addition, the European Commission has published numerous detailed guidelines interpreting the EU Treaty provisions on competition (EU anti-trust/cartels, mergers and State aid). These guidelines bind only the European Commission officially, limiting its discretion and reflecting current EU enforcement practice.[28] However, informally, they also provide important guidance to national institutions as well as practitioners, e.g., lawyers advising in matters falling under EU competition law. In the area of administrative enforcement, the European Commission only takes up selected cases outside the areas of merger and state aid control which require pre-notification.

Within the (semi-formal) **European Competition Network** (ECN), the Member State agencies have competences to enforce the EU competition rules in parallel to the European Commission, but they also enforce the national competition rules. In Germany, for instance, there is even a two-layered structure with the Federal Cartel Office (FCO; *Bundeskartellamt*) and the *Länder* Cartel Offices. In France, the competence to enforce the competition rules is centralized at the Autorité de la concurrence. In Italy, it lies with the Autorità Garante della Concorrenza e del Mercato (AGCM), and in Spain, with the Comisión Nacional de los Mercados y la Competencia (CNMC). Private litigation exists as well and is mostly regulated by the EU Member States (although an EU Cartel Damages Directive exists as well).[29]

In the EU, the structure of the enforcement system and the fact that the competences for court procedures generally continue to lie with the Member States could, like in the U.S., lead to divergent enforcement policies. However, the **system** is, in reality, **again mostly homogeneous**. Similar to the situation in the U.S., this is for two reasons:

(1) One reason is that **EU law overrides national law** and, moreover that the competition rules, in particular, apply directly without further

---

[28] Cf. ECJ, Judgment of 13 December 2012, Expedia (C-226/11) ECLI:EU:C:2012:795, §§ 28–30 (*re* the European Commission's de-minimis notice).

[29] Directive 2014/104/EU of the European Parliament and of the Council of 26 November 2014 on certain rules governing actions for damages under national law for infringements of the competition law provisions of the Member States and of the European Union, OJ L 349 of 5 December 2014, p. 1.

transformation.[30] Competition law overrides national law whenever the EU's internal market (or "single market") may be affected, which can essentially only be excluded in purely local cases.[31]

(2) In addition, also in the EU, court review is centralized and stream-lined in competition matters: The EU has a two-tiered court system. One tier is the Court of the European Union, which is composed of the General Court (GC; previously, Court of First Instance, CFI) and the European Court of Justice (ECJ) as the appeals court.[32] The ECJ also provides **binding interpretations of EU law** and even of national law if it is designed on EU law and a divergent interpretation could lead to a fragmentation of the EU legal system.[33] In ensuring the homogeneity of EU law, the ECJ is supported by an Advocate General (AG), who submits opinions before a decision of cases before the ECJ. The second tier is formed of the courts in the EU Member States, which apply the directly applicable EU rules alongside the national competition rules.

3. Japan

It is noted above that it was the U.S. interest to reshape the Japanese post-war economy that brought the AMA into being. For this reason, the **Japan Fair Trade Commission** (JFTC) is organized in a way resembling more of an independent administrative agency in the U.S. than other Japanese agencies. Notably, it is organized as a commission and shielded from

---

[30]ECJ, Judgment of 5 February 1963, *Van Gend en Loos/Administratie der Belastingen* (26/62, ECR 1963 p. 1), ECLI:EU:C:1963:1; Judgment of 15 July 1964, Costa/E.N.E.L. (6-64, ECR 1964 p. 585), ECLI:EU:C:1964:66.

[31]Commission Notice — Guidelines on the effect on trade concept contained in Articles 81 and 82 of the Treaty, OJ C 101, 27 April 2004, p. 81; accessible: https://eur-lex.europa.eu/legal-content/EN/ALL/?uri=CELEX:52004XC0427(06); see also European Commission, Decision of 23 July 2014, C(2014) 5077 final, SA.33045 — *Germany (Kristall Bäder)*, §40; press release of 29 April 2015, IP/15/4889 (both regarding Article 107 TFEU).

[32]Article 19 TEU.

[33]See Article 267 TFEU *re* EU law. Moreover, see ECJ, Judgment of 7 July 2011, *Agafiţei and others* (C-310/10, ECR 2011 p. I-5989) ECLI:EU:C:2011:467, §39; Judgment of 28 October 2010, *Volvo Car Germany* (C-203/09, ECR 2010 p. I-10721) ECLI:EU: C:2010:647, §25 *re* national law.

cabinet interference in its area of competences. Moreover, the JFTC enjoys exceptionally broad powers and can issue its own **delegated legislation** (notably "General Designations"). However, this does not exclude that the Ministry of Economy, Trade and Industry (METI) engages in activities potentially even counteracting the AMA, e.g., when METI takes a political interest in certain measures for industrial policy reasons.

Japan is a civil law jurisdiction. The Japanese Constitution abolished the specialized court system that existed formerly for administrative matters. Today, judgments (including Supreme Court judgments) do **not operate as binding precedents**. The courts can, however, not quash agency decisions. The interpretation of the Supreme Court of Japan and other high courts' interpretation of the law also have a strong impact on the JFTC's enforcement in subsequent cases. For instance, the Tokyo High Court interpreted AMA Article 3, second part, as only covering horizontal violations, and the JFTC has ceased to apply the provision in vertical scenarios ever since.[34] In addition, the Japanese courts can also adjudicate standalone civil cases (i.e., cases without prior JFTC decisions).

Good to know: The Brussels effect and international convergence

In terms of competition regulation, both EU competition law and U.S. antitrust law have set an example for other jurisdictions around the globe. By now, the EU and U.S. rules have been exported and transplanted into numerous other legal systems. However, in recent years, the EU rulebook seems to have become even more influential than the U.S. rules. One reason is certainly that the **U.S. rules are legally more demanding** because they generally require a finding of anticompetitive market effects. Another reason may lie in the so-called "Brussels Effect".[35] This term was coined to describe the mechanism of large companies designing their internal

---

[34] See Tokyo High Court, Judgment of 9 March 1953 (*Newspaper Distribution*); moreover Wakui, Intellectual Property and Antitrust in Japan, 138, 139.

[35] Bradford, *The Brussels Effect: How the European Union Rules the World.* Oxford University Press, New York, 2020.

(Continued)

compliance rules according to the **strictest standard they cannot evade** in international operations. Since the EU single market is important for foreign exporters, and since the EU competition rules are only one set of rules in an overall very comprehensive rulebook (giving rise to significant compliance risks), companies have started to adapt their own compliance rules to what is demanded under the EU standard and to follow that standard in international operations. This, in turn, has made it attractive for legislation and regulators in other jurisdictions to adapt (and tighten) their own national rules, such that they become aligned with EU rules.

The third factor contributing to international convergence — first under the U.S., but now increasingly under the EU standard — is the **regulatory cooperation** in specialized institutions such as UNCTAD, the OECD or the International Competition Network (ICN), in which officials from the U.S. and the EU have been playing an active and an important role. China, however, has started to engage in standard setting as well. It remains to be seen whether Chinese officials will also make themselves heard in dealing with competition regulation in the future.

Chapter 2

Horizontal Collusion

Introductory note

The following **Chapters 2 and 3 are best read together**. Chapter 2 deals with cartels bringing about horizontal collusion, which is regarded as a problem that is particularly harmful to the economy and to society. Chapter 3 deals with other types of horizontal or vertical collaborations. In the EU, the U.S. and Japan, Article 101 TFEU, §1 Sherman Act and AMA Articles 2(6) and 3 respectively **cover** all these cases where companies coordinate their market activities. The exception is that AMA Articles 2(6) and 3 are not used with regard to vertical collaboration, but instead AMA Articles 2(5), 2(9), 3 and 19 cover it. A legal differentiation only takes place when it comes to the requisite legal standard for establishing a cartel violation and to rules providing for justifications. Regarding the **legal standard for violations**, EU law distinguishes, on the one hand, between violations "by object" and "by effect", and between narrow exceptions and exemptions for cartels, and wider safe harbors for various other types of horizontal and vertical coordination. In the U.S., a key distinction is made between restraints of trade *per se* and restraints falling under a middle standard ("truncated rule of reason") or assessed under a flexible "rule of reason" standard. In Japan, although the relevant provision does not make any distinction, a hardcore cartel, or a clearly anticompetitive horizontal collusion, is deemed to be generally unlawful and does not require detailed analysis on competitive effect, while the rest is subject to in-depth case-by-case analysis to assess whether it creates or enhances market power.

(Continued)

(Continued)

Horizontal collusion can take place in a **trade association**. Article 101 TFEU and §1 Sherman Act cover both enterprise agreements and trade association decisions (the latter being a type of agreement where individual objections can be overcome according to the association's charter). Meanwhile, Japanese competition law has a special provision for trade associations, AMA Article 8, and they are subject to more stringent regulations.

I. The law

The relevant statutory provisions covered in this chapter are the following:

1. Article 101 TFEU

1. *The following shall be prohibited as incompatible with the internal market: all agreements between undertakings, decisions by associations of undertakings and concerted practices which may affect trade between Member States and which have as their object or effect the prevention, restriction or distortion of competition within the internal market, and in particular those which:*
   (a) *directly or indirectly fix purchase or selling prices or any other trading conditions;*
   (b) *limit or control production, markets, technical development, or investment;*
   (c) *share markets or sources of supply;*
   (d) *apply dissimilar conditions to equivalent transactions with other trading parties, thereby placing them at a competitive disadvantage;*
   (e) *make the conclusion of contracts subject to acceptance by the other parties of supplementary obligations which, by their nature or according to commercial usage, have no connection with the subject of such contracts.*
2. *Any agreements or decisions prohibited pursuant to this Article shall be automatically void.*

3. *The provisions of paragraph 1 may, however, be declared inapplicable in the case of:*
   — *any agreement or category of agreements between undertakings,*
   — *any decision or category of decisions by associations of undertakings,*
   — *any concerted practice or category of concerted practices, which contributes to improving the production or distribution of goods or to promoting technical or economic progress, while allowing consumers a fair share of the resulting benefit, and which does not:*
       (a) impose on the undertakings concerned restrictions which are not indispensable to the attainment of these objectives;
       (b) afford such undertakings the possibility of eliminating competition in respect of a substantial part of the products in question.

In addition, the following EU Regulations and guidelines are important for the interpretation of this provision:

- On the notion of an "agreement" or "concerted practice" (including information exchanges) in Article 101(1) TFEU and the considerations to be taken into account for an individual exemption of horizontal cooperation agreements under Article 101(3) TFEU: Guidelines on Horizontal Cooperation.[1]
- On the effect on "trade between Member States" in Article 101(1) TFEU: Guidelines on the effect on trade.[2]

---

[1] Communication from the Commission — Guidelines on the applicability of Article 101 of the Treaty on the Functioning of the European Union to horizontal cooperation agreements, OJ C 259, 21 July 2023, p. 1; accessible: https://eur-lex.europa.eu/legal-content/EN/TXT/?uri=uriserv%3AOJ.C_.2023.259.01.0001.01.ENG&toc=OJ%3AC%3A2023%3A259%3ATOC.

[2] Commission Notice — Guidelines on the effect on trade concept contained in Articles 81 and 82 of the Treaty, OJ C 101, 27 April 2004, p. 81; accessible: https://eur-lex.europa.eu/legal-content/EN/ALL/?uri=CELEX:52004XC0427(06). See Chapter 1, Section III.2.

- On the question of what constitutes a competition restriction "by object" or "by effect" and when a restriction is disregarded as an ancillary restraint: Guidelines on the application of Article 81(3) of the Treaty (§§8–31).[3]
  - o Additionally, on the question of what constitutes a competition restriction "by object": The Commission staff document, "by-object" guidance.[4] Note, however, that the legal relevance of this guidance paper is currently unclear as it was not included in the list of legislative notices available on the revised European Commission website.
- On the question of what constitutes an "appreciable" (sufficient) restriction of competition under Article 101(1) TFEU: De Minimis Notice.[5]
- On the question of under which conditions a practice serves to "limit or control production" in the context of subcontracting agreements under Article 101(1) lit. b TFEU: Notice on subcontracting agreements.[6]

---

[3]Communication from the Commission — Notice — Guidelines on the application of Article 81(3) of the Treaty, OJ C 101, 27 April 2004, p. 97; accessible: https://eur-lex.europa.eu/legal-content/EN/ALL/?uri=CELEX%3A52004XC0427%2807%29.

[4]Commission Staff Working Document, Guidance on restrictions of competition "by object" for the purpose of defining which agreements may benefit from the De Minimis Notice, Accompanying the Notice on agreements of minor importance which do not appreciably restrict competition under Article 101(1) of the Treaty on the Functioning of the European Union (De Minimis Notice), SWD(2014) 198 final, revised version of 3 June 2015; accessible: https://ec.europa.eu/competition/antitrust/legislation/de_minimis_notice_annex_en.pdf.

[5]Communication from the Commission — Notice on agreements of minor importance which do not appreciably restrict competition under Article 101(1) of the Treaty on the Functioning of the European Union (De Minimis Notice), OJ C 291, 30 August 2014, p. 1; accessible: https://eur-lex.europa.eu/legal-content/EN/TXT/PDF/?uri=OJ:C:2014:291:FULL.

[6]Commission notice of 18 December 1978 concerning its assessment of certain subcontracting agreements in relation to Article 85(1) of the EEC Treaty, OJ C 1, 3 January 1979, p. 2; accessible: https://eur-lex.europa.eu/legal-content/EN/ALL/?uri=CELEX:31979Y0103(01).

- On the relevant "market" within the meaning of Article 101(1) lit. c TFEU and generally within the meaning of EU competition law: Notice on the relevant market.[7]
- On the individual exemption of agreements under Article 101(3) TFEU (no block exemption is available for collusive horizontal arrangements): Guidelines on the application of Article 81(3) of the Treaty (§§1–12, 32 ff.).[8]

The European Commission has also issued temporary guidelines and "comfort letters" providing for a benevolent treatment of certain types of cooperation due to the COVID pandemic.[9] However, the guidelines only concerned enforcement priorities while the comfort letters were case-specific. They have no practical effect for any new transactions.

2. §1 of the Sherman Act (15 U.S.C. §1)

Every contract, combination in the form of trust or otherwise, or conspiracy, in restraint of trade or commerce among the several States, or with foreign nations, is declared to be illegal. Every person who shall make any contract or engage in any combination or conspiracy hereby declared to be illegal shall be deemed guilty of a felony, and, on conviction thereof, shall be punished by fine not exceeding $100,000,000 if a corporation, or, if any other person, $1,000,000, or by imprisonment not exceeding 10 years, or by both said punishments, in the discretion of the court.

In addition, the FTC/DOJ Joint Antitrust Guidelines for Collaboration Among Competitors are important for the interpretation of this provision. They set out the analytical framework for violations of §1 Sherman Act.[10]

---

[7]Commission Notice on the definition of relevant market for the purposes of Community competition law, OJ C 372, 9 December 1997, p. 5; accessible: https://eur-lex.europa.eu/legal-content/EN/ALL/?uri=CELEX:31997Y1209(01) . This Notice is currently under review; see here: https://competition-policy.ec.europa.eu/public-consultations/2022-market-definition-notice_en.
[8]See fn. 3 in this chapter.
[9]See: https://competition-policy.ec.europa.eu/antitrust/legislation/coronavirus_en.
[10]FTC/DOJ, Antitrust Guidelines for Collaborations Among Competitors, April 2000; see https://www.ftc.gov/sites/default/files/documents/public_events/joint-venture-hearings-antitrust-guidelines-collaboration-among-competitors/ftcdojguidelines-2.pdf.

3. Articles 2(5), 2(6), 3 and 8 of the Japanese Antimonopoly Act (AMA)

Article 2(5) *The term "private monopolization" as used in this Act means such business activities, by which any enterprise, individually or by combination, in conspiracy with other enterprises, or by any other manner, excludes or controls the business activities of other enterprises, thereby causing, contrary to the public interest, a substantial restraint of competition in any particular field of trade.*

Article 2(6) *The term 'unreasonable restraint of trade' as used in this Act means such business activities, by which any enterprise, by contract, agreement or any other means irrespective of its name, in concert with other enterprises, mutually restrict or conduct their business activities in such a manner as to fix, maintain or increase prices, or to limit production, technology, products, facilities or counterparties, thereby causing, contrary to the public interest, a substantial restraint of competition in any particular field of trade.*

Article 3 *An enterprise must not effect private monopolization or unreasonable restraint of trade.*

Article 8 *A trade association must not engage in any act which falls under any of the following items*

(i) substantially restraining competition in any particular field of trade, [...]

(iii) limiting the present or future number of enterprise in any particular field of business.

(iv) unjustly restricting the functions or activities of the constituent enterprise.

In addition, the JFTC has published guidelines which are relevant for the assessment of collusive behavior, especially the Guidelines Concerning the Activities of Trade Associations under the Antimonopoly Act (1995, revised 2020).

II. Collusion and liability

As shown in Chapter 1, **antitrust/competition law reflects economic principles**, which themselves may be understood as a set of rules determining the behavior of the market participants. That being said, economists and antitrust lawyers look at the respective rules from different perspectives.

This is also relevant when it comes to horizontal collusion. The term **collusion** has long been used in the legal context; in Anglo-American criminal law, it indicates "an agreement between two or more persons, to defraud a person of his rights by the forms of law, or to obtain an object forbidden by law".[11] Identifying collusion has thus to begin with the finding of such agreement. However, today, collusion is more prominently known as an **economic concept**. Horizontal collusion may be defined as the parallel behavior of suppliers leading to high prices or reduced output. In the view of economists, it is not the individual behavior of suppliers that counts but rather the production of a **market outcome** harming consumers.[12]

Lawyers, in turn, have difficulties in dealing with market outcomes as such. This is because **liability can only attach to market behavior** that can be **attributed to individual market participants**. In the U.S., first, it is hard to condemn and remedy parallel behavior as *J. Breyer* (U.S.) aptly pointed out in *Clamp-All v. Cast Iron Soil Pipe Institute*:

> *Courts have noted that the Sherman Act prohibits agreements, and they have almost uniformly held, at least in the pricing area, that [...] individual pricing decisions [...] do not constitute an unlawful agreement [...] That is not because such pricing is desirable (it is not), but because it is close to <u>impossible to devise a judicially enforceable remedy for</u> <u>'interdependent' pricing</u>.* (Emphasis added.)[13]

Second, prohibiting parallel behavior may inhibit dynamics in the marketplace and harm consumers. This is because, where parallel price increases are prohibited, companies may be more reluctant to lower prices fearing that, once they do, later price increases may be found to be a violation of the law. Thus, **unintended consequences** of such prohibition could be stable high prices.

Horizontal collusion condemned by the law is conventionally called **cartel** behavior, and market participants are liable for very specific

---

[11] Bouvier Law Dictionary (1853).

[12] See, e.g., European Commission, first version of the Guidelines on horizontal cooperation OJ C 11, 14 January 2011, p. 1, §§65 ff. These passages were removed from the current version of the guidelines, which generally does not address the market outcome separately anymore. See §21 in these Guidelines (fn. 1) for an exception.

[13] *Clamp-All v. Cast Iron Soil Pipe Institute*, 851 F.2d 478, 484 (1st Cir. 1988).

actions which result in collusion. In the European Commission's definition, cartels are agreements or other types of collaborations *between two
or more competitors aimed at coordinating their competitive behavior on
the market and/or influencing the relevant parameters of competition.*[14]
Cartels, thus, have two important elements: (i) the intentional and active
coordination of competitors and (ii) a restriction of trade or competition
(collusive element).

As said before, both **Article 101(1) TFEU and §1 Sherman Act** only
apply when the cartel **affects the EU's internal market or U.S. interstate commerce**, respectively. In contrast, the AMA is not subject to such
limitations. The same holds in relation to cartel laws of EU Member States
and U.S. State's antitrust laws. This also implies that there may be exemptions and exceptions applicable only within a particular (Member) State.
In Germany, for example, a special exception from liability exists for
Small and Medium Enterprise (SME) cartels.[15] However, this exception is
only available for purely local cartels.[16]

III. The liable actors

In order to capture the underlying economic issues accurately, EU law,
U.S. law and Japanese law define the addressees of the competition/anti-
trust rules as economic actors, using different terms. Note, though, that the
ECJ uses the concept of an economically active unit not only to define the
addressee of conduct prohibitions but also to define the addressee of
sanctions. In contrast, both §1 Sherman Act and the AMA include differentiated provisions on who may be held liable for violating the cartel
prohibition. In relation to criminal sanctions, they are also applicable to
individuals who work for the relevant enterprise (different, Article 101
TFEU in conjunction with Article 23 Reg. 1/2003).

The rest of **this chapter** deals only with the question as to **who can
commit** cartel and other offenses relating to horizontal collusion (i.e., the
substance of the law) and not with the question of who is the addressee

---

[14]European Commission, Commission Notice on Immunity from fines and reduction of
fines in cartel cases, OJ C 298, 8 December 2006, p. 17, §1.
[15]§3 GWB.
[16]See Chapter 1, Section IV.1–2 for the limitations of local rules diverging from EU law
or federal U.S. law.

of a sanctioning decision or a claim for damages (i.e., procedural aspects).[17]

1. EU law

In EU law, the Treaty provides that "undertakings" are the addressees of the competition rules (here, Article 101 TFEU). As the ECJ has consistently held:

> *The authors of the Treaties chose to use the concept of an undertaking to designate the perpetrator of an infringement of competition law, who is liable to be punished pursuant to Articles [101 and 102 TFEU], and not other concepts such as the concept of a company or firm or of a legal person [...].*
>
> *When such an* <u>*economic entity*</u> *infringes the competition rules, it is for that entity,* <u>*in accordance with the principle of personal responsibility*</u>*, to answer for that infringement.* (Emphasis added.)[18]

Thus, the ECJ defines undertakings as "economic entities" (in some judgments, "economic units") and does **not** use the concept of a **legal person**, although this concept is well established in all Member States. This bars the EU Member States from deciding themselves on the scope of application of the EU competition rules.[19] Moreover, the ECJ attributes the actions (or failures to act) of **employees** strictly to the undertaking and does not look for individual liability on the part of those employees.[20]

---

[17] See Chapter 6 on these issues.

[18] ECJ, Judgment of 10 April 2014, *Commission/Siemens Österreich and others* and *Siemens Transmission & Distribution and others/Commission* (C-231/11 P, C-232/11 P and C-233/11 P) ECLI:EU:C:2014:256, §§42, 44.

[19] ECJ, Judgment of 14 March 2019, *Skanska Industrial Solutions and others* (C-724/17) ECLI:EU:C:2019:204, §§46–47.

[20] ECJ, Judgment of 18 September 2003, *Volkswagen/Commission* (C-338/00 P, ECR 2003 p. I-9189) ECLI:EU:C:2003:473, §98; Judgment of 7 June 1983, *Musique Diffusion française/Commission* (100 to 103/80, ECR 1983 p. 1825) ECLI:EU:C:1983:158, §§97–98 (there with respect to Article 15 Reg. No 17). The legal situation in the EU Member States is different to the extent that authorities may also impose sanctions on individuals there; see, e.g., §81(1) GWB in conjunction with §§2, 9, 130 OWiG in Germany.

An **economic** entity can exist even when the entity is not operating for profit as long as it is at least engaging in market conduct. As an "entity", the legal persons forming the economic entity are irrelevant for finding a violation of the cartel prohibition. That being said, they are not wholly irrelevant, given that the legal addressee of an agency decision or a court judgment must be either a legal or a natural person. Over time, the ECJ clarified the relationship between the "economic entity" considered as an "undertaking" for the purposes of applying the substantive rules and the legal persons that belong to that "economic entity".

More specifically, the ECJ held that an "undertaking" ("economic entity") may be formed by **several natural and legal persons**.[21] However, no cartel violation in terms of Article 101 TFEU is possible **within** one and the same economic entity.[22] Moreover, the fact that the "economic entity" is the addressee of Article 101 TFEU means that competition agencies are allowed to impose fines for competition infringements (e.g., participation in a cartel) also on a legal entity which was **no active participant** in the infringement but to which relevant market behavior can be **attributed**.[23] This may occur if, for example, the owner of the entity directly participating in a cartel decides to dissolve that entity and to reallocate its assets within the corporate group.

In corporate groups, also **holdings or the parents of a joint venture** may be held liable, at least to the extent that they direct the management of the "economic entity". It does not matter which legal form the parents have themselves, i.e., whether they are separate legal or natural persons. Indeed, also an SOE and even a **state authority** as controlling shareholders may form or belong to an undertaking. This is at least the case if they either have their own market operations or if they direct the management of the "economic entity".[24]

---

[21] ECJ, Judgment of 28 June 2005, *Dansk Rørindustri and others/Commission* (C-189/02 P, C-202/02 P, C-205/02 P to C-208/02 P and C-213/02 P, ECR 2005 p. I-5425) ECLI:EU:C:2005:408, §113.

[22] ECJ, Judgment of 24 October 1996, *Viho/Commission* (C-73/95 P, ECR 1996 p. I-5457) ECLI:EU:C:1996:405, §§50–51.

[23] ECJ, Judgment of 10 September 2009, *Akzo Nobel and others/Commission* (C-97/08 P, ECR 2009 p. I-8237) ECLI:EU:C:2009:536, §59; Judgment of 29 September 2011, *Elf Aquitaine/Commission* (C-521/09 P, ECR 2011 p. I-8947) ECLI:EU:C:2011:620, §63 (98%).

[24] ECJ, Judgment of 11 December 2007, *ETI and others* (C-280/06, ECR 2007 p. I-10893) ECLI:EU:C:2007:775, §§49–50. Regarding the application of the EU competition rules to the state, see also Chapter 8.

However, managing the undertaking generally requires an **active exercise of influence regarding the strategic business decisions** of the undertaking.[25] This is particularly true for holding entities (including state holdings or family offices) that do have any market activities themselves. *The mere fact that the share capital of two separate commercial companies is held by the same person or the same family is insufficient, in itself, to establish that those two companies are a single economic unit.*[26] The GC requires that influence be exercised even in day-to-day operations.[27]

However, a relaxed standard applies when an entity holds 100% or at least **nearly all of the shares of a subsidiary** engaged in a competition violation. In this case, the holding entity is presumed to exercise an influence in the aforementioned sense.[28] It even does not matter that the parent company is non-operational: This fact alone is insufficient to rebut the presumption that it actually exercises decisive influence over the commercial policy of subsidiaries, given the close connection between the holding and the subsidiaries.[29] Other than that, the presumption can be rebutted by showing that the subsidiaries conducted their business completely independently.

A **change in the legal form and name** of an undertaking does not create a new undertaking free of liability either. This is true if the two undertakings are identical at least from an economic point of view.[30] In contrast, in cases where one company takes over another, the question arises whether this change in corporate structure is relevant for the purposes of imputing liability. Here, the rules are as follows: A subsidiary violating Article 101 TFEU which continues to exist remains the addressee of a fine despite its transfer to another group of companies. In addition,

---

[25] ECJ, Judgment of 26 September 2013, *EI du Pont de Nemours/Commission* (C-172/12 P) ECLI:EU:C:2013:601, §52.

[26] ECJ, Judgment of 28 June 2005, *Dansk Rørindustri and others/Commission* (C-189/02 P, C-202/02 P, C-205/02 P to C-208/02 P and C-213/02 P, ECR 2005 p. I-5425) ECLI:EU:C:2005:408, §118.

[27] GC, Judgment of 11 July 2014, *Sasol and others/Commission* (T-541/08) ECLI:EU:T:2014:628, §108 ff.

[28] ECJ, Judgment of 10 September 2009, *Akzo Nobel and others/Commission* (C-97/08 P, ECR 2009 p. I-8237) ECLI:EU:C:2009:536, §60.

[29] ECJ, Judgment of 29 September 2011, *Arkema/Commission* (C-520/09 P, ECR 2011 p. I-8901) ECLI:EU:C:2011:619, §48.

[30] ECJ, Judgment of 28 March 1984, *CRAM/Commission* (29/83 and 30/83, ECR 1984 p. 1679) ECLI:EU:C:1984:130, §§8–9.

the former parent company is liable if it formed an economic unit with the former subsidiary at the time of the infringement.[31] In contrast, the fact that the new parent (acquirer) could not have been unaware during the relevant period that the subsidiary participated in a cartel (even if the new parent participated in this cartel) cannot suffice to impute liability to the new parent for the subsidiary's violation before the acquisition. Finally, if the subsidiary no longer exists, it is necessary to determine the legal successor that carries on the economic activity of the legal entity that no longer exists (so-called principle of **economic continuity**).[32]

If an "economic entity" composed of several legal persons commits a competition violation (e.g., participates in a cartel), then **all persons forming the "economic entity" are jointly and severally liable**.[33] The same rule applies if several legal persons are liable as parents under the principle of "economic continuity". Liability is enforced under the national procedural rules of the EU Member States.[34]

2. U.S. law

In U.S. law, the Supreme Court has held that conspiracy within the meaning of §1 Sherman Act may only take place between *separate economic actors pursuing separate economic interests*.[35] Thus, officers or subsidiaries of the same company cannot conspire with each other in general because no cartel may be formed within a single economic actor. However, this is not always the case *when the parties to the agreement act on interests separate from those of the firm itself, and the intrafirm agreements may simply be a formalistic shell for ongoing concerted action*.[36]

Where a company engaged in a cartel is part of a corporate group, the parents can be liable only if the plaintiff is able to **pierce the corporate veil** because the subsidiary operates as the *alter ego* of the parent or as an agent. In relation to joint ventures, depending on the circumstances,

---

[31] ECJ, Judgment of 16 November 2000, *Cascades/Commission* (C-279/98 P, ECR 2000 p. I-9693) ECLI:EU:C:2000:626, §§75 ff.

[32] ECJ, Judgment of 16 December 1975, *Suiker Unie and others/Commission* (40 to 48, 50, 54 to 56, 111, 113 and 114-73, ECR 1975 p. 1663) ECLI:EU:C:1975:174, §§84 ff.

[33] ECJ, Judgment of 10 April 2014, *Areva and others/Commission* (C-247/11 P and C-253/11 P) ECLI:EU:C:2014:257, §122.

[34] Article 299 TFEU.

[35] *Copperweld v. Independent Tubes*, 467 US 752, 769 (1984).

[36] *American Needle, Inc. v. NFL*, 560 U.S. 183 (2010).

parties to a joint venture may, or may not, be seen as separate economic entities.[37] Moreover, collaborative structures can be separate economic actors, irrespective of the structure being a **state-chartered entity**.[38]

3. Japanese law

The provisions of the AMA are generally applicable to enterprises as defined by AMA Article 2(1) or associations of enterprises (trade associations) as defined by AMA Article 2(2). An **enterprise** is any individual or legal person who operates a business.[39] The term "business" includes any continuous economic activities in which something carrying an economic value is provided for a certain price.[40]

The JFTC has established the practice that AMA Article 2(6), which defines "unreasonable restraint of trade" and covers typical horizontal collusion, applies only to enterprises which are in a competitive relationship. Conventionally, horizontal collusion is found among **enterprises that are independent** of **each other**.[41] Yet, enterprises belonging to the same group and ultimately having the same parent company may commit an AMA Article 2(6) violation where they separately participate in public tendering as if they were independent enterprises.[42]

Another actor potentially liable under cartel rules is a **trade association**. AMA Article 2(2) defines trade association as an association of enterprises or a federation of such associations. Where such an association or federation operates businesses, it is deemed to be an enterprise as defined in AMA Article 2(1) and regulated in the same manner as an enterprise.

4. Comparison

The definition of the addressees of the cartel prohibitions is very similar in the EU, the U.S. and Japan. If anything, there is less controversy over

---

[37] *United States v. Terminal Railroad Ass'n*, 224 U.S. 383 (1912); *Texaco, Inc. v. Dagher*, 547 U.S. 1 (2006).
[38] *Board of Trade of Chicago v. United States*, 246 US 231, 238.
[39] Supreme Court, 14 December 1989, 43 Minshu 2078 (*Tokyo Slaughterhouse*).
[40] *Idem.*
[41] Tokyo High Court, 9 March 1953, 3 Shinketsu-shu 4 (*Newspaper Distribution*).
[42] JFTC Cease and Desist Order, 11 May 2007, 54 Shinketsu-shu 461 (*Eco-station*).

the question of what an "economic actor" is in terms of U.S. and Japanese law than the question of what an "economic entity" is in terms of EU law. This may be due to the fact that the question of liability can be approached either from a substantive or from a procedural perspective. In the EU, especially in Germany, it was unclear for a long time whether national legislature enjoyed any scope (which it does not) to define the entities that may be held liable and sanctioned for a competition violation committed by an "economic entity" (substance). An argument for this position was that it is procedural law that defines the addressees of sanctions. However, the ECJ ruled that the addressee of substantive competition law prohibitions and of sanctions for violation are the same.[43] Moreover, since fines are imposed on legal entities, cartel violators have attempted to evade liability in the EU by means of corporate group restructurings. However, cartel violations in the U.S. can lead to criminal penalties and not only to administrative fines imposed on the company. It is therefore more difficult for responsible management to evade liability through corporate restructurings.

IV. The coordination of behavior

Article 101(1) TFEU, §1 Sherman Act and AMA Articles 2(6) and 3 address various types of collaboration among competitors. However, the legal distinctions between these types of collaboration are only of limited practical importance if **any competitor collaboration** falling under the rules can be established. The competitive significance of the relevant types of collaboration is discussed in **Section V**.

We ask three interrelated questions in the following sections: What are the legal requirements for finding a relevant coordination of behavior **(Subsection 1)**? What is the requisite standard of proof **(Subsection 2)**? And how do we deal with atypical scenarios such as cartels in public, working partnerships or hub-and-spoke scenarios involving up- or downstream companies **(Subsection 3)**?

---

[43] See Monopolies Commission, Special Report No. 72, Strafrechtliche Sanktionen bei Kartellverstößen, 1st ed. 2015, §§27 ff., 133 ff., referring particularly to ECJ, Judgment of 10 April 2014, *Siemens Österreich and others and Siemens Transmission & Distribution and others/Commission* (C-231/11 P bis C-233/11 P) ECLI:EU:C:2014:256, paras. 42–44. The ECJ meanwhile clarified that parallel liability exists toward private claimants; see Judgment of 6 October 2021, *Sumal* (C-882/19) ECLI:EU:C:2021:800, §§41–42, 48.

1. Legal requirements

(a) EU law

Article 101 TFEU applies where an agreement between undertakings, a decision by an association of undertakings or a concerted practice exists, regardless of whether the collaboration takes place between competitors (i.e., horizontally), between companies along the distribution chain (i.e., vertically) or between companies acting in wholly unconnected markets (conglomerally).[44]

An agreement within the meaning of Article 101 TFEU is present where there is a *faithful expression* of the *joint intention* of the parties to the agreement with regard to their conduct in the common market.[45]

This definition consists of two elements: (i) a joint (or common) intention and (ii) a faithful expression of that joint intention between the cartel members. The joint intention must be about each cartel member's competitive behavior. It conditions that behavior (at least implicitly) on how the other cartel members will act on the market: "I will raise my prices because you are going to raise your prices". The required faithful expression means that the cartel members communicate their intention and that they plan to abide by that communicated intention.[46]

What was said in the previous paragraph means that the joint intention must encompass a restraint of competition. This is confirmed in the case law; see, e.g., ECJ C-49/92 P — *Anic Partecipazioni*, §87: *The Commission must [...] show that the undertaking intended to contribute by its own conduct to the common objectives pursued by all the participants and that it was aware of the actual conduct planned or put into effect by other undertakings in pursuit of the same objectives or that it*

---

[44] See also Chapter 3, Sections IV and V on other collaboration. The issue of conglomeral agreements mostly comes up in the context of takeovers (see Chapter 7, Section IV.3), but it may also become relevant with regard to cartel facilitators (see Section IV.3.c in this chapter).

[45] ECJ, Judgment of 15 July 1970, *Chemiefarma/Commission* (41/69, ECR 1970 p. 661) ECLI:EU:C:1970:71, §112.

[46] See ECJ, Judgment of 7 January 2004, *Aalborg Portland and others/Commission* (C-204/00 P, C-205/00 P, C-211/00 P, C-213/00 P, C-217/00 P and C-219/00 P, ECR 2004 p. I-123) ECLI:EU:C:2004:6, §§330, 335; GC, Judgment of 24 October 1991, *Rhône-Poulenc/Commission* (T-1/89, ECR 1991 p. II-867) ECLI:EU:T:1991:56, §§109, 120–122.

could reasonably have foreseen it and that it was prepared to take the risk. (Emphasis added.) However, the communicated intention does not need to explain all the details of the cartel violation.[47]

Moreover, the fact that there must be a "faithful expression" means that the concept of an agreement is an objective concept. It is crucial how other participants interpreted the conduct.[48] This also explains why a cartel member may be liable even if it only attended a cartel meeting passively.[49] To escape liability, the company representatives must show, in relation to the agreement, that the company had *indicated to its competitors that it was participating in those meetings in a spirit that was different from theirs [=pursuing different objectives] or that it later publicly distanc[ed] itself from its content or report[ed] it to the administrative authorities.*[50]

A **decision of an association** is a particular form of an agreement. Where such a decision is found, the cartel's liability extends to those association members that did not expressly agree to the decision or even objected to it, assuming that the association is empowered to regulate the market conduct of its members.[51]

The concept of **concerted practice** is another peculiarity of EU law. In the ECJ's words, that concept *implies, besides undertakings' concerting with each other, subsequent conduct on the market, and a relationship of cause and effect between the two.* (Emphasis added.)[52] This means that a

---

[47]ECJ, Judgment of 8 July 1999, *Commission/Anic Partecipazioni* (C-49/92 P, ECR 1999 p. I-4125) ECLI:EU:C:1999:356, §§79, 90.

[48]ECJ, Judgment of 7 January 2004, *Aalborg Portland and others/Commission* (C-204/00 P, C-205/00 P, C-211/00 P, C-213/00 P, C-217/00 P and C-219/00 P, ECR 2004 p. I-123) ECLI:EU:C:2004:6, §§330, 335.

[49]ECJ, Judgment of 25 January 2007, *Sumitomo Metal Industries/Commission* (C-403/04 P, and C-405/04 P, ECR 2007 p. I-729) ECLI:EU:C:2007:52, §§47–48.

[50]ECJ, Judgment of 7 January 2004, *Aalborg Portland and others/Commission* (C-204/00 P, C-205/00 P, C-211/00 P, C-213/00 P, C-217/00 P and C-219/00 P, ECR 2004 p. I-123) ECLI:EU:C:2004:6, §§81, 84.

[51]ECJ, Judgment of 29 October 1980, *Van Landewyck/Commission* (209 to 215 and 218/78, ECR 1980 p. 3125) ECLI:EU:C:1980:248. The association may itself considered to be an "undertaking" within the meaning of Article 101 TFEU if it pursues a market activity of its own; see ECJ, Judgment of 9 June 1977, *Van Ameyde/UCI* (90/76, ECR 1977 p. 1091) ECLI:EU:C:1977:101.

[52]ECJ, Judgment of 8 July 1999, *Hüls/Commission* (C-199/92 P, ECR 1999 p. I-4287) ECLI:EU:C:1999:358, §161.

concerted practice also requires some sort of joint or common intention. However, a concerted practice does not require any expression of will *vis-à-vis* the other cartel participants but instead an activity implementing the common intention on the market. In this context, the *subsequent conduct on the market* is only an element of the coordination among the cartel members and must be distinguished from the additionally required competition restriction. The ECJ has made this express by holding the following: *[A]lthough the very concept of a concerted practice presupposes conduct by the participating undertakings on the market, it does not necessarily mean that that conduct should produce the specific effect of restricting, preventing or distorting competition.* This is understandable considering that otherwise it would be impossible to discern the concerted practice as such.

However, in practice, the finding of a concerted practice frequently falls together with the finding of a competition restriction. This is because the concerted practices between competitors which the competition authorities pursue most are exchanges of strategic information (e.g., information on price elements and capacities). In this context, the ECJ clarified the concept of a "concerted practice" further in the seminal *T-Mobile Netherlands* judgment. Regarding the question of proving a joint intention in cases of information exchange, but without any communication indicating a concurrence of wills, the ECJ held that it is necessary to take into account the market situation[53]: *On a highly concentrated oligopolistic market, [it must be examined whether] the exchange of information [is] such as to enable traders to know the market positions and strategies of their competitors and thus to impair appreciably the competition which exists between traders.*

(b) U.S. law

Under the Sherman Act §1, a collaboration is a contract, combination or conspiracy. In the U.S. Supreme Court's jurisprudence, the differences between these types of collaborations are insignificant and they tend to be called simply agreements. Such an agreement is found *where the circumstances are such as to warrant a jury in finding that the conspirators had a unity of purpose or a common design and understanding, or a meeting*

---

[53] ECJ, Judgment of 4 June 2009, *T-Mobile Netherlands and others* (C-8/08, ECR 2009 p. I-4529) ECLI:EU:C:2009:343, §§34 ff.

of the minds in an unlawful arrangement. (Emphasis added.)[54] Thus, neither opportunity to collude nor the profitability of the agreement alone is sufficient to prove collusion.[55] On the other hand, the standard does not presuppose or require any formal agreement.[56] When an agreement, or meeting of minds, is present, it does not matter whether it is explicit or based on tacit understanding.

However, in addition to circumstantial evidence indicating an agreement, the plaintiff also needs to prove that *the actions are rational only when contracting parties mutually understand their actions are in a similar fashion.* (Emphasis added.)[57] Here again, *[t]he crucial question is whether respondents' conduct toward petitioner stemmed from independent decision or from an agreement, tacit or express.*[58]

U.S. law does not distinguish between agreements and decisions of trade associations.

(c) **Japanese law**

(1) **Agreements**

AMA Article 2(6) regards enterprises' concerted action to mutually restrict their business activities as an unreasonable restraint of trade. Concerted action exists only where participants communicate their intentions to each other, either explicitly or implicitly.[59] Such communication resulting in concerted actions is often termed an "agreement".

The mutual "restriction of business activities" is generally deemed to exist where there is an agreement, as participants would act in line with such an agreement, restraining the parties' business activities in a way that would have been otherwise nonexistent.[60] Beginning with the Tokyo High Court Judgment in 1953 (*Newspaper Distribution*), this element was interpreted narrowly to require that the activities of competitors be

---

[54] *American Tobacco v. United States*, 328 US 781, 810 (1946).

[55] *Blomkest Fertilizer v. Potash Corp. of Saskatchewan*, 203 F.3d 1028, 1036 (8th Cir. 2000).

[56] *Ibid.*, at 809.

[57] *Starr v. Sony BMG Music Entertainment*, 592 F.3d 314 (2nd Cir. 2010).

[58] *Theatre Enterprises v. Paramount Distributing*, 346 U.S. 537, 540 (1954).

[59] Tokyo High Court, 25 September 1995, 906 Hanrei Times 136 (*Toshiba Chemical*).

[60] *Araigumi.* Supreme Court, 20 February 2012, 58-II Shinketsu-shu 148.

restricted in the same manner).[61] Over time, the practice changed, and currently, the restriction need not be the same in substance; the unity of purpose suffices.

Restriction must be mutual, implying that a ringleader orchestrating cartel-like behavior among other enterprises without being subject to any restriction itself does not fall under AMA Article 2(6); such an action is instead sanctioned as private monopolization (controlling activity) under AMA Articles 2(5) and 3.

(2) Trade associations

More stringent rules apply under AMA Article 8 to the activities of trade associations. Horizontal collusion realized as a decision of trade association is prohibited by AMA Article 8(i) when it causes substantial restraint of competition in a relevant market. Additionally, trade association's actions leading to reduction in the number of enterprises active in a particular business field or unfairly restricting members' activities or functions are prohibited under AMA Article 8(iii) and (iv), respectively. This implies that trade associations are more stringently regulated than enterprises. Such stringent regulation reflects the prewar and wartime Japanese economy under which business associations would suppress economic activities and the free market, as well as tend to organize anticompetitive activities.

(d) Comparison

Overall, there is significant convergence between EU, U.S. and Japanese law when it comes to defining the coordination covered by the relevant cartel prohibitions. If we look closer, differences do still exist. For instance, in comparison with EU law, it is notable that U.S. law does not make a distinction between an "agreement" and a "concerted practice". It does not require any specifically defined behavior, neither a *faithful expression* of a common will nor any *conduct on the market*. Instead, it is sufficient that there is a "meeting of minds" taking place in the context of an unlawful arrangement. Under Japanese law, two differences spring to mind: first, the required *restriction of business activities*,

---

[61] Tokyo High Court, 9 March 1953, 3 Shinketsu-shu 4 (*Newspaper Distribution*).

although this requirement does not have substantial meaning if a communication of intentions leading to an agreement can be found, and second, the special rules for trade associations, which go beyond the rules existing in EU and U.S. law.

2. Proving the requirements of coordination

Proving the existence of a cartel can be a daunting task as cartels are usually formed in secret. Thus, applying a stringent legal standard for establishing the required collaboration carries the risk of encouraging illegal competition infringements.[62] The courts have consequently relaxed the burden of proof of public enforcers or private claimants.

(a) EU law

The ECJ has eased the European Commission's burden of proving a cartel through presumptions of facts that operate in the European Commission's favor.[63] When it comes to proving concertation (i.e., a joint intention) in cases of an information exchange, the Court held in *Hüls*[64]:

> [S]ubject to proof to the contrary, which the economic operators concerned must adduce, the presumption must be that the undertakings taking part in the concerted action and remaining active on the market take account of the information exchanged with their competitors for the purposes of determining their conduct on that market. (Emphasis added.)[65]

Moreover, in so far as the undertaking participating in the concerted action remains active on the market in question, the ECJ held in *T-Mobile*

---

[62]This concern was referred to also in: ECJ, Judgment of 7 January 2004, *Aalborg Portland and others/Commission* (C-204/00 P, C-205/00 P, C-211/00 P, C-213/00 P, C-217/00 P and C-219/00 P, ECR 2004 p. I-123) ECLI:EU:C:2004:6, §84.

[63]It may be recalled here that the exercise of influence is (rebuttably) presumed in cases where a parent holds 100% of the shares in a subsidiary; see Section III.1 in this chapter.

[64]ECJ, Judgment of 8 July 1999, *Hüls/Commission* (C-199/92 P, ECR 1999 p. I-4287) ECLI:EU:C:1999:358, §162.

[65]ECJ, Judgment of 8 July 1999, *Hüls/Commission* (C-199/92 P, ECR 1999 p. I-4287) ECLI:EU:C:1999:358, §162.

Netherlands that there is a presumption of the required causal connection between the concerted practice and the conduct of the undertaking on that market, even if the concerted action is the result of a meeting held by the participating undertakings on a single occasion.[66]

(b) U.S. law

The U.S. Supreme Court has been cautious in developing legal presumptions. That said, also the Supreme Court has eased the burden of proving a "meeting of minds" by holding that *conspiracies [...] may be inferred from proof of the things actually done.*[67] Thus, public enforcers or private claimants may have to prove parallel pricing behavior or other forms of conduct pointing to a "meeting of minds" but not the meeting of minds itself. In practice, the fact that the parties are acting largely inconsistently with unilateral conduct but largely consistently with explicitly coordinated action (e.g., fixed relative market shares, declining market share of leaders, market-wide pricing patters with only regional variations and ongoing exclusionary practices) and so-called **plus factors** helps prove a conspiracy.[68] On the other hand, "conduct as consistent with permissible competition as with illegal conspiracy does not, standing alone, support an inference of antitrust conspiracy".[69]

(c) Japanese law

The existence of a hardcore cartel agreement is mostly established through circumstantial evidence. There is no rigid rule as to the evidential rules, apart from the fact that a parallel price increase alone is considered insufficient. Information exchanges are often considered part of the relevant evidence. Indeed, the Tokyo High Court announced that the communication of intentions is presumed where the participants meet and exchange price information and, subsequently, increase the price, unless

---

[66]ECJ, Judgment of 4 June 2009, *T-Mobile Netherlands and others* (C-8/08, ECR 2009 p. I-4529) ECLI:EU:C:2009:343, §§58 ff.

[67]*Eastern States Retail Lumber Dealers' Ass'n v. U.S.*, 234 U.S. 600, 612 (1914).

[68]Kovacic *et al.*, Plus Factors and Agreement in Antitrust Law, 110 Mich. L. Rev. 393 (2011), regarding the examples, with reference to Posner, Antitrust Law 79-93 (2nd ed., 2001), on p. 415 with fn. 89.

[69]*Matsushita v. Zenith Radio Corp.*, 475 U.S. 574 (1986).

it is established that such an increase is based on participants' independent business judgments.[70]

Horizontal collusion often takes place in relation to public tendering. When enterprises rig the bid, they normally agree that they would coordinate their bids in relation to a particular type of public tendering in advance. The existence of such framework agreements is established by the fact that participants engaged in coordination many times in relation to a particular type of public tendering.

Good to know: What about mere attempts to bring about collusion?

Mere attempts to collude are an issue that in practice often stays under the enforcement agencies' radar. This is because the agencies usually limit their resources where they can prove a cartel violation and defend their findings in court. Nevertheless, a notorious case involving this issue was *U.S. v. American Airlines*, which included findings of the following conversation between two competitors[71]:

Putnam: Do you have a suggestion for me?
Crandall: Yes. I have a suggestion for you. Raise your goddamn fares twenty percent. I'll raise mine the next morning.
Putnam: Robert, we–
Crandall: You'll make more money and I will too.
Putnam: We can't talk about pricing.
Crandall: Oh bull****, Howard. We can talk about any goddamn thing we want to talk about.

According to the court, Putnam did not raise Braniff's fares in response to Crandall's proposal; instead, he presented the government with a tape recording of the conversation. In such circumstances, the laws requiring coordinated behavior (e.g., Article 101 TFEU, §1 Sherman Act and Article 6 AMA) do not apply because the parties did not reach a common understanding (no "meeting of minds"). That does not mean that a conversation like the one above is admissible. However, how to approach it under the

---

[70]Tokyo High Court, 25 September 1995, 906 Hanrei Times 136 (*Toshiba Chemical*).
[71]*United States v. American Airlines*, 743 F.2d 1114 (5th Cir. 1984).

(Continued)

law is a question that needs to be answered in each individual case. In the case at hand, the court held that "the government's complaint sufficiently alleged facts that if proved would permit a finding of attempted [unilateral] monopolization" within the meaning of §2 Sherman Act.[72] Additionally, Crandall's attempt may well be considered an unfair trade practice under §5 of the U.S. FTC Act.[73] In view of the broad rules on fraud in the U.S., the conversation might also be caught by the wire fraud and mail fraud statutes.[74] Finally, the U.S. states' civil laws and unfair competition statutes may apply.[75]

In Europe, it is questionable whether Crandall's unilateral suggestion could be captured by the rules on abuse of dominance (Article 102 TFEU): No market player involved effectively took action to exclude/foreclose competitors. It is true that Crandall talked about exploiting customers, but it remains unclear also whether that exploitation took place at some point. However, in European jurisdictions that treat competition violations as administrative offenses or as torts, the suggestion of anticompetitive conduct may still be considered as a form of "attempted participation".[76] This would be similar to the "attempted monopolization" claim under §2 of the U.S. Sherman Act.

3. Atypical scenarios

In this section, we deal with atypical scenarios of cartel collaboration, i.e., cartels in public, working partnerships to achieve a competitively neutral purpose and hub-and-spoke scenarios involving up- or downstream companies. The issue of cartels in the context of a joint venture is discussed later in the context of merger control.[77]

---

[72] *Ibid.*

[73] *Du Pont De Nemours v. FTC*, 729 F.2d 128 (2nd Cir. 1984).

[74] *United States v. Ames Sintering*, 927 F.2d 232 (6th Cir. 1990).

[75] *Liu v. Amerco*, 677 F.3d 489 (1st Cir. 2015).

[76] This is, e.g., possible in Germany because violations of Article 101, 102 TFEU are subject to enforcement under the administrative offense rules (§14 OWiG) and also considered to be torts (§§33 ff. GWB).

[77] See Chapter 7, Section IV.4.

(a) Cartels in public (signaling)

Even though cartels are usually formed in secret, that need not be the case. A public announcement can give rise to cartel liability as well. However, a unilateral announcement that is also genuinely public, such as the announcement of new prices in a newspaper advertisement, is likely not only to inform consumers but also to promote competition. Thus, it is necessary to distinguish genuine price announcements from information activities that allow competitors to collude in an anticompetitive fashion.

In that regard, the European Commission Guidelines on horizontal agreements note the following[78]:

> *The fact that an undertaking discloses commercially sensitive information through a public announcement [...] does not in itself exclude the possibility that the announcement may constitute a concerted practice [...]. Indeed, public disclosure may in some cases form part of a communication channel between competitors to signal future intentions to behave on the market in a specific way, or to provide a focal point for coordination between competitors and thereby fall within Article 101(1).*

In U.S. and Japanese law, what matters is whether such signaling leads to a meeting of minds (U.S.) or communication of intentions (Japan), without which it is impossible to find a §1 Sherman Act and AMA Article 2(6) violation. However, in the U.S., the FTC charged U-Haul with a violation of §5 of the Federal Trade Commission Act (15 U.S.C. §45) because U-Haul's chairman repeatedly instructed regional managers and dealers to raise their own or undercut the rival's rates and to let the rival Budget know their decisions in advance.[79] Such practice is known as an invitation to collude and is subject to §5 of the Federal Trade Commission Act.[80]

---

[78] European Commission, Guidelines on horizontal cooperation (fn. 1), §398.

[79] Complaint *In the matter of U-Haul International, Inc., and AMERCO*, FTC 081 0157 (July 20, 2010).

[80] Policy Statement Regarding the Scope of Unfair Methods of Competition Under Section 5 of the Federal Trade Commission Act (Commission File No. P221202) November 10, 2022; accessible: https://www.ftc.gov/system/files/ftc_gov/pdf/P221202Section5Policy Statement.pdf.

(b) Working partnerships to achieve a competitively neutral purpose

When companies claim that they pursue goals different from colluding, it is necessary to distinguish two scenarios: In one scenario, the question is whether the collaboration is either intended to serve a purpose unrelated to competition or whether it is collusion in the guise of such collaboration. In the other scenario, the question is whether collaboration not falling in the first category restrains competition to an extent that requires legal intervention. Regarding both scenarios, EU law, on the one hand, and U.S. law and Japanese law, on the other hand, differ to varying degrees. This section deals with the first scenario while the second scenario is discussed in depth in Chapter 3.

In **EU law**, in line with the concept of "immanence" (as German lawyers call it), restraints on competition may be deemed necessary to achieve a legitimate purpose which is neutral in terms of antitrust law. Under Article 101 TFEU, collaborations of this type are considered not to "appreciably" restrain competition.[81] However, in the instances where the parties pursue an objective outside competition, it may also be necessary to discern to what extent the competition rules apply at all.[82] Thus, in sports, for example, it is first necessary to distinguish economics from sporting competition.[83] To exclude an indirect effect of sporting rules on competition, it is necessary that the parties apply those rules in an objectively transparent and non-discriminatory manner. Moreover, the competition restriction associated with the application of the rules must be directly related to and necessary for the pursuance of the legitimate objective, i.e., it must be excluded that other ways of action are available that would

---

[81] ECJ, Judgment of 13 December 2012, *Expedia* (C-226/11) ECLI:EU:C:2012:795, §§16–17; Judgment of 12 September 2000, *Pavlov and others* (C-180/98, C-181/98, C-182/98, C-183/98 and C-184/98, ECR 2000 p. I-6451) ECLI:EU:C:2000:428, §§94–97.

[82] See European Commission, Guidelines on Article 81(3) of the Treaty (fn. 3), §§17–18 with general guiding principles in that regard.

[83] ECJ, Judgment of 18 July 2006, *Meca-Medina and Majcen/Commission* (C-519/04 P, ECR 2006 p. I-6991), ECLI:EU:C:2006:492, §§22, 29–31.

burden competition less.[84] Similar principles shield collective labor agreements from the European cartel prohibition.[85]

In **U.S. law**, it is likewise accepted that activities may be excepted from the ambit of §1 Sherman Act. As a general rule, an agreement cannot be regarded as being unlawful *per se* if it is *necessary to market the product at all*.[86] Similarly, activities such as setting up a sports league, which requires a limited group of participants, are permissible since, without such restraints, the desired activity cannot take place.[87]

Japanese law expressly requires a finding of anticompetitive effect, or a substantial restriction of competition in the market, as discussed above, and an agreement concluded to achieve a competitively neutral purpose is likely to lack such effect. By definition, an agreement of that type is never a hardcore cartel and is examined on a case-by-case basis.

(c) Hub-and-spoke scenarios

In some cases, not only do competitors come together to form a cartel, but they do that with the help of suppliers or customers, or external service providers (occasionally, this is also called an A-B-C structure).[88] In these cases, one question is whether the competitors (A and B) may enter into a cartel without directly communicating with each other. Another question is whether the third party (C) may be liable as well.

(1) EU law

In cartel cases in EU law, the basic rule is that Article 101 TFEU only requires some kind of market activity by undertakings. However, Article

---

[84]European Commission, Guidelines on Article 81(3) of the Treaty (fn. 3), §18(2).

[85]ECJ, Judgment of 21 September 1999, *Albany* (C-67/96, ECR 1999 p. I-5751) ECLI:EU:C:1999:430, §§60–64.

[86]*Broadcast Music, Inc. v. CBS, Inc.*, 441 U.S. 1, 23 (1979).

[87]*National Collegiate Athletic Ass'n v. Board of Regents of the University of Oklahoma*, 468 U.S. 85, 101 (1984); *National Hockey League Players' Ass'n v. Plymouth Whalers Hockey Club*, 325 F.3 d 712, 719 (6th Cir. 2003). Furthermore, federal labor laws shield from antitrust attack an agreement among several employers who bargain together to implement after an impasse the terms of their last best good-faith wage offer. Note that in this context, the employees are not considered to be economic actors although they market their labor power.

[88]*Argos Limited v. OFT and JJB Sports v. OFT* (2006) EVCA Civ 1318, §141.

101 TFEU can be infringed regardless of whether the undertakings concerned are active in the market affected by the restrictions of competition or in any other market.[89]

Thus, **third parties** (cartel facilitators) may be liable if they participated actively and in full knowledge of the facts in the implementation or supervision of a cartel.[90] In addition, cartel members may **coordinate via a third party** if the *concerted practice at issue may be attributed to [each] undertaking using the services [because] the undertaking* <u>was aware</u> *of the anticompetitive objectives pursued by its competitors and the service provider* <u>*and intended to contribute*</u> *to them by its own conduct.* (Emphasis added.)[91]

An open question still is whether the horizontally active cartel members (A and B) must consider the third party to be an active member of the cartel itself or whether it is sufficient, e.g., that they simply buy information about the other cartel members' conduct from a disinterested third party. However, the ECJ's *Eturas* judgment may allow one to infer that it is sufficient if the horizontally active cartel members are aware that a coordination of conduct is taking place between each other.[92]

(2) U.S. law

The U.S. Supreme Court had to deal with a hub-and-spoke scenario in its landmark *Interstate Circuit* judgment.[93] This case was quite close to the scenario in the European *Eturas* case: Interstate, a movie theater operator ("exhibitor"; i.e., the "hub"), sent letters to groups of movie studios ("distributors") urging them to fix a price for second-run movies. Each letter indicated that the same letter had been sent to other distributors. The distributors complied. The Supreme Court held:

---

[89]ECJ, Judgment of 22 October 2015, *AC-Treuhand/Commission* (C-194/14 P) ECLI:EU:C:2015:717, §34.

[90]ECJ, Judgment of 22 October 2015, *AC-Treuhand/Commission* (C-194/14 P) ECLI:EU:C:2015:717, §§26, 36.

[91]ECJ, Judgment of 21 July 2016, *VM Remonts and others* (C-542/14) ECLI:EU:C:2016:578, §30; see also European Commission Guidelines on horizontal cooperation (fn. 1), §368, 401 ff.

[92]See ECJ, Judgment of 21 January 2016, *Eturas and others* (C-74/14) ECLI:EU:C:2016:42, §§43–45, esp. §44: "concertation between the travel agencies" (not between those agencies and the "administrator").

[93]U.S. law: *Interstate Circuit, Inc. v. United States*, 306 U.S. 208 (1939).

> *Acceptance by competitors, knowing that concerted action is contem-
> plated, of an invitation to participate in a plan the necessary conse-
> quence of which, if carried out, is restraint of interstate commerce is
> sufficient to establish an unlawful conspiracy under the Sherman Act.*
> (Emphasis added.)[94]

In this case, the Supreme Court found the distributors to be liable for
a violation of §1 Sherman Act. In addition, the Supreme Court held that
Interstate violated §1 and could not defend its participation in the cartel
scheme with the interest to protect its movie copyrights: *An agreement
illegal because it suppresses competition is not any less so because the
competitive article is copyrighted.* Different from the ECJ's holding cited
above, the Supreme Court only stressed that each distributor knew the
anticompetitive objectives pursued by its competitors, but it did not
equally stress that they were also aware of the exhibitor's role as the hub.
This may have been due to the fact that the exhibitor's orchestrating role
was clear in this case, anyway.

In any event, similar to what was noted in EU law, *Interstate Circuit*
is not conclusive on the role of the hub. This is because Interstate actively
orchestrated the cartel, in pursuance of its own interest in dominating the
business of its competitors. It remains unclear whether Interstate, as the
hub, would have been considered part of the cartel if it had been a disinterested third party.

(3) Japanese law

As long as participants are in a competitive relationship and communicate
their intentions and mutually restrict their business activities, the way to
achieve such a situation does not matter: the JFTC and courts will find an
unreasonable restraint of trade.[95]

---

[94] *Interstate Circuit, Inc. v. United States*, 306 U.S. 208 (1939).
[95] The JFTC Study Group on Competition Policy in Digital Markets, Algorithms/AI and
Competition Policy (March 2021) 26–27 <https://www.jftc.go.jp/en/pressreleases/
yearly-2021/March/210331004.pdf>.

V. Restraint of competition or trade

A cartel only exists if competitors collaborate in a way that restrains competition (in terms of Article 101 TFEU and AMA Article 2(6)) or trade (in terms of §1 Sherman Act).[96]

1. EU law

To fall under Article 101(1) TFEU, the coordination of the cartel members prevents competition by raising structural barriers, restricting competition through anticompetitive behavior or distorting competition by restricting it or any other way. It is generally not necessary to distinguish between these types of restraints. The term "restraint" is used here as a general and all-encompassing term.

(a) Restraints "by object" and "by effect"

In order to distinguish between the seriousness of the restraints, the restraint can be classified as "by object" or "by effect". Restraints "by object" are *types of coordination between undertakings which reveal a sufficient degree of harm to competition that it may be found that there is no need to examine their effects.*[97] These are types of restraints that are serious "by their very nature".[98] Given their *high potential of negative effects on competition, [...] it is unnecessary for the purposes of applying Article 81(1) [= Article 101(1) TFEU] to demonstrate any actual effects on the market.*[99] This includes, in particular, the restraints listed in Article 101(1) lit. a–e TFEU. The presumption of negative market effects

---

[96]Note that the term trade is used in EU law to refer to transactions of trade in goods or services whereas the term is used in U.S. law as a synonym of competition.

[97]ECJ, Judgment of 26 November 2015, *Maxima Latvija* (C-345/14) ECLI:EU:C:2015:784, §18.

[98]See ECJ, Judgment of 11 September 2014, *CB/Commission* (C-67/13 P) ECLI:EU:C:2014:2204, §50.

[99]European Commission, Guidelines on the application of Article 81(3) of the Treaty (fn. 3), §21.

in the case of a restraint "by object" means that the collaboration is always deemed to have an appreciable effect on the market (no *de-minimis* exemption!) and that an agreement or association decision including such restraints may be void in its entirety under Article 101(2) TFEU in conjunction with national law.

The list of restraints "by object" in Article 101(1) TFEU is not exclusive. Note that a restraint may only be considered as "by object" if there is *sufficiently reliable and robust experience for the view to be taken that that agreement is, by its very nature, harmful to the proper functioning of competition.* (Emphasis added.)[100] To assess whether this condition is met, the courts may not ignore *strong indications that [absent the agreement], upwards pressure on [prices] would have ensued.*[101]

The European Commission has extended the list of restraints "by object" in Article 101(1) TFEU by defining so-called **hardcore restraints** in the BERs and its Guidelines. An agreement or decision including hardcore restrictions, as defined by the European Commission, falls outside the BERs in its entirety. This, however, does not exclude an individual exemption.[102]

Restraints "by effect" are all restraints not falling into the "by object" category and not being considered to be "hardcore" restraints. *In the case of restrictions of competition by effect, there is no presumption of anti-competitive effects.*[103] Instead, the ECJ has held that *it is necessary to assess competition within the actual context in which it would occur if that agreement had not existed* (counter-factual analysis).[104] That being said, agreements producing anticompetitive effects may likewise be void in their entirety under Article 101(2) TFEU in conjunction with national law.

In cases of information exchanges, in particular, it may be questionable whether the exchange constitutes a restraint "by object" or "by effect", considering that information exchanges aiming at price collusion

---

[100]ECJ, Judgment of 2 April 2020, *Budapest Bank and others* (C-228/18) ECLI:EU:C:2020:265, §76.

[101]*Ibid.*, §§82–83.

[102]ECJ, Judgment of 29 June 2023, Super Bock Bebidas (C-211/22) ECLI:EU:C:2023:529, §37.

[103]European Commission, Guidelines on Article 81(3) of the Treaty (fn. 3), §24.

[104]ECJ, Judgment of 2 April 2020, *Budapest Bank and others* (C-228/18) ECLI:EU:C:2020:265, §55.

do not necessarily require a direct exchange of pricing information. An exchange of information related to pricing elements may be sufficient. However, the ECJ has developed a strict standard for classifying restraints as "by object". In *T-Mobile Netherlands*, it held the following:

> as to whether a concerted practice may be regarded as having an anti-competitive object even though there is <u>no direct connection between that practice and consumer prices</u>, it is <u>not possible</u> on the basis of the wording of Article 81(1) EC to conclude <u>that only concerted practices which have a direct effect on the prices paid by end users are prohibited.</u> (Emphasis added.)[105]

Good to know: Do agreements fall under Article 101(1) TFEU if they harm parties to the agreement only?

In relation to agreements to discriminate or bundle, Article 101(1) lit. d–e TFEU, it is unclear whether they must aim at harming market participants outside the agreement. That is to say, is it also a "by object" violation of Article 101 TFEU if a (potentially) dominant supplier discriminates between its customers or forces customers to accept a bundle of products or services? The general question is whether it may constitute anticompetitive conduct if one party to the agreement harms the other one. A related question was put to the ECJ in *Courage & Crehan*: In a setting where both the plaintiff and the defendant were parties to a potentially anticompetitive supply agreement, could a pub owner sue a brewery for damages? The ECJ answered this question indeed in the affirmative.[106] In U.S. law, it is unclear whether the described scenario would be considered to amount to an agreement. In Japanese law, it would not because the plaintiff pub owner would be considered rather a victim than a perpetrator. Instead, Article 19 on unfair trade practices would apply. However, it would be unclear also in this context whether the plaintiff, as a party to the agreement, could claim damages based on detriments it incurred due to the agreement.

---

[105] ECJ, Judgment of 4 June 2009, *T-Mobile Netherlands and others* (C-8/08, ECR 2009 p. I-4529) ECLI:EU:C:2009:343, §36.

[106] ECJ, Judgment of 20 September 2001, *Courage and Crehan* (C-453/99, ECR 2001 p. I-6297) ECLI:EU:C:2001:465, §§34–35.

(b) Restraints of competition and efficiencies to the consumers' benefit

Where an agreement or decision restrains competition within the meaning of Article 101(1) TFEU, it is void as a matter of principle (Article 101(2) TFEU). However, it can be exempted either *en bloc* (block exemption) or individually if it comes along with overriding benefits for consumers, meeting the criteria of Article 101(3) TFEU. Thus, in EU law, there is a clear legal separation in the assessment of anti- and procompetitive effects pursuant to Article 101(1) and (3) TFEU.

This legal separation is relevant for the burden of coming forward with evidence. Article 2 Regulation 1/2003 provides the following: *In any [...] proceedings for the application of Articles [101 and 102 TFEU], the burden of proving an infringement [...] shall rest on the party or the authority alleging the infringement. The undertaking or association of undertakings claiming the benefit of Article [101(3) TFEU] shall bear the burden of proving that the conditions of that paragraph are fulfilled.*

Moreover, the ECJ takes the legal requirements for assessing the anti-competitive and procompetitive effects of collaboration in Articles 101(1) and (3) TFEU very seriously. Therefore, the ECJ has rejected the proposal to make a general balancing already in the determination of whether there is a competition restraint: *EU competition law does not recognise a 'rule of reason', by virtue of which there should be undertaken a weighing of the pro- and anticompetitive effects of an agreement when it is to be characterised as a 'restriction of competition' under Article 101(1) TFEU.*[107]

Finally, a **public interest justification** outside Article 101(3) TFEU is not excluded, but it is only allowed within the scope of the EU Treaties. To date, such a justification has been discussed, e.g., for competition restraints intended to benefit the environment.[108] Article 106(2) TFEU contains a special exception for providers of "services of general economic interest". That exception is discussed in **Chapter 8**.

---

[107] ECJ, Judgment of 30 January 2020, *Generics (UK) and others* (C-307/18) ECLI:EU:C:2020:52, §104.

[108] See Monopolies Commission, Symposium 40. Jahre Monopolkommission, conference report, 1st ed., 2014.

2. U.S. law

Although the language of §1 of the Sherman Act may seem to prohibit all agreements *in restraint of trade or commerce among the several States, or with foreign nations*, it actually only condemns unreasonable restraint of trade. Reasonableness is assessed in light of the effect on competition, and only agreements that suppress competition are condemned.[109] Thus, the U.S. courts need to determine whether the agreement has anti- or pro-competitive effects.[110] Still, an agreement *formed for the purpose and with the effect of raising, depressing, fixing, pegging, or stabilizing the price of a commodity in interstate or foreign commerce is illegal per se.*[111] On the other hand, the agreement is considered lawful if the agreement promotes competition.[112]

Over time, the U.S. courts have developed *two complementary categories of antitrust analysis.*[113] Certain types of conduct are considered to be harmful and to lack a procompetitive justification to such a degree that they are conclusively presumed to be illegal.[114] These types of conduct are called *per se* violations and cannot be justified in case of horizontal collusion. *It is only after considerable experience with certain business relationships that courts classify them as per se* illegal.[115] At the time of writing, *per se* violations include naked horizontal price-fixing, output limitation, bid rigging and market division. The restraints of trade subject to the *per se* rule overlap with EU restraints "by object" and types of horizontal agreements that are generally assumed to substantially restrict competition to a large extent.

---

[109] *Chicago Board of Trade v. United States*, 246 U.S. 231, 238 (1918).

[110] *Ibid.*; *Standard Oil Co. of New Jersey v. United States*, 221 U.S. 1 (1911).

[111] *United States v. Socony-Vacuum Oil Co., Inc.*, 310 U.S. 150, 223 (1940).

[112] *National Soc'y of Prof. Engineers v. United States*, 435 U.S. 679, 691 (1978); *Polk Brothers v. Forest City Enters.*, 776 F.2d 185 (7th Cir. 1985).

[113] *National Soc'y of Prof. Engineers*, 453 U.S., 692 (1978).

[114] See *United States v. Socony-Vacuum Oil Co., Inc.*, 310 U.S. 150 (1940), 310 U.S. 150; *Northern Pacific R. Co. v. United States*, 356 U.S. 1 (1958).

[115] *United States v. Topco Assocs., Inc.*, 405 U.S. 596, 607–608 (1972).

> ## Good to know: The case law on group boycotts
>
> A notable difference between U.S. and Japanese law, on the one hand, and EU law, on the other hand, is the treatment of "group boycotts". In the U.S. and Japan, a group boycott is assumed if two or more firms conspire to restrict the ability of another firm to compete (concerted refusal to deal). In **U.S. law**, a group boycott falls into the *per se* category but — different from, e.g., price fixing — only if market power exists.[116] According to *Nynex Corp. v. Discon, Inc.*, the group boycott must also be based on a direct agreement between competitors.[117] Finally, §1 Sherman Act is not violated if the conspiracy is justified. In **Japan**, group boycotts are an important category of joint violations besides cartels and may be captured as private monopolization, unfair trade practices or unreasonable restraints of trade. Although no *per se* violation for group boycotts exists, these practices are presumed to be anticompetitive.
>
> In **EU law**, the category of group boycott is virtually **non-existent** as a separate category under Articles 101 and 102 TFEU (although collective boycotts are considered to fall into the "by object" category, and the issue has been raised in individual cartel cases).[118] Yet, **Member States** are free to create their own rules on boycott; for instance, §21(1) of the German Competition Code prohibits undertakings from requesting other undertakings to "refuse to supply to or purchase from certain undertakings, with the intention of unfairly impeding these undertakings". This provision has not played a substantial role in many cases to date.

In other cases, the "rule of reason" standard applies, meaning that the *competitive effect can only be evaluated by analyzing the facts peculiar to the business, the history of the restraint, and the reasons why it*

---

[116] *FTC v. Indiana Fed'n of Dentists*, 476 U.S. 447, 458 (1986).

[117] *Nynex Corp. v. Discon, Inc.*, 525 U.S. 198 (1998) (direct agreement). Note that in *FTC v. Indiana Federation of Dentists*, 476 U.S. 447, 459–61 (1986), the Supreme Court treated an agreement between several suppliers and a customer interested in the same way (but under a rule of reason standard).

[118] See, e.g., ECJ, Judgment of 28 June 2005, Dansk Rørindustri and others/Commission (C-189/02 P, C-202/02 P, C-205/02 P to C-208/02 P and C-213/02 P, ECR 2005 p. I-5425) ECLI:EU:C:2005:408, §§146 ff. and European Commission, Guidance on restrictions of competition "by object" (fn. 4), §2.5.

was imposed.[119] Depending on these, the court may reach the conclusion that the restraint actually enhances competition.

In some cases, the courts also apply an abbreviated (or, quick-look) rule-of-reason analysis (middle standard), under which they *can determine the competitive effects of a challenged restraint in the 'twinkling of an eye'.*[120] Such an abbreviated analysis may be used if *an observer with even a rudimentary understanding of economics could conclude that the arrangements in question would have an anticompetitive effect on customers and markets* or if *the great likelihood of anticompetitive effects can easily be ascertained*[121] or the restraints at issue are *so obviously incapable of harming competition that they require little scrutiny.*[122]

When a restraint of trade is found, on principle, the rule-of-reason standard allows for a justification (in both cases of a full or abbreviated analysis alike). As factors offsetting the restraint, it is possible to take into account procompetitive or efficiency-enhancing effects. Other justifications, particularly the assertion that the competition is ill-suited to achieve a social goal, are unlikely to be recognized. In the U.S., considering that *[t]he statutory policy precludes inquiry into the question whether competition is good or bad,*[123] the *'orderly way' to temper that [Sherman] Act's policy of competition is 'by legislation and not by court decision'.*[124]

3. Japanese law

(a) Unreasonable restraint of trade (AMA Articles 2(6) and 3)

AMA Article 2(6) does **not** have a *per se* concept, and the JFTC must demonstrate the effect of substantial restriction of competition in a

---

[119] *National Soc'y of Prof. Engineers v. United States*, 435 U.S. 679, 692 (1978).

[120] *National Collegiate Athletic Assn. v. Alson*, 594 U.S. (2021); *FTC v. Indiana Federation of Dentists*, 476 U.S. 447, 459 (1986).

[121] *California Dental Ass'n v. FTC*, 526 U.S. 756 (1999) (which limits the application of the quick-look rule to cases where anticompetitive effects are obvious to people who have only a rudimentary understanding of economics).

[122] *National Collegiate Athletic Assn. v. Alson*, 594 U.S. (2021).

[123] *National Soc'y of Prof. Engineers.*

[124] *National Collegiate Athletic Assn. v. Alson*, 594 U.S. (2021).

particular field of trade in every case. However, the decisional practices at the JFTC and courts differ between a horizontal agreement that is very likely to have an anticompetitive effect without any redeeming virtue (called hardcore cartels) and other types of horizontal collaborations. The former include price fixing, output limitation, market allocation and bid rigging. For these, the **relevant market** is defined based on the product and the geographic scope of the agreement. Typically, participants collectively have more than 50% in such a "market" and are thus considered to have market power. Additionally, outsiders (non-participants) follow the lead of cartelists and also increase the prices. Such an effect is enough to prove a substantial restriction of competition, which is understood to mean the establishment, maintenance and enhancement of market power. By definition, such activities lack any procompetitive justification; if they have any, it is no longer a question of a hardcore cartel and is dealt with as other types of horizontal collaborations.

AMA Article 2(6) also requires that the enterprise's action be **contrary to public interest**. This is interpreted to mean the competitive economic order in general, yet it may encompass the broader interest of general consumers as well as the benevolent impact on the wholesome growth of the national economy. The Japan Supreme Court announced that, once such broader interest or impact is shown, it would balance that broader interest or impact and the competitive effects against each other.[125] However, the courts have never concluded that a hardcore cartel is justified in light of such broader societal interests at the time of writing.

(b) Trade associations (AMA Article 8)

AMA Article 8(i) requires a substantial restriction of competition in a relevant market. When price fixing, output limitation, market allocation and bid rigging occur within a trade association, the effect will be analyzed in the **same manner as in a hardcore cartel**. Even if the market share is extremely small, or the trade association's coordination fails to cause any substantial effect, AMA Article 8(iii) or (iv) would still apply.

---

[125] Supreme Court, Judgment of February 24, 1984, 38-IV Keishu 1287 (*Oil Cartel [Criminal]*).

4. Comparison

In all three jurisdictions covered in this book, the most important part of the competition analysis is about whether the relevant coordination is prohibited due to its **(likely) contribution to a collusive market outcome**. Depending on the market, various factors may increase or decrease the likelihood of such a collusive outcome. The jurisdictions covered in this book use different concepts to distinguish the relevant cases.

Regarding the question of when there is a **restraint of competition or trade**, all three jurisdictions generally require a case-specific analysis of market effects. At the same time, they prohibit price fixing, output limitation, market allocation and bid rigging given the great likelihood of serious harm to competition and — to a varying degree — limit the requirement of an in-depth analysis in these cases. According to the case law, other types of conduct may fall into this category of strictly prohibited behavior in individual jurisdictions as well. Moreover, particularly U.S. law finely adapts the assessment standard under its "rule of reason" depending on how likely the relevant coordination is to lead to a collusive market outcome. The EU approach is more formal in that regard, whereas Japan follows the U.S. example.

Major differences exist when it comes to taking into account **potentially justifying factors**. Here, U.S. law requires a balancing of anti- and procompetitive factors under the rule of reason. That is to say, a (prohibited) restraint of trade can only be found if the anticompetitive factors outbalance the procompetitive ones. Moreover, U.S. law only leaves limited scope for other potential grounds for justification. In EU law, the TFEU provides an explicit framework for the analysis of procompetitive factors, leaving no room for a general balancing exercise. That said, it can be assumed that the results of the assessment under EU law will often come close to those under U.S. law. A public interest justification is possible under EU law but only within the ambit of the EU Treaties. Japanese law again generally follows the U.S. approach but also has a fleshed-out public interest exception in the law.

VI. Explicit *v.* tacit (implicit) collusion

Depending on the market situation, the products involved and other factors, it may not be necessary for companies to collude explicitly. Instead, it may be possible to reach the same market outcome implicitly, i.e., by each company adapting silently to the market. Such tacit collusion does not meet the requirement of coordination within the meaning of Article 101 TFEU, §1 Sherman Act or Article 2(6) AMA. However, it may constitute a violation of the rules on abusive conduct at least in the EU (Article 102 TFEU). Both in the U.S. and Japan, it would not be captured by §2 Sherman Act and Article 2(5).

Good to know: Do computer algorithms collude tacitly?

Algorithms are instructions in the form of a program code that solves certain problems. The algorithms used in e-commerce can serve as tools to derive information from large amounts of data that could not be obtained using conventional methods. More specifically, merchants on online platforms can employ pricing algorithms to analyze the pricing behavior of competitors beyond the level of transparency which is available in conventional markets. It has been argued that pricing algorithms can facilitate collusion and that this collusion may even not be explicit but rather tacit collusion in many cases. Hence, a debate has arisen about whether the competition rules should be modified to better tackle the specific competition problems associated with pricing algorithms.

While it is true that collusion in e-commerce is difficult to demonstrate due to the fast-moving nature of online markets, it may be questioned whether the algorithms require additional specific rules. This is because the algorithms are mere tools to analyze pricing patterns and to implement pricing decisions. Behind the algorithm, there is always a traditional market participant deciding to use the algorithm. If that is taken into consideration, the algorithm should not be regarded differently from pens and paper used for a traditional cartel arrangement.

---

1. The rules

(a) EU law

In EU law, the ECJ's jurisprudence provides guidance on how to distinguish explicit and tacit collusion. In *ICI*, a judgment addressing this issue, the ECJ held that market behavior restricts competition through anticompetitive coordination within the meaning of **Article 101 TFEU** if

*by the way in which they ac[t], the undertakings [...] **eliminat[e]** with
respect to prices **some of the preconditions** for competition on the market
which [stand] in the way of the achievement of parallel uniformity of
conduct.* (Emphasis added.)[126]

Thus, the companies involved may not have agreed on any **tampering
with the market forces**. However, in *Suiker Unie*, another case dealing
with a similar scenario, the ECJ made clear that *[...] this requirement of
independence does not deprive economic operators of the right to adapt
themselves intelligently to the existing and anticipated conduct of their
competitors [...].* (Emphasis added.)[127] Thus, even (tacit) collusion of
firms adapting themselves intelligently (and unilaterally) to the market
would not be captured by Article 101 TFEU.

However, where several firms engage in individual behavior leading
to a collusive market outcome, this behavior could still be found to violate
Article 102 TFEU. This would be the case where there is a joint abuse of
dominant positions in an oligopoly situation. In *Compagnie maritime
belge transports*, the ECJ set out how several firms may be regarded as
enjoying a **joint dominant position**. It held the following:

> *a dominant position may be held by two or more economic entities
> legally independent of each other, provided that from an economic point
> of view they present themselves or act together on a particular market
> as a **collective entity**. [...] In order to establish the existence of [such]
> collective entity [...], it is necessary to examine the **economic links** or
> factors which give rise to a connection between the undertakings con-
> cerned [and] **which enable them to act together independently of their
> competitors, their customers and consumers**.* (Emphasis added.)[128]

The Court also held that the existence of an agreement within the
meaning of Article 101 TFEU is not decisive in this context, although
such an agreement may contribute to the links that are relevant under

---

[126]ECJ, Judgment of 14 July 1972, *ICI/Commission* (48/69, ECR 1972 p. 619)
ECLI:EU:C:1972:70, §103.

[127]ECJ Judgment of 16 December 1975, *Suiker Unie and others/Commission* (40 to 48, 50,
54 to 56, 111, 113 and 114–73, ECR 1975 p. 1663) ECLI:EU:C:1975:174, §174.

[128]ECJ, Judgment of 16 March 2000, *Compagnie Maritime Belge Transports and others/
Commission* (C-395/96 P and C-396/96 P, ECR 2000 p. I-1365) ECLI:EU:C:2000:132,
§§36, 41–44.

Article 102 TFEU.[129] Additional criteria for analyzing the economic links or factors giving rise to a connection between the undertakings concerned have been set out in the Commission's Horizontal Merger Guidelines.[130]

Furthermore, regarding the potentially abusive behavior, the ECJ held, again in *Compagnie maritime belge transports,* that abuse may occur if the relevant **conduct strengthens that position structurally** in such a way *that the degree of dominance reached substantially fetters competition.* This may be the case where the relevant firms *eliminat[e] the only means of competition (**exclusionary** aspect), thus allowing the firms to require [their] users to pay higher prices for the services which are not threatened by that competition (**exploitative** aspect).*[131]

(b) U.S. and Japanese law

A meeting of minds and the communication of intentions are necessary in the U.S. and Japan. As noted earlier, such a state of mind could be achieved by any means and this can be inferred through circumstantial evidence which may include information exchanges, plus factors and price increases as explained earlier.

Beyond that, U.S. and Japanese law diverge substantially from EU law when it comes to tacit collusion where there is no way to find a meeting of minds or the communication of intentions. This is particularly true for Japanese law. In Japan, the communication of intentions and mutual restrictive elements clearly indicate that a parallel price increase alone does not constitute an AMA infringement. Indeed, the AMA once had special reporting rules to address parallel price increases caused by an oligopolistic market situation. Under the system, an enterprise was obliged to inform the JFTC of the price increase in advance when it raised its prices following its competitors' increase. The system was considered

---

[129]ECJ, Judgment of 16 March 2000, *Compagnie Maritime Belge Transports and others/ Commission* (C-395/96 P and C-396/96 P, ECR 2000 p. I-1365) ECLI:EU:C:2000:132, §§43–44.

[130]European Commission, Guidelines on the assessment of horizontal mergers under the Council Regulation on the control of concentrations between undertakings, OJ C 31, 5 February 2004, p. 5, §§39 ff. (on coordinated effects).

[131]ECJ, Judgment of 16 March 2000, *Compagnie Maritime Belge Transports and others/ Commission* (C-395/96 P and C-396/96 P, ECR 2000 p. I-1365) ECLI:EU:C:2000:132, §§113, 117. See also Chapter 4, Section VI on the potentially anticompetitive conduct.

ineffective, lacking any deterrent effect and instead merely burdening the enterprises and the JFTC. For these reasons, it was abolished.[132]

In the U.S., the Supreme Court has constantly held that **parallel behavior** does **not constitute an agreement in terms of §1 Sherman Act**.[133] However, an agreement may be found if the actions are contrary to the individual interests of the actors.[134] The application of **§2 Sherman Act to oligopolies** has likewise remained controversial. §2 Sherman Act requires the willful acquisition and maintenance of monopoly power or such dangerous probability (see Chapter 4, Sections II.2 and III.2). The prevailing view is that "**shared monopoly**" **power does not provide a cause of action** for an antitrust offense. The U.S. courts have consistently rejected the "shared monopoly" theory and held that *a firm can only be liable for monopolization [...] where it can monopolize the relevant market while acting on its own*.[135]

The idea that an oligopoly could **conspire to violate §2** remains controversial as well.[136] The conspiracy to monopolize under §2 Sherman Act is possible under basically the same conditions as a conspiracy under §1 Sherman Act. In addition, §2 requires an "overt act" in furtherance of the conspiracy.[137] However, *§2 Sherman Act [...] applies to the conduct of single firms only rather than to the conduct of a small number of firms engaged in tacit collusion*.[138] Thus, also a "conspiracy" theory of harm in terms of §2 cannot specifically be used to address oligopoly conduct.

---

[132] *Shiteki dokusen no kinshi oyobi kôsei torihiki no kakuhô ni kansuru hôritsu no ichibu o kaisei suru hôritsu* [Act to Partially Amend the Act on Prohibition of Private Monopolization and Maintenance of Fair Trade], Law No. 35/2005.

[133] *Williamson Oil v. Philip Morris USA*, 346 F.3d 1287 (11th Cir. 2003); *Reserve Supply Corp. v. Owens-Corning Fiberglas Corp.*, 971 F.2d 37, 50 (7th Cir. 1992).

[134] *Interstate Circuit, Inc.*, 306 U.S. 208, 59 S. Ct. 467 (1939).

[135] *Foam Supplies, Inc. v. The Dow Chemical Co.*, 2008–1 Trade Case. (CCH) ¶ 76027, 2007 WL 4210354 (E.D. Mo. 2007); as quoted in: Robinson/Koley, Antitrust enforcement against oligopolies, October 2019, fn. 73.

[136] Robinson/Koley, Antitrust enforcement against oligopolies, October 2019, p. 13.

[137] *American Key Corp. v. Cole Nat'l Corp.*, 762 F.2d 1569, 1579 n. 8 (11th Cir. 1985); *Todorov v. DCH Healthcare Authority*, 921 F.2d 1438, 1460 (11th Cir. 1991).

[138] *ID Security Systems Canada, Inc. v. Checkpoint Systems, Inc.*, 249 F. Supp. 2d 622, 649 (E.D. Pa. 2003), as quoted in: Robinson/Koley, Antitrust enforcement against oligopolies, October 2019, fn. 73.

This rigid interpretation of §2 Sherman Act makes sense, considering that monopolization within the meaning of the law requires exclusionary conduct and not the (joint) exploitation of consumers.

2. The factual issue: Information flows in the market

The issue of tacit collusion may arise where the market situation contributes to such an extent to a collusive outcome that it is not necessary for competitors to collude explicitly. Particularly the market structure is of great importance in this context. As the European Commission noted in its Guidelines on horizontal concentrations:

> *In some markets the <u>structure</u> may be such that firms would consider it possible, economically rational, and hence preferable, to adopt on a sustainable basis a course of action on the market aimed at selling at increased prices. <u>[F]irms [may be] able to</u> coordinate their behaviour in this way and <u>raise prices, even without entering into an agreement or resorting to a concerted practice</u> within the meaning of Article [101 TFEU].* (Emphasis added.)[139]

Thus, the question under the cartel provisions is when information readily available in the market is likely to further coordination through individual conduct, and when firms will resort to (explicit) cartelization. The question of cartelization can come up specifically when firms exchange information actively with each other, potentially even without agreeing on specific market conduct.

(a) The EU approach

In the EU, the assessment of information exchanges under the rules for concerted practices has been a topic of hot debate. This has not been with a view to distinguishing explicit and implicit collusion. Rather, it has proved to be difficult to distinguish pro- and anticompetitive information

---

[139]European Commission, Guidelines on the assessment of horizontal mergers under the Council Regulation on the control of concentrations between undertakings, OJ C 31, 5 February 2004, p. 5, §39.

exchanges. Therefore, the European Commission has published guide-lines setting out which factors are relevant for the assessment, whether an information exchange amounts to a concerted practice restraining competition and whether the restraint is of a type that is unlikely to benefit from a procompetitive justification. In its Guidelines on horizontal cooperation, the Commission explained that such a risk exists if the information is, in the eyes of the competitors, commercially sensitive (i.e., "strategic") because its exchange allows one to draw inferences on an individual competitor's future market behavior.[140] That type of risk may be obvious, for example, when the parties share information relating to future prices or individual customers.

In other cases, and in line with the above, the Commission's Guidelines require practitioners to consider also the likely effect on competition, depending on the market structure, the information value and the characteristics of the exchange. In that regard, the Guidelines on horizontal cooperation overlap with the previously mentioned Guidelines on horizontal concentrations. In those Guidelines, the Commission explained that market structure characteristics (e.g., high or low market concentration or more or less homogeneous goods) are important because coordination is more likely in markets where it is relatively simple to reach a common understanding on the terms of coordination. In addition, however, coordination must be sustainable. Whether this is the case depends on three conditions: (i) the ability for firms to monitor coordination, (ii) the existence of a credible deterrent mechanism for deviations and (iii) the fact that reactions of outsiders should not jeopardize the results of coordination.

Thus, market transparency proves to be one of the deciding market characteristics when it comes to distinguishing explicit and tacit collusion. This is because the competitors' ability to monitor coordination depends on the quality of relevant data and surrounding information and the quantity of available information flows. If market transparency is high, firms may collude tacitly because it does not make commercial sense to deviate from a common course of conduct (assuming that deterrence mechanisms are available). If market transparency is not high enough, firms may decide to collude explicitly to remove the last obstacles to their coordination.

---

[140] European Commission, Guidelines on horizontal cooperation (fn. 1), §§366 ff.

(b) The U.S. and Japanese approaches

The U.S. Supreme Court has approached the issue from a different angle. In its jurisprudence, the Court proceeded from the rule that an agreement on prices (price fixing) is a *per se* violation under §1 Sherman Act. In contrast to that, it held the following: *The dissemination of price information is not itself a per se violation of the Sherman Act.*[141] The confidential reciprocal exchange of most recent prices charged or quoted to identified customers may permit an inference of a price-fixing agreement, but this is useful to prove the anticompetitive conspiracy and only under limited circumstances such that the following are present: (i) The exchange involves a fungible product in a highly concentrated industry, (ii) the exchange has a "chilling" effect on the vigor of price competition and (iii) no lawful "controlling circumstances" are present, such as the parties' interest to prevent buyers' fraud.[142]

Similarly, in Japan, sharing information may be useful to demonstrate the existence of a hardcore cartel (see Section V.3 in this chapter) but is rarely condemned on its own. The JFTC Trade Association Guidelines explain that information exchange may restrain competition where it enables competitors to *mutually predict the specific contents of such important competition-related factors as pricing concerning present or future business activities.*[143]

The U.S. approach to the issue of tacit collusion appears in fact in line with the approach in the EU: The Supreme Court pays attention primarily to the structure of the market and the products traded there; it considers the transparency of the market and potential of deterrence by requiring a "chilling effect" and excludes additional factors that are not relevant for the assessment. The main difference to EU law is that the Supreme Court requires proof of a chilling market "effect", which is more demanding than the required proof of a credible deterrent mechanism in EU law.

---

[141] *Northwest Wholesale Stationers, Inc. v. Pacific Stationery & Printing Co.*, 472 U.S. 284 (1985).

[142] *United States v. Container Corp.*, 393 U.S. 333 (1969).

[143] JFTC, Guidelines Concerning the Activities of Trade Associations under the Antimonopoly Act (1995, last amended 2020).

Good to know: Gas stations — Explicit collusion, tacit collusion or nothing?

In the EU and the U.S., gas retail is a frequently cited example of a market where it is unclear whether collusion takes place. As a general matter, the distribution chain for gasoline is marked by few suppliers and a high level of vertical integration. The market is concentrated at the level of refinement (production), wholesale (distribution) and retail (gas stations). Moreover, the quality of information flows between competitors is high due to homogeneous products and price columns (high market transparency). Likewise, the quantity of information flows is high due to structural links and many interactions between suppliers. For these reasons, it is unclear whether companies adapt intelligently to the market or coordinate market conduct. In a merger proceeding concerning the East German market, the involved parties argued that they were competing on quality but that they avoided price advances to prevent a downward price spiral. Indeed, a factor potentially indicating competition is that gas retail prices are not stable. Instead, gas stations constantly adjust their prices, sometimes several times a day.

Chapter 3

Other Collaboration

I. The law

The main relevant statutory provisions covered in this chapter are the same as for horizontal collusion in the EU and the U.S., while they are mostly different in Japan. In the EU, other types of collaboration subject to Article 101 TFEU and in the U.S. to §1 Sherman Act, regardless of whether it is collusive or not. That being said, when it comes to applying the rules in relation to agreements between two companies active at different levels in the supply chain (vertical agreements), particular attention must be placed on the finding of coordinated conduct meeting the requirements of Article 101(1) TFEU or §1 Sherman Act because unilateral behavior is not captured by these rules. In Japan, in contrast, horizontal cooperation is subject to AMA Articles 2(6) and 3, as in the case of horizontal collusion. Meanwhile, vertical agreements are mostly dealt with under AMA Articles 2(9) and 19, which regulate unfair trade practices.

Moreover, the rules for justifying a potential restraint of competition or trade under Article 101(3) TFEU, §1 Sherman Act and the relevant provisions of AMA differ considerably from the rules applied in the context of horizontal collusion.

1. EU law

In the EU, the following additional rules apply for the block exemption or individual exemption of agreements under Article 101(3) TFEU:

- Regarding horizontal cooperation agreements in the field of **Research and Development (R&D)**: Council Regulation No. 2821/71[1] regarding the scope of any Commission Regulation on that matter; Commission Regulation (EU) 2023/1066 on R&D (R&D Block Exemption Regulation — BER)[2]; particularly regarding individual exemptions: Horizontal Cooperation Guidelines (§§51 ff., 523–524 ff., 111 ff.).[3]
- Regarding horizontal cooperation agreements with the purpose of **specialization**: Council Regulation No. 2821/71 regarding the scope of any Commission Regulation on that matter[4]; Commission Regulation (EU) 2023/1067 (Specialization BER)[5]; particularly regarding individual exemptions: Horizontal Cooperation Guidelines (§§187 ff., 523–524).
- Regarding **vertical agreements (in general)**: Council Regulation No. 19/65/EEC, as amended by Council Regulation (EC) No. 1215/1999 (regarding the scope of any Commission Regulation on that matter)[6];

---

[1] Council Regulation No. 2821/71 on application of Article 85(3) [now 81(3)] of the Treaty to categories of agreements, decisions and concerted practices, OJ L 285, 29 December 1971 p. 46; accessible: https://eur-lex.europa.eu/legal-content/EN/ALL/?uri=CELEX:31971R2821.

[2] Commission Regulation No. (EU) 2023/1066 of 1 June 2023 on the application of Article 101(3) of the Treaty on the functioning of the European Union to certain categories of research and development agreements, OJ L 143, 2 June 2023, p. 9.

[3] See fn. 1 in Chapter 2.

[4] See fn. 1 above.

[5] Commission Regulation (EU) 2023/1067 of 1 June 2023 on the application of Article 101(3) of the Treaty on the Functioning of the European Union to certain categories of specialisation agreements, OJ L 143, 2 June 2023, p. 20.

[6] Council Regulation No. 19/65/EEC of 2 March 1965 on application of Article 85(3) of the Treaty to certain categories of agreements and concerted practices, OJ 36, 6 March 1965, p. 533; accessible: https://eur-lex.europa.eu/legal-content/EN/ALL/?uri=CELEX:31965R0019; as amended by Council Regulation (EC) No. 1215/1999 of 10 June 1999 amending Regulation No. 19/65/EEC on the application of Article 81(3) of the Treaty to certain categories of agreements and concerted practices, OJ L 148,

Commission Regulation (EU) 2022/720 (replacing Commission Regulation 330/2010; Vertical BER)[7]; Guidelines on vertical restraints.[8]

- Regarding **licensing agreements for the transfer of technology**: Commission Regulation (EU) No. 316/2014 (TTBER)[9] and the Guidelines for the assessment of technology transfer agreements (TT Guidelines).[10]
- Regarding **standardization** agreements and standard terms: Horizontal Cooperation Guidelines (§§436 ff.).[11]
- Particularly regarding **individual exemptions**: Guidelines on the application of Article 81(3) of the Treaty (§§1–12, 32 ff.).[12]

In addition, rules exist for the distribution of **motor vehicles** (BER),[13] and regarding the application of the competition and market-related rules

---

15 June 1999, p. 1; accessible: https://eur-lex.europa.eu/legal-content/EN/ALL/?uri=CELEX:31999R1215.

[7]Commission Regulation (EU) 2022/720 of 10 May 2022 on the application of Article 101(3) of the Treaty on the Functioning of the European Union to categories of vertical agreements and concerted practices (VBER); accessible: https://eur-lex.europa.eu/legal-content/EN/TXT/?uri=CELEX%3A32022R0720&qid=1652368074897. The Regulation succeeds Reg. 330/2010 and is accompanied by revised Guidelines (Ch. 2 fn. 1); on the history of the current rules, see generally also European Commission, Review of the VBER and the Vertical Guidelines, htps://hbfm.link/111317.

[8]European Commission, Guidelines on vertical restraints; accessible: https://ec.europa.eu/competition-policy/system/files/2022-05/20220510_guidelines_vertical_restraints_art101_TFEU_.pdf.

[9]Commission Regulation (EU) No. 316/2014 of 21 March 2014 on the application of Article 101(3) of the Treaty on the Functioning of the European Union to categories of technology transfer agreements (TTBER), OJ L93, 28 March 2014, p. 17; accessible: https://eur-lex.europa.eu/legal-content/EN/TXT/?uri=uriserv:OJ.L_.2014.093 January 0017 January ENG.

[10]Communication from the Commission — Guidelines on the application of Article 101 of the Treaty on the Functioning of the European Union to technology transfer agreements (Guidelines), OJ C89, 28 March 2014, p. 3; accessible: https://eur-lex.europa.eu/legal-content/EN/TXT/?uri=uriserv:OJ.C_.2014.089 January 0003 January ENG.

[11]See fn. 1 in Chapter 2.

[12]See fn. 3 in Chapter 2.

[13]Commission Regulation (EU) No. 461/2010 of 27 May 2010 on the application of Article 101(3) of the Treaty on the Functioning of the European Union to categories of vertical agreements and concerted practices in the motor vehicle sector, OJ L 129,

in **sectors subject to special regulation** under the TFEU (agricultural and food, insurance, postal services, professional services, telecommunications and transport).[14] These sector-specific rules are not covered in any more detail in this book.

2. U.S. law

In the U.S., §1 Sherman Act is complemented by §3 Clayton Act (15 U.S.C. §14) for instances of non-collusive vertical agreements (e.g., for tying cases):

> *It shall be unlawful for any person engaged in commerce, in the course of such commerce, to lease or make a sale or contract for sale of goods, wares, merchandise, machinery, supplies, or other commodities, whether patented or unpatented, for use, consumption, or resale within the United States or any Territory thereof or the District of Columbia or any insular possession or other place under the jurisdiction of the United States, or fix a price charged therefor, or discount from, or rebate upon, such price, on the condition, agreement, or understanding that the lessee or purchaser thereof shall not use or deal in the goods, wares, merchandise, machinery, supplies, or other commodities of a competitor or competitors of the lessor or seller, where the effect of such lease, sale, or contract for sale or such condition, agreement, or understanding may be to substantially lessen competition or tend to create a monopoly in any line of commerce.*

Moreover, the following **additional guidance** exists to help the assessment of agreements and set out safety zones under §1 Sherman Act:

- Antitrust Guidelines for **collaboration among competitors**,
- Antitrust Guidelines for the Licensing of **Intellectual Property**.

The Statements of Antitrust Enforcement Policy in **Health Care** were withdrawn in 2023 as both the DOJ and the FTC considered them to be outdated.

---

28 May 2010, p. 52; accessible: https://eur-lex.europa.eu/legal-content/EN/ALL/?uri=CELEX:32010R0461.

[14] See: https://ec.europa.eu/competition-policy/antitrust/legislation/block-exemption-regulations_en.

3. Japanese law

Horizontal collaborative agreements are subject to AMA Articles 2(6) and 3 where the parties are enterprises. Where collaboration takes place within a trade association, that association is subject to AMA Article 8. Although AMA Articles 2(6) and 3 do not distinguish between **horizontal and vertical agreements** expressly, these types of collaboration are **dealt with differently**. Vertical agreements are subject to AMA Article 2(9) and Article 19, which regulate a series of practices termed unfair trade practices. Unfair trade practices are defined under AMA Article 2(9)(i)–(v) and designated by the JFTC as such under AMA Article 2(9)(iv), which encompasses vertical restraints and agreements, unilateral actions to exclude competitors or exploit trading partners as well as misleading practices. In relation to vertical agreements, the following provisions are most relevant.

AMA Article 2(9)
The term "unfair trade practices" as used in this Act means an act falling under any of the following items:

AMA Article 2(9)(iv) [Resale Price Maintenance]
Supplying goods to another party who purchases the relevant goods from oneself while imposing, without justifiable grounds, one of the restrictive terms listed below:

(a) *causing the party to maintain the selling price of the goods that one has determined, or otherwise restricting the party's free decision on the selling price of the goods,*
(b) *having the party cause an enterprise that purchases the goods from the party maintain the selling price of the goods that one has determined, or otherwise causing the party to restrict the relevant enterprise's free decision on the selling price of the goods.*

The AMA delegates to the JFTC the power to designate the Unfair Trade Practices (AMA Article 2(9)(vi)), which include the following:

JFTC General Designation Para. 11
Unjustly trading with another party on condition that the said party shall not trade with a competitor, thereby tending to reduce trading opportunities for the said competitor.

JFTC General Designation Para. 12
In addition to any act falling under the provisions of Article 2, paragraph (9), item (iv) of the Act and the preceding paragraph, trading with another party on conditions which unjustly restrict any trade between the said party and its other transacting party or other business activities of the said party.

The JFTC constantly issues and revises the guidelines to help businesses assess whether their actions would constitute an AMA violation. Outside specific sectors, the most important of these are as follows:

- Guidelines Concerning the **Activities of Trade Associations under the Antimonopoly Act** (1995, revised 2020),
- Guidelines Concerning **Joint Activities for Recycling** under the Antimonopoly Act (2001),
- Guidelines for the **Use of Intellectual Property** under the Antimonopoly Act (2007, revised 2016),
- Guidelines on **Standardization and Patent Pool Arrangements** (2005),
- Guidelines Concerning **Joint Research and Development** under the Antimonopoly Act (1993),
- Guidelines Concerning **Distribution Systems and Business Practices** (1991, revised 2017).

II. Non-collusive collaboration and liability

Companies collaborate not only to jointly raise prices or reduce output but also to achieve other business goals. These other forms of collaboration are often legitimate and generally viewed favorably from an economic standpoint. However, exceptions requiring a closer assessment do exist. One exception is *Agreements that [...] create or increase market power or facilitate its exercise*; another one consists in agreements that *reduce the ability or incentive to compete independently*.[15] The main reason for these exceptions is that increases in market power or the reduced capacity of others to compete may raise the risk of or facilitate collusive practices.

Although the need to distinguish anticompetitive and procompetitive collaboration or restriction is recognized in all jurisdictions covered in this book, the approaches to other types of collaboration diverge to a much

---

[15] See FTC/DOJ, Antitrust Guidelines for Collaborations Among Competitors (Ch. 2, fn. 10), §3.31.

greater extent than for explicit horizontal collusion. This is at least partly due to the fact that Article 101 TFEU requires practitioners to distinguish in the assessment between the anti- and the procompetitive aspects of the collaboration. In contrast, §1 Sherman Act and AMA only provide for a combined analysis under a review standard that is, however, tightened the more likely the collaboration is to produce an anticompetitive market outcome. Further complications relate to Japanese practices, which apply a different set of rules to vertical collaborations.

III. Agreements considered to not even restrain competition

When companies claim that they pursue goals different from colluding (and do not merely collude under the guise of pursuing such goals),[16] the general question is whether the collaboration restrains competition to an extent that requires legal intervention. In dealing with this issue, **EU law defines certain categories** where companies may show that they meet the defined criteria to evade a competition analysis altogether. In **U.S. and Japanese law**, the collaboration meeting these criteria would generally be assessed under the **"rule of reason"** standard. In this section, we discuss the most prominent examples where this divergence can be seen.

1. Agreements not restricting competition (in all jurisdictions)

Thus, in EU law, companies may argue that their agreement may — depending on the circumstances — be considered to not even restrain competition within the meaning of Article 101(1) TFEU. This is accepted, e.g., for competition restraints covering such a small fraction of the market that they may be considered to restrain competition not "appreciably" (*de minimis* **restraints**).[17] Another important example of agreements excepted from Article 101(1) TFEU are certain distribution agreements. This is because suppliers may have an interest in limiting the number of

---

[16]See Chapter 1, Section IV.
[17]See European Commission, Commission Notice on agreements of minor importance which do not appreciably restrict competition under Article 101(1) of the Treaty on the Functioning of the European Union (*De Minimis* Notice), OJ C 291 30 August 2014, p. 1.

sales outlets or in prescribing the appearance of sales outlets in order to strengthen their own brand in competition with other brands. Thus, so-called **selective distribution** may be admissible because it limits "intra-brand" competition between sales outlets to the benefit of "inter-brand" competition at the level of suppliers. Indeed, purely qualitative selective distribution is not even considered to restrain competition, however, provided that three conditions are satisfied:

- First, the nature of the product in question must necessitate a selective distribution system, in the sense that such a system must constitute a legitimate requirement.
- Second, resellers must be chosen on the basis of objective criteria of a qualitative nature which are laid down uniformly for all and made available to all potential resellers and are not applied in a discriminatory manner.
- Third, the criteria laid down must not go beyond what is necessary.[18]

In contrast, a limitation of the number of sales outlets (quantitative selective distribution) is considered to restrain competition. However, it may be exempted from the prohibition of Article 101(1) TFEU if it meets the conditions of Article 101(3) TFEU.

In the U.S. and Japan, once falling outside the category of *per se* violations or hard-core cartels respectively, the effect of the collaboration categories mentioned before on competition is generally analyzed on a case-by-case basis taking into account the participants' goals and other activities carried out at the same time. Notably, selective distribution is rarely considered to raise any competitive concerns to begin with, and there is no case in which such a violation has been found.

2. Ancillary restraints as part of a larger collaboration

When the relevant agreement is part of a larger collaboration, it may be considered to be an ancillary restraint. In EU law, *"any alleged restriction of competition which is directly related and necessary to the implementation of a main non-restrictive transaction and proportionate to it"* is

---

[18]European Commission, Guidelines on vertical restraints (fn. 6), §§148 ff.; see also ECJ, Judgment of 25 October 1977, Metro/Commission (26/76, ECR 1977 p. 1875) ECLI:EU:C:1977:167, §§20–21.

excepted from Article 101(1) TFEU as an ancillary restraint.[19] A potential example (where these conditions were not fulfilled, though) was an agreement between banks on the rate of interbank fees for credit card transactions.[20] §1 Sherman Act is similarly not violated in the context of *an efficiency-enhancing integration of economic activity* where the agreement *is reasonably related to the integration and reasonably necessary to achieve its procompetitive benefits.* This may be the case where *practical, significantly less restrictive means* are available.[21] The same standard applies in Japanese law. In direct comparison, U.S. and Japanese law here appear to be more flexible than EU law because they apply a rule-of-reason analysis and not a proportionality test.

IV. Horizontal agreements restraining competition/trade

It was set out above that horizontal cartels restraining competition "by object" (EU law) or falling into the category of *per se* restraints of trade (U.S. law) are subject to a very strict standard of assessment. Although the AMA has neither a "by object" nor *per se* category, price fixing and other outrightly anticompetitive horizontal agreements are subject to similar strict regulation. This is different for other horizontal agreements which may restrain competition or trade.

1. EU law

Horizontal agreements not amounting to "by object" restraints are subject to differentiated rules under EU law. It must first be assessed whether the agreement restrains competition under Article 101(1) TFEU **appreciably**. This is not the case if it falls into one of the safe harbors based on market shares in the European Commission's *de minimis* notice, which is mentioned above.[22] Where an agreement exceeds these market shares, it is

---

[19] European Commission, Guidelines on Article 81(3) of the Treaty (Ch. 2 fn. 3), §29.

[20] However, this was rejected for interbank fees: ECJ, Judgment of 11 September 2014, *MasterCard and others/Commission* (C-382/12 P) ECLI:EU:C:2014:2201, ECLI:EU:C:2014:2201, §§87 ff.

[21] DOJ/FTC, Antitrust Guidelines for Collaborations Among Competitors, §3.2.

[22] European Commission, Commission Notice on agreements of minor importance which do not appreciably restrict competition under Article 101(1) of the Treaty on the Functioning of the European Union (*De Minimis* Notice), OJ C 291 30 August 2014, p. 1.

considered to restrain competition under Article 101(1) TFEU and must be exempted under Article 101(3) TFEU in order to be legal.

The exemption may be either a "block exemption" of certain types of agreements or an individual exemption based on an individual assessment. As noted in **Section I**, the European Commission has enacted three **Block Exemption Regulations (BER)**, which are complemented by Guidelines for agreements of the relevant type but which require an individual assessment. Thus, Regulation (EU) 2023/1066 block exempts R&D agreements and Regulation (EU) 2023/1067 for specialization agreements. These two BERs are supplemented in the European Commission's guidelines on horizontal agreements for agreements necessitating an individual assessment. In addition, Regulation 316/2014 and another set of guidelines deal with licenses granted to the transfer of industrial or Intellectual Property (IP).

Whenever the agreement does not fall into any block-exempted category of agreements, the **Guidelines on horizontal agreements** may provide additional safe harbors and include other rules for the assessment of such agreements. These guidelines deal with joint production, joint purchasing, the joint marketing of products ("commercialization") and standardization if they are based on agreements.

Finally, if the agreement cannot be considered under the guidelines on horizontal agreements, it may still be exempted under an individual assessment of the criteria of Article 101(3) TFEU. An individual exemption requires that the parties to the agreement be able to show that any competition restraint associated with the collaboration is outweighed by **efficiencies** to the benefit of **consumers**. In order to find out whether this is the case, some guidance may be drawn from another set of guidelines which the European Commission published for Article 81(3) EC, the predecessor provision to Article 101(3) TFEU.[23] Two aspects are noteworthy regarding this assessment: One is the term "consumer", which always covers the direct customers of the collaborating parties, regardless of whether the distribution chain also includes indirect customers (e.g., if it consists of suppliers, distributors and consumers). Moreover, an outer limit to competition restraints exists if the agreement harms the competitive process as such, e.g., by precluding any further market entries or innovation ("elimination" of competition).

---

[23] Guidelines on Article 81(3) of the Treaty; see §§48 ff. re the required efficiency gains, §§83 ff. re the necessary fair share for "consumers", §§73 ff. re the indispensability of restrictions and §§105 ff. re the requirement that there be no elimination of competition (§§105 ff.).

2. U.S. law

In U.S. law, horizontal agreements not prohibited *per se* must be assessed under a **rule of reason**.[24] Under the rule of reason, *competitive effect can only be evaluated by analyzing the facts peculiar to the business, the history of the restraint, and the reasons why it was imposed*[25] to determine whether the challenged agreement is one that promotes competition or one that suppresses competition.[26] In the Antitrust Guidelines for Collaborations among competitors, as applied by the U.S. federal agencies, the latter situation is described as *harm[ing] competition by increasing the ability or incentive profitably to raise price above or reduce output, quality, service, or innovation below what likely would prevail in the absence of the relevant agreement.*[27] The density of the analysis carried out in the name of the rule of reason differs, as was noted in *California Dental Ass'n v. FTC*, 526 U.S. 756, 779 (1999): *[E]very case attacking a less obviously anticompetitive restraint (like this one) is a candidate for plenary market examination.* For example, competitors' blanket ban on advertisements will be more readily determined unlawful than an agreement relating to joint R&D.

The U.S. DOJ & FTC Antitrust Guidelines set out the **analytical framework** as follows:

(i) First, the nature of the agreement is examined. Thus, *where the likelihood of anticompetitive harm is evident from the nature of the agreement, or anticompetitive harm has resulted from an agreement already in operation, then, absent overriding benefits that could offset the anticompetitive harm, the Agencies challenge such agreements without a detailed market analysis.* On the other hand, *the nature of the agreement and the absence of market power together may demonstrate the absence of anticompetitive harm.*

(ii) Second, *[i]f the initial examination of the nature of the agreement indicates possible competitive concerns, but the agreement is not one that would be challenged without a detailed market analysis,* the agreement is subject to a detailed analysis to determine the overall

---

[24]See Chapter 2.

[25]*National Soc'y of Prof. Engineers v. United States*, 435 U.S. 679, 692 (1978).

[26]*National Soc'y of Prof. Engineers v. United States*, 435 U.S. 679, 691 (1978).

[27]Antitrust Guidelines for Collaborations Among Competitors, §3, March 2020.

competitive effect. At this stage, *the Agencies typically define relevant markets and calculate market shares and concentration as an initial step in assessing whether the agreement may create or increase market power or facilitate its exercise. The Agencies examine the extent to which the participants and the collaboration have the ability and incentive to compete independently. The Agencies also evaluate other market circumstances, e.g., entry, that may foster or prevent anticompetitive harms.* Then, *if the examination of these factors indicates no potential for anticompetitive harm, the Agencies end the investigation without considering procompetitive benefits.* Otherwise, the Agencies move on to the third stage.

(iii)   At the third stage, the Agencies examine whether the relevant agreement is reasonably necessary to achieve procompetitive benefits that would likely offset anticompetitive harms.

Also in the U.S., the applicable guidelines on horizontal agreements provide **safe harbors** or include other rules for horizontal collaboration (cf. **Section I**). This includes the aforementioned **Antitrust Guidelines for Collaborations Among Competitors**, which provide for safety zones (safe harbors) for collaborations in general and R&D collaborations.[28] The Statements of Antitrust Enforcement Policy in Health Care with safety zones for various types of collaboration (healthcare equipment, services, etc.) were recently withdrawn.[29] In addition, like in the EU, there are also **Antitrust Guidelines for the Licensing of Intellectual Property**.

Finally, note that the scope of **justification** tends to be **limited to procompetitive effect or greater efficiency**, where the courts are reluctant to engage in a balancing exercise between anticompetitive effect and greater social issues under antitrust law: The latter is generally left to the special legislations and regulators.

---

[28] DOC/FTC, Antitrust Guidelines for Collaborations Among Competitors, April 2000; accessible: https://www.ftc.gov/sites/default/files/documents/public_events/joint-venture-hearings-antitrust-guidelines-collaboration-among-competitors/ftcdojguidelines-2.pdf.
[29] FTC, press release of 14 July 2023; DOJ, press release of 3 February 2023.

3. Japanese law

Like in the U.S., the JFTC and the Japanese courts are expected to carry out a **competitive effects analysis on a case-by-case basis** where such effect is not obvious before applying AMA Articles 2(6) and 3. The analysis is similar to the one that is carried out in relation to mergers, for which the analysis begins with the delineation of relevant markets and the calculation of market shares, except that the degree of integration of economic activities largely differs depending on the matter the parties collaborate on. Thus, jointly setting a voluntary standard which does not anyway restrict the parties' business activities tends to be seen as unproblematic. In contrast, agreements to integrate sales activities by establishing a common sales agent tend to give rise to concerns under the AMA. Ultimately, the test is whether the horizontal collaboration results in the establishment, maintenance or enhancement of market power in a relevant market. Any procompetitive effects associated with the respective agreement are taken into account in the assessment. The JFTC established a safe harbor in relation to joint research and development in its Guidelines Concerning Joint Research and Development under the AMA (1993).

A slightly stricter standard applies to **trade associations** under AMA Article 8. Not only practices which create or cement market power but also practices limiting the number of enterprises or unreasonably restricting the activities or functions of the members of an association are prohibited under AMA Article 8(iii) and (iv). Furthermore, trade associations are prohibited to cause enterprise to engage in unfair trade practices under AMA 8(v).

Under AMA Articles 2(6)/3 and 8, **procompetitive effects** are taken into account as well. However, a controversy exists as to whether also interests of the general public, such as sustainability and social security, may be taken into account. The difficulty is whether broader societal and economic issues, which are difficult to characterize as procompetitive effects, may provide a justification for an — otherwise — anticompetitive agreement. Although the courts have accepted such a possibility in light of the goals of AMA set out under AMA Article 1, there has been no court case in which the defendants successfully justified their anticompetitive horizontal agreements on the ground of social justice.

4. Comparison

In comparison, the U.S. and Japanese systems appear more flexible than the EU system. Both those systems provide for a case-specific or rule-of-reason review. Further, where the guidelines provide for safety zones, these are defined rather broadly. The market share threshold set for Competitor Collaboration in general is set at 20% in the U.S. Although there are no general guidelines in Japan, the JFTC Joint R&D guidelines adopt the same thresholds. This at least mirrors the combined market share threshold for specialization agreements in the context of production in the EU's R&D BER.[30] In contrast, the market share thresholds for joint purchasing and joint commercialization are set at 15% in the EU, whereas higher (e.g., 20%) or no specific market share thresholds are set for other agreements and jointly negotiated standard terms.[31] Having said all of that, the increased flexibility means also less legal certainty for collaborations that may entail restraints of trade. When it comes to non-economic values, Japanese law sets out explicitly when these may be considered relevant in the assessment. In the EU, a case-by-case analysis under the Treaties would be necessary in these instances.[32]

V. Vertical agreements

1. Introduction

Vertical agreements, as covered in this section, are agreements where two companies active at different levels in the production and distribution chain (supply chain) agree that one will supply (or purchase) goods or services (henceforth products) from the other for the purpose of resale.[33] Vertical agreements are legally defined in EU law but not in U.S. and

---

[30]DOC/FTC, Antitrust Guidelines for Collaborations Among Competitors, April 2000, Section 4.2; Article 3 Reg. 1218/2010; Horizontal Cooperation Guidelines, §§169–170.
[31]European Commission, Horizontal Cooperation Guidelines, §§202, 230–231 (joint production), 291 (joint purchasing), 339 (joint commercialization); §§472, 502, 509 (standardization agreements/standard terms), 549 (sustainability agreements).
[32]See Chapter 2, Section V.2.
[33]See ECJ, Judgment of 30 June 1966, *Société Technique Minière/Maschinenbau Ulm* (56/65, ECR 1966 p. 235), ECLI:EU:C:1966:38, at p. 248.

Japanese law.[34] In the EU, these agreements are subject to Article 101 TFEU just like horizontal agreements. In U.S. law, it must (only) be examined whether the conditions of §1 Sherman Act are met while in Japan, vertical agreements are mostly dealt with as a trade on restrictive conditions.

The rules on agreements and single-company conduct may apply in parallel under the circumstances. However, in the EU, where an arrangement seemingly involving a vertical agreement is actually unilateral behavior, Article 101(1) TFEU does not apply and the arrangement must be assessed under Article 102 TFEU.[35] In contrast, where a dominant party imposes its will on another and the existence of an agreement is difficult to establish, agencies may limit their assessment to Article 102 TFEU and leave open the assessment under Article 101 TFEU. In the U.S., many of the vertical arrangements in the latter scenario would be examined under §1 of the Sherman Act in practice, considering that the U.S. antitrust rules for contracts, combinations or conspiracies are more stringent than those for unilateral conduct. In addition, §3 Clayton Act may apply, which makes it unlawful to sell goods [not services!] on condition that the purchaser does not buy competing goods if the effect is to substantially lessen competition. The general prohibition of unfair trade in §5 FTC Act may apply as well, (potentially) also as a standalone provision.[36] In Japan, vertical agreements are assessed in light of AMA Article 19 (prohibition of unfair trade practice) mostly, although they can constitute private monopolization when they cause serious harm to competition.

The assessment of vertical agreements diverges in EU, U.S. and Japanese law much more than for horizontal agreements. In line with what is stated above **(Section II)**, this is because, in the EU, vertical agreements are subject to detailed rules specifying the criteria of Article 101(3) TFEU for types of cases (block exemption) or individual cases. In Japan, a variety of provisions exists which is specifically tailored to each type of practice. Furthermore, the EU and Japan still consider vertical agreements on

---

[34] See Article 1(1) Regulation No 19/65/EEC of 2 March 1965 of the Council on application of Article 85(3) of the Treaty to certain categories of agreements and concerted practices, OJ 036, 6 March 1965 P. 0533; Article 1(1) lit. a Reg. (EU) 2022/720.

[35] See Chapter 4, Section 1 on Article 102 TFEU. A "decision" or "concerted practice" is generally not to be expected in a vertical setting.

[36] *In re Intel Corp*, FTC Dkt No. 9341.

prices to be restraints "by object" (EU) or to generally constitute an AMA Article 19 violation (Japan). Under §1 Sherman Act, as a matter of principle, a rule-of-reason analysis applies in most of those instances.[37]

The policy adopted toward vertical agreements is developing constantly and has been doing so particularly in recent years, due to the increasing relevance of online distribution. In the EU, while the basic rules in Article 101 TFEU continue to be the same, the European Commission recently passed a new Vertical Block Exemption Regulation (EU) 2022/720 (VBER) and associated guidelines.[38] The pre-existing Regulation 330/2010 expired in May 2022.[39] In the U.S., major changes have been brought about by the jurisprudence, which is adapting the law continuously to the evolution and understanding of market economics. In Japan, the JFTC revised its Guidelines Concerning Distribution Systems and Business Practices in 2015, 2016 and 2017 to reflect changes in the digital environment better and deal with platform-related issues more. In the following, we address also the changes that were brought about through the review of the EU vertical rules or have been brought about through U.S. case law as well as the JFTC revision of guidelines and decisional practices so far.

This section first sets out when vertical business relations are actually considered to crystallize in an agreement for the purposes of Article 101 TFEU, §1 Sherman Act and AMA provisions **(Subsection 1)**. It then examines various settings requiring a closer analysis **(Subsection 2)**. After that, it deals with the rules for the assessment of restraints and (potential) justifications **(Subsection 3)**.

2. Agreements and other types of trading practices

(a) The general requirements

In the EU and the U.S., the assessment of vertical coordination starts similar to the assessment of coordination in horizontal cases. In the **EU**, the

---

[37] EU: Article 4(a) Reg. (EU) 2022/720; *Leegin Creative Leather Products, Inc. v. PSKS, Inc.*, 551 U.S. 877 (2007).

[38] Reg. (EU) 2022/720; European Commission, Guidelines on vertical restraints (fn. 5–6).

[39] The European Commission conducted a sector inquiry into e-commerce in the years 2015–2017 and reviewed the existing rules as of 2018.

European Commission stated in its Vertical Guidelines that *For there to be an **agreement** within the meaning of Article 101 of the Treaty, it is sufficient that the parties have expressed their joint intention to conduct themselves on the market in a specific way.*[40] This definition, while certainly being correct, omits to explain when parties active at two levels in the supply chain express a joint intention in contrast to one party simply imposing its will on the other.

However, the ECJ clarified that *it is necessary that the manifestation of the wish of one of the contracting parties to achieve an anticompetitive goal constitute an invitation to the other party, whether express or implied, to fulfil that goal jointly [...]. Therefore, [it is necessary to establish that one party had required] of the [other one], as a condition of their future contractual relations, that they should comply with its new commercial policy.*[41] Thus, the joint intention must be about the one party's competitive behavior and condition that behavior (at least implicitly) on how the other party will act on the market: *I am aware that you will supply goods on condition that I maintain my resale price.*

In **U.S. law**, the application of §1 Sherman Act in vertical settings crucially depends on the *distinction between concerted and independent action.*[42] In order to find the former, *there must be evidence that tends to exclude the possibility that the [parties] were acting independently"* or *"direct or circumstantial evidence that reasonably tends to prove that the manufacturer and others had a **conscious commitment to a common scheme** designed to achieve an unlawful objective.*[43] Meanwhile, no such concerted action exists where a manufacturer makes an announcement with regard to, e.g., its resale prices and terminates contracts with a distributor who does not comply with the imposed conditions.[44] This is even true where such an announcement lets a distributor *acquiesce in the manufacturer's demand in order to avoid termination.*[45]

---

[40] European Commission, Guidelines on vertical restraints (fn. 6), §53.

[41] ECJ, Judgment of 6 January 2004, *BAI and Commission/Bayer* (C-2/01 P and C-3/01 P, ECR 2004 p. I-23) ECLI:EU:C:2004:2, §§102–103; in national practice, see also German FCO, Decision of 25 October 2009, B3-123/08, *Ciba Vision*, §§52 ff., 56–57 (2009); FCO/BDB, Hinweispapier: Preisbindung im Lebensmitteleinzelhandel (food retail guidelines), 12 July 2017, §11.

[42] *Monsanto Co. v. Spray-Rite Svc. Corp.*, 465 U.S. 752, 761 (1984).

[43] *Monsanto Co. v. Spray-Rite Svc. Corp.*, 465 U.S. 752, 764, 768 (1984).

[44] *United States v. Colgate & Co.*, 250 U.S. 300, 307 (1919).

[45] *Monsanto*, 465 U.S., 761.

In **Japan**, in contrast, the primary provisions applicable to vertical restraints, namely AMA Article 2(9)(iv) and JFTC GD paras 11 and 12, require that the defendant **impose certain restrictive conditions**. Where such restrictive conditions are part of contractual terms, this requirement is obviously fulfilled. Otherwise, the Court and the JFTC examine whether the defendant implemented measures to ensure that its counterparties would comply with its request. Such measures are typically suggesting imposing economic disadvantages on non-complying parties, while a leading company's termination of the contract typically constitutes such a disadvantage.

Consequently, Japanese law would apply also to practices that might not be captured by EU law or U.S. law. A **unilateral imposition of trading conditions**, i.e., a scenario where the supplied firm does not accept the terms as a condition for supply would not trigger Article 101 TFEU and would arguably constitute also "independent action" falling out of the scope of §1 Sherman Act.

(b) Coordination requiring a closer analysis

In some instances, it is particularly difficult to decide whether vertical coordination falling under Article 101 TFEU, §1 Sherman Act or a vertical business relationship falling under AMA (Article 3 or 19) exists. In that regard, particularly the following two scenarios merit closer analysis: (i) agency relationships and (ii) platform relationships.

(1) Agreement between undertakings/economic actors: The agency problem

Companies enter into vertical agreements not only with independent resellers but also with resellers that are economically dependent on the supplier. In **EU law**, Article 101(1) TFEU only applies if the reseller is free to act independently. Thus, the reseller must be free to accept or reject the terms of that agreement. Moreover, a mere **"agent" not bearing any financial or commercial risk** is not considered to be an independent economic entity. Thus, coordination between a supplier and its agents would not constitute an agreement for the purposes of Article 101(1) TFEU.[46]

---

[46]European Commission, Guidelines on vertical restraints (fn. 6), §§30 ff. See also Article 1 lit. k Reg. (EU) 2022/720: *"buyer" includes an undertaking which, under an*

In the most recent revision of the EU Vertical Guidelines, it was made clear that the relevant risks include contract-specific risks, risks related to market-specific investments and risks related to other activities which the agent undertakes on the principal's demand on its own risk on the same product market.[47]

In **U.S. and Japanese law**, there is a corresponding rule that no anti-trust issue arises in case of genuine agency contracts.[48] In 2009, the U.S. Court of Appeals for the Fourth Circuit developed a three-part test for agency in the context of resale price maintenance: It must first be examined whether the potential agent *"bear[s] most or all of the traditional burdens of ownership"*, which is not the case if the agent is relieved of bearing financial or commercial risks. Then, it must be assessed whether the agency arrangement has *"a function other than to circumvent the rule against price fixing"*. Finally, an agency arrangement falls outside §1 Sherman Act if it is *"a product of coercion"*, removing any freedom to act independently. In addition, there is a general requirement that an agent may only be exempted from the application of the antitrust rules if it acts *bona fide*.[49]

(2) Vertical agreements in the case of intermediation: Online platforms

The traditional distinction between horizontal and vertical agreements reaches its limits where operators of online platforms are present. Online platforms have been developed over the past 20 years. They act as intermediaries either between users of the same type (**one-sided** network; e.g., a social network) or users of different groups (**two- or multi-sided**; e.g., a marketplace for buyers and sellers).

Online platforms may allow users to exchange dealings via the platform infrastructure; as does, for example, an online marketplace (e.g., a flight booking portal) or an online search platform allowing one to search for or offer content (**transaction platforms**). But online platforms may

---

agreement falling within [Article 101 TFEU], sells goods or services on behalf of another undertaking.

[47] Guidelines on vertical restraints (fn. 6), §31.

[48] *United States v. General Electric Co.*, 272 U.S. 476 (1926); ADD Japanese reference.

[49] *Valuepest.com of Charlotte v. Bayer Corp.*, 561 F.3d 282, 290–291 (Fourth Circuit 2009).

also allow one side to attract (positive/negative) attention from the other side of the platform (e.g., advertisers on search platforms; **attention platforms**). Some platforms also have a hybrid structure because the operator offers a marketplace and is also selling itself at the same time (dual role).

In any event, online platforms stand **between user groups but not necessarily between distinct "relevant markets"**. Moreover, platforms target their intermediation service at the relevant user groups **in parallel** and allow the users to **directly interact** with each other. That is to say, the platforms do not buy something from one group of users and resell it to other users. This characteristic of online platforms makes it difficult to decide how platform intermediation should be viewed where products are sold and resold within a supply chain.

In EU law, the **revised Vertical BER and Guidelines of 2022** have brought various clarifications, as the pre-existing rules were not conclusive as regards online platforms. Under the revised rules, online platforms are **regarded as part of the supply chain**. This had been unclear before given the narrow express definition of vertical agreements in EU law.[50] Further, platforms generally cannot be regarded as agents as this would require showing that the platform is integrated into the supply/demand side of the transaction.[51] In reality, it may happen that the platform operator (i.e., the potential agent) is so powerful that it can dictate its own commercial interests on the users, e.g., the product suppliers (i.e., the supposed "principal").[52] The platform also bears commercial risks of its own (at least platform-specific risks).[53] The Vertical BER now solves these problems by stating expressly that, for the purposes of the BER, the term *"supplier" includes an undertaking that provides online intermediation services.*[54]

---

[50]This definition has remained unchanged; see Article 1(1) lit. a Reg. (EU) 2022/720.

[51]Cf. Article 1 lit. k Reg. (EU) 2022/720; European Commission, Guidelines on vertical restraints (fn. 6), §46.

[52]See European Commission, Decision of 25 July 2013, AT.39847 — *Ebooks*.

[53]With regard to the question of whether platforms may be regarded as agents, it had been unclear before whether the platform must bear risks arising specifically in the context of the service where competition is restrained; see OLG Düsseldorf, Judgment of 4 December 2017, *Expedia*, VI-U (Kart) 5/17, ECLI:DE:OLGD:2017:1204. VI.U.KART5.17.00, §34.

[54]Article 1 lit. d, e Reg. (EU) 2022/720; see also European Commission, Guidelines on vertical restraints (fn. 6), §§62 ff.

The revised Vertical BER and Guidelines had to solve another issue in relation to online platforms, given the narrow scope of application of the previous rules: The block exemption under the BER generally depends on **market share thresholds of 30%** on any supplier/buyer market.[55] However, it is difficult to identify a supplier/buyer market for intermediators although it is true that online platforms offer a service. Moreover, the intermediation power of online platforms builds on user dependence and not on the characteristics of the platform product. Thus, the power of online platforms does not depend on the existence of substitutable alternative offers. The new Vertical Guidelines now specify that the market share of undertakings providing *"online intermediation services is calculated on the relevant market for the supply of those services"*.[56] However, the Guidelines still remain rather generous regarding the calculation of market shares rising over time.[57] It may be questioned whether this approach allows one to capture accurately the competition issues in cases where online platforms grow fast to make the market tip in their favor.

However, it should also be noted that the Guidelines take a rather **strict approach** when it comes to evaluating **competition restraints**: As a general matter, restraints imposed by platforms are treated as equivalent to restraints imposed by suppliers.[58] The Guidelines now also provide specific guidance for restraints imposed by the operators of online marketplaces and price-comparison sites.[59] Moreover, at the level of platform users, the Guidelines address the fact that online platforms may incentivize bundles of similar vertical restraints (as part of their growth strategy). The Guidelines now include rather strict rules also for price-parity clauses.[60]

---

[55] Article 3 Reg. (EU) 2022/720.

[56] European Commission, Guidelines on vertical restraints (fn. 6), §67 lit. b. In the case of online platforms, it may not be possible to use a "small but significant and non-transitory increase in price" (SSNIP Test) to define the relevant market as platforms may provide their services to one platform side for free. In this case, other tests must be used, e.g., the Unique Visitor Test.

[57] Article 8 lit. d Reg. (EU) 2022/720.

[58] European Commission, Guidelines on vertical restraints (fn. 6), §67 lit. c.

[59] See European Commission, Guidelines on vertical restraints (fn. 6), §§332 ff. (*re* online marketplaces) and §§343 ff. (*re* price-comparison sites).

[60] European Commission, Guidelines on vertical restraints (fn. 6), §§67 lit. d, 356 ff. Note that the DMA bars price parity clauses completely for designated Gatekeepers

Hybrid platforms raise additional questions under the EU rules for vertical agreements restraining competition. This is because the Vertical BER includes a specific exception for dual distribution: The block exemption does not apply to vertical agreements entered into between competitors unless the agreement is non-reciprocal and (i) the firms only compete at the distribution level, but not upstream, or (ii) the supplier provides services at several levels of trade and the buyer is active at the retail level and does not compete at the level of trade where it purchases the contract services.[61] An operator of a hybrid platform may actually meet these criteria based on the wording of the exception. However, if it does, it does not meet the criteria with one business model alone. Rather, it pursues two distinct business models at the same time, i.e., the business model of a (retail) seller and the business model of an intermediator (upstream service?) that enable other retailers to complete their (downstream?) transactions. The revised Vertical BER and the Guidelines make clear now that this is insufficient to trigger the dual distribution exception, meaning that the hybrid platform operator cannot rely on the block exemption.[62]

In **U.S. and Japanese law**, all these challenges brought about by the particular structure of the EU rules on vertical restraints virtually do not exist. Neither Sherman Act §1 nor the AMA defines vertical agreements as a type of agreement for the purchase and resale of goods or services. Therefore, both distribution agreements and arrangements involving online platforms are subject to the same assessment under §1 Sherman Act or AMA Article 19. In that assessment, no *per se* standard applies, which allows one to consider the individual setting of the arrangement.

3. Anticompetitive effects and (potential) justifications

(a) General notes

In comparison with horizontal agreements, vertical agreements are generally viewed more favorably due to potential efficiencies associated with

---

(Article 5(3)). See also Section V.3.d in this chapter on price parity clauses and Chapter 5, Section II.1, 2(b) on the rules for Gatekeepers.

[61] Article 2(4) Reg. (EU) 2022/720.

[62] Article 2(6) Reg. (EU) 2022/720; European Commission, Guidelines on vertical restraints (fn. 6), §67 lit. e.

vertical business relationships. By way of example, if lemonade is being supplied to retailers for resale, more people can get the lemonade than if the producer had to distribute all the lemonade on its own.

However, vertical agreements can also bring about competition restraints. Here it is possible to distinguish two broad categories:

1. Vertical agreements may **restrain competition by raising market entry barriers, or partitioning markets artificially**, or engaging in other practices with similar effect. Depending on the situation, such practices can carry the risk of foreclosure leading to the permanent exclusion of one party's rivals (upstream or downstream).
2. However, vertical agreements may also include restraints that can only be successfully implemented in a **market structure where alternative suppliers are already hindered from entering the market**. An example of this would be Resale Price Maintenance (RPM) agreements. RPM agreements allow individual suppliers to limit intra-brand competition on resale prices and to impose a minimum price level without having to fear price-cutters. RPM may come along with further risks to competition (e.g., risks of reseller collusion).

Meanwhile, practices such as Most-Favored Nation (MFN; price parity) clauses have the potential to exclude rivals and to facilitate collusion alike. The following subsection deals with competition restraints that are possible regardless of market entry barriers **(Subsection b)** and the subsection following afterward with RPM and similar restrictions **(Subsection c)**. Price parity is discussed in a third subsection **(Subsection d)**.

(b) Competition restraints by raising market entry barriers, by partitioning markets or through other practices with similar effect

As noted above, vertical agreements may restrain competition by foreclosure of one party's rivals, by partitioning markets artificially or using other practices with similar effect. They may also entail a softening of competition at one of the supply levels and/or create obstacles to innovation. The reduced competition may open the door for price discrimination and other practices harming subsequent supply levels as well as consumers.

However, the propensity of the market to produce such effects is amplified the more foreclosure occurs in the first place. In this context, **foreclosure** may be **defined** as follows:

> *any instance where actual or potential rivals' access to supplies or markets is hampered or eliminated [...], thereby reducing these companies' ability and/or incentive to compete.*[63]

In the assessment of a vertical agreement between two parties on two different levels of the production or distribution chain, we may distinguish upstream and downstream foreclosure. **Upstream foreclosure** exists if the following question must be answered positively: Is a customer denied access to *suppliers*? (Alternatively: Is sale denied to competing *suppliers*?). An example would be if a producer of lemonade were to agree with its main supplier not to buy lemon syrup from *other suppliers*. In that case, the other suppliers might effectively be foreclosed from the lemon syrup market. And this could have detrimental effects on distributors further downstream because these distributors would lose alternatives for sourcing lemonade.[64]

Downstream foreclosure exists if the following question must be answered positively: Is a supplier denied access to *customers*? (Alternatively: Is sourcing denied to competing *customers*?). An example would be if a producer of lemonade were to agree with its supplier that the supplier should only provide lemon syrup to that producer of lemonade and not to other soft drink producers (as *customers*). In that case, other producers might be foreclosed from the soft drink market.[65]

In both cases, the foreclosure may **pave the way for** building up **market power**. Typically, this has been achieved by exclusive dealing and tying. The rules on exclusive dealing are detailed in the following, while Chapter 4 explains the rule on tying.

---

[63] See European Commission, Guidelines on the assessment of non-horizontal mergers under the Council Regulation on the control of concentrations between undertakings, OJ C 265 of 18 October 2008, §§18, 29.

[64] See European Commission Guidelines on non-horizontal mergers (fn. 62), §§58 ff., on "customer foreclosure".

[65] See European Commission Guidelines on non-horizontal mergers (fn. 62), §§31 ff., on "input foreclosure".

(1) EU law

In EU law, foreclosure is regarded to be virtually a synonym for **exclu-sionary effects**. When a supplier enters into an agreement with resellers, it must be examined above all whether the agreement allows one of the parties to foreclose (exclude) competition (although a full analysis must certainly go beyond that and include also other effects on competition). This risk may exist **whenever the agreement provides for exclusive sell-ing or purchasing**. A similar risk may exist if the seller forces the buyer to accept several products in bundles (tying). However, when a supplier restricts the resale of products by agreement or is itself restricted in its sourcing or sales, the restraint may be block-exempted if it falls under the Vertical BER, or it can be exempted individually. The same applies if the parties agree that products should be sold only in bundles. A tightened assessment is required whenever there is market power.

(a) Exclusivity and the balancing of effects under the European Commission's guidelines

The European Commission **Vertical Guidelines** include specific guidance on different groups of restraints providing for some sort of **exclusivity**:

- right of a buyer (distributor) to buy products exclusively for resale (**exclusive distribution**, §§117 ff.),[66]
- right of a qualified group of buyers to buy products exclusively for resale (**selective distribution**, §§143 ff.), potentially in the context of a **franchising** agreement (§§165 ff.),
- direct/indirect obligation for a buyer to concentrate its orders with one supplier (**exclusive purchasing**/single sourcing/"single brand-ing", §§298 ff.),
- direct/indirect obligation of a supplier to sell products only or mainly to one buyer (**exclusive supply**, §§321 ff.).

In addition, the same Guidelines include guidance on **related types** of competition restraint, namely:

---

[66]This includes guidance on the right of a buyer to buy products exclusively for resale to a particular group of customers (exclusive customer allocation, §§139 ff.). This type of restraint had been discussed in a separate section in the preceding Guidelines on vertical restraints.

- direct/indirect obligation of the buyers of one product (the tying product) to also purchase another distinct product (the tied product) from the same/a designated supplier (**tying**, §§214 ff.),[67]
- other restraints when there is already some kind of exclusivity in place: **payments** by manufacturers **for access** to distribution infrastructure (§§379 ff.) and the transfer of marketing functions from distribution to manufacturers (**category management**, §§385 ff.).

Moreover, the European Commission **Communication on exclusionary abuses** also includes guidance on the following:

- unilaterally imposed direct/indirect obligations for a buyer to concentrate orders with one supplier (**exclusive purchasing**, §§33 ff.),
- unilaterally imposed **tying/bundling** (§§47 ff.).[68]

The approach for dealing with unilateral exclusionary abuses through exclusivity and tying is discussed in Chapter 4.

The main features of the European Commission guidelines above are that any type of exclusivity is usually acceptable absent market power, but it may require closer analysis if it is combined with other restrictions. This makes sense, particularly regarding the distribution of branded goods or services: Here, the connection between the brand and the product is important and may justify that a brand manufacturer imposes product-related restraints (**intra-brand**) to further competition between brands (**inter-brand**).

(b) Specifically: Selective distribution

A selective distribution system is a system where the supplier sells the contract products only to distributors selected on the basis of specified criteria and where these distributors undertake not to sell those products to unauthorized distributors within the territory reserved by the supplier to operate the system.[69] Thus, a selective distribution system establishes

---

[67] European Commission, Guidelines on vertical restraints (fn. 6).

[68] European Commission, Guidance on its enforcement priorities in applying Article 82 of the European Commission Treaty to abusive exclusionary conduct by dominant undertakings, OJ C 45, 24 February 2009, pp. 7–20.

[69] Article 1(1)(g) Reg. (EU) 2022/720.

exclusivity regarding dealer characteristics. In the EU, selective distribution is subject to special rules, as is highlighted already in Section III. The allocation of customers to certain dealers is treated similarly.

As is stated above, in the EU, selective distribution is considered to not even restrain competition if (i) the product justifies limitations on the dealership (e.g., to maintain quality/advice on right use), (ii) the selection of dealers is based on qualitative criteria and (iii) the restraint is proportionate.[70] If the selection of dealers is based on quantitative criteria, the distribution system is considered to restrain competition in terms of Article 101(1) TFEU, but it may be block-exempted under Article 101(3) TFEU. Under the previous rules, the system could even require dealers to operate at least one physical point of sale.[71] The revised Guidelines provide for differentiated rules in that regard, depending on the foreclosure risks.[72]

However, some restrictions may not be imposed on dealers in a block-exempted selective distribution system because they are considered as **hardcore restraints** (territorial restrictions, restrictions of active or passive sales to end users and restrictions of cross-supplies between distributors) or at least they can only be exempted individually (restrictions of sales of competing brands).[73]

Against the background of the special prohibition in Article 101(1)(c) TFEU on market-sharing agreements, some of the **territorial restrictions** considered as hardcore restraints under the Vertical BER are actually prohibited regardless of whether the distribution system is selective or not.[74] Moreover, if a supplier uses its selective distribution system to monitor **price-aggressive dealers**, this monitoring may provide a context where dealers are no longer independent in their pricing and therefore amounts to resale price maintenance.

---

[70] ECJ, Judgment of 25 October 1977, *Metro/Commission* (26/76, ECR 1977 p. 1875) ECLI:EU:C:1977:167, §§20–21; Judgment of 11 December 1980, *L'Oréal/De Nieuwe AMCK* (31/80, ECR 1980 p. 3775) ECLI:EU:C:1980:289, §§15–16; see also Section III.1 in this chapter.

[71] European Commission, Guidelines on Vertical Restraints, OJ C 130, 19 May 2010, p. 1, §54.

[72] See European Commission, Guidelines on vertical restraints (fn. 6), §§155, 164, 208 lit. d.

[73] Article 4 lit. b-d, Article 5(1)(c) Reg. (EU) 2022/720.

[74] Article 4 lit. c(i) Reg. (EU) 2022/720.

(c) Specifically: Restraints of online distribution

The evolution of online trade has opened up new possibilities for the distribution of products, but it also has put established distribution systems in question and may even undermine systems where the supplier limits resale outlets, e.g., to preserve a certain brand image (as in an exclusive or selective distribution system). Suppliers therefore have sought to establish **exclusivity regarding distribution channels** to the benefit of either online or offline distribution, at first particularly by prohibiting online reselling.

In the EU, the ECJ has made clear that it is considered to be a **restraint "by object"** if the supplier **excludes the online sales channel completely**.[75] This type of restraint can never be considered to be block-exempted, meaning that the supplier always bears the burden of proving that the restraint is justified in the individual case.

However, in many cases, suppliers do not exclude online sales completely nowadays but merely seek to impose **restraints to protect the quality** of their distribution system. In that regard, terms excluding sales via third-party platforms have proved to be particularly challenging in terms of assessment. The ECJ has ruled that even where the exception criteria for selective distribution do not apply in the individual case, at least an exemption must be available for this type of restraint, considering that notably an aura of luxury may be *essential in that it enables consumers to distinguish [branded goods] from similar goods and, therefore, [...] an impairment to that aura of luxury is likely to affect the actual quality of those goods.*[76] Thus, the ECJ acknowledges that the distribution system may contribute to the distinguishing power of the brand as a quality signal. However, it may be necessary to consider the market characteristics (e.g., the market participants' share of online sales) to decide whether the exclusion of sales via third-party platforms really matters for the brand image.

In its revised vertical rules, the European Commission has consequently decided to explicitly allow **bans of third-party platforms**, depending on the circumstances.[77] They may, hence, be accepted as a

---

[75] ECJ Judgment of 13 October 2011, *Pierre Fabre Dermo-Cosmétique* (C-439/09, ECR 2011 p. I-9419) ECLI:EU:C:2011:649: objective restraint within the meaning of Reg. 330/2010.

[76] ECJ, Judgment of 6 December 2017, *Coty Germany* (C-230/16) ECLI:EU:C:2017:941, §25.

[77] This would mean that the strict approach of some national competition authorities has to be abandoned. See, e.g., FCO, case report of 24 October 2013 on case B7-1/13-35 —

legitimate qualitative criterion for selective distribution systems. This would mean that even a block exemption is available.[78] However, the restraint must not be used to effectively foreclose the online sales channel completely.[79] Broad bans on the collaboration with price comparison sites or other much-used advertisement tools may have to be viewed more critically as well because those bans may likewise be used to foreclose the online sales channel to a substantial extent.[80]

(2) U.S. law

(a) Exclusive dealing in the Supreme Court's jurisprudence

In the U.S., restraints associated with exclusive dealing are **generally** subject to a **rule of reason analysis** with a focus on the percentage of commerce foreclosed. However, the Supreme Court has developed its jurisprudence on exclusive dealing only in a small number of cases so far. In its early *Standard Oil* judgment (1949), the Court held — here under the Clayton Act — that where *"the affected proportion of retail sales of petroleum products [was] substantial"*, the contract violated the law and there was no room for potential procompetitive justifications.[81] In *Tampa Electric Co. v. Nashville Coal Co.* (1961), the Supreme Court then held more nuancedly the following:

> *[t]o determine substantiality in a given case, it is necessary to weigh the probable effect of the contract on the relevant area of effective competition, taking into account the relative strength of the parties, the proportionate volume of commerce involved in relation to the total*

Sennheiser (re high-quality headsets) on the German practice. This strict stance originally had its basis in the EU policy of enforcing equal treatment between online and offline sales in order to further online sales and, thus, the integration of the EU internal market. However, in its revised Vertical BER and Guidelines, the European Commission has aligned the assessment criteria, meaning that one sales channel may now be favored over the other where an economic justification exists.

[78] European Commission, Guidelines on vertical restraints (fn. 6), §150.

[79] European Commission, Guidelines on vertical restraints (fn. 6), §208.

[80] European Commission, Guidelines on vertical restraints (fn. 6), §206 lit. g; see also Fed. Ct. of Justice (Germany), Order of 12 December 2017, *Asics*, KVZ 41/17, ECLI:DE: BGH:2017:121217BKVZ41.17.0.

[81] *Standard Oil Co. of California v. United States (Standard Stations)*, 337 U.S. 293, 314 (1949).

volume of commerce in the relevant market area, and the probable immediate and future effects which pre-emption of that share of the market might have on effective competition therein.[82]

However, in *FTC v. Brown Shoe Co.* (1966), the Court held that also an exclusivity arrangement with approximately one percent of U.S. shoe retailers could violate the law (here, §5 of the FTC Act) if the arrangement required *shoe retailers [...] substantially to limit their trade with [the supplier's] competitors.*[83] Since the Supreme Court did not have to rule on exclusive dealing after this case, the courts of appeals have developed the law further on their own and have considered a variety of competitive factors when assessing exclusive dealing.[84]

In the context of **tying**, the Supreme Court has held that *exclusive-requirements contract [...] could be unlawful if it foreclosed so much of the market from penetration by [...] competitors as to unreasonably restrain competition in the affected market.*[85] This may indicate that also in the U.S., the underlying concerns associated with exclusive dealing and tying are of a similar nature.

Finally, note again that U.S. law does not have a rule prohibiting the *abuse of a dominant provision.* This makes it necessary to apply a stricter standard for some practices under §1 Sherman Act if these practices do not meet the strict conditions of monopolization/attempted monopolization under §2 Sherman Act.

(b) Exclusivity in intra-brand competition to the benefit of inter-brand competition

The question of whether a brand manufacturer imposes product-related restraints **(intra-brand)** to further competition between brands **(inter-brand)** was also brought before the U.S. Supreme Court.

---

[82] *Tampa Electric Co. v. Nashville Coal Co.*, 365 U.S. 320, 329 (1961).

[83] *FTC v. Brown Shoe Co.*, 384 U.S. 316, 321 (1966).

[84] See, e.g., *Barry Wright Corp. v. ITT Grinnell Corp.*, 724 F.2d 227 (1st Cir. 1983); *Roland Mach. Co. v. Dresser Indus., Inc.*, 749 F.2d 380 (7th Cir. 1984); *U.S. Healthcare, Inc. v. Healthsource, Inc.*, 986 F.2d 589 (1st Cir. 1993); *Omega Envtl., Inc. v. Gilbarco, Inc.*, 127 F.3d 1157 (9th Cir. 1997); *United States v. Microsoft Corp.*, 253 F.3d 34 (D.C. Cir. 2001); *United States v. Dentsply Int'l, Inc.*, 399 F.3d 181 (3d Cir. 2005).

[85] *Jefferson Parish Hospital District No. 2 v. Hyde*, 466 U.S. 2, 30 n.51 (1984).

The Supreme Court originally made a distinction between sale and non-sale restrictions in *United States v. Arnold, Schwinn & Co.*, a case concerning a three-tier distribution system comprising *Schwinn* (i.e., the supplier), intermediate distributors and a network of franchised retailers.[86] The Supreme Court held that *where a manufacturer sells products to his distributor subject to **territorial restrictions** upon resale, a per se violation of the Sherman Act results.*[87]

However, in ***GTE Sylvania***, the U.S. Supreme Court overruled the *Schwinn per se* rule and gave up the distinction between sale and non-sale restrictions.[88] Instead, the Court held that restrictions should be distinguished on the basis of their individual potential for **intra-brand** harm or **inter-brand** benefit. The Court reasoned that *[v]ertical restrictions reduce intra-brand competition by limiting the number of sellers of a particular product competing for the business of a given group of buyers.* ***Location restrictions** have this effect because of practical constraints on the effective marketing area of retail outlets. Although intrabrand competition may be reduced, the ability of retailers to exploit the resulting market may be limited both by the ability of consumers to travel to other franchised locations and, perhaps more importantly, to purchase the competing products of other manufacturers.* At the same time, vertical restrictions may *promote interbrand competition by allowing the manufacturer to achieve certain efficiencies in the distribution of his products.*[89]

The Supreme Court's holding in *GTE Sylvania* paved the way for a consumer-oriented economic assessment of vertical restraints which is on principle **agnostic on how suppliers organize their business vertically**. Therefore, a supplier has also the right to terminate a discounting dealer to prevent free riding. In that respect, the Supreme Court confirmed later that a supplier *has a right to deal, or refuse to deal, with whomever it likes as long as it does so independently.*[90] Moreover, it held that *since price cutting and some measure of service cutting usually go hand in hand*, a supplier may reduce the number of dealers due to its *legitimate desire to*

---

[86] *United States v. Arnold, Schwinn & Co.*, 388 U.S. 365 (1967).

[87] *United States v. Arnold, Schwinn & Co.*, 388 U.S. 365, 379 (1967).

[88] *Continental T.V., Inc. v. GTE Sylvania, Inc.*, 433 U.S. 36 (1977).

[89] *Continental T.V., Inc. v. GTE Sylvania, Inc.*, 433 U.S. 36, 54 (1977) (Emphasis added).

[90] *Monsanto Co. v. Spray-Rite Service Co.*, 465 U.S. 752, 760–61 (1984).

have dealers provide services and with a view to preventing *price cutting [which] is frequently made possible by 'free riding' on the services provided by other dealers.*[91]

(3) Japanese law

Exclusive dealing that causes impediments to fair competition is designated as an Article 19 violation under GD para. 11. Such impediments are found where such practice **lessens free competition** by making it difficult for new entrants or existing competitors to find alternative trading partners and access to the markets (foreclosure). The effect to lessen competition is more readily found where the defendant has stronger market positions and the number of trading partners subject to exclusive conditions is large. The effect is also more likely where several existing suppliers implement the exclusive dealing in parallel. In contrast, such an effect is unlikely to be found when the market share of the defendant does not exceed 20%.

In a case where the defendant prohibits **dealing with a particular competitor**, such practice is assessed in light of GD para. 12. In such a case, too, foreclosure is the issue and the analytical framework is the same as in the case of GD para. 11. The JFTC may issue a cease-and-desist order against the GD paras. 11 and 12 violations.

Where the anticompetitive effect of exclusive dealing, or prohibition of dealing with a particular competitor, is so serious that it establishes or maintains market power, the same practice constitutes private monopolization as defined by AMA Article 2(5) and prohibited by AMA Article 3. The JFTC issues a cease-and-desist order and orders the infringing company to pay an administrative fine called a surcharge.

Any foreclosure is subject to these rules, be it about downstream, upstream or platforms. In all cases, procompetitive effect is taken into account. The erosion of confidential information and know-how, which would discourage investment and information flow between the supplier and its trading partners, is a typical justification.

(4) The EU/U.S./Japanese approaches compared

When comparing the three systems, it must first be noted that all three jurisdictions allow for exclusivity, but all of them also subject exclusivity

---

[91] *Business Elec. Corp. v. Sharp Elec. Corp.*, 485 U.S. 717, 728, 731 (1988).

arrangements to **more stringent conditions the more such arrangements tend to exclude other firms** from the market or from entry to the market. This risk of foreclosure is perceived the greater, the more market power the firm enjoys that imposes the exclusivity requirement. The rules for tying are similar in that respect.

When one looks more closely, the **EU approach to exclusivity appears more rigid** than the approach prevailing in the U.S. and Japan. The European Commission has defined certain vertical restraints as hardcore restraints in its Vertical BER, meaning that a block exemption and, at least in the European Commission's view, even an individual exemption is not available for these restraints.[92] That definition of hardcore restraints is much farther-reaching than the categories of restraints considered anticompetitive under the U.S. rule of reason analysis. A key difference between EU and U.S. law is **that EU law submits potentially all types of exclusivity to stringent review**, given the potential that supplier attempts to foreclose resellers might fragment the internal market, and to preserve the freedom of resellers in competition. In contrast, as noted above, **U.S. law is principally agnostic on how suppliers organize their business vertically** as long as consumers retain the possibility to buy products in other locations or from other manufacturers.[93]

Consequently, **EU law** foresees a **structured** and sometimes even formalistic **assessment for all categories of agreements resulting in any form of exclusivity**. This includes selective distribution and restraints regarding the online distribution channel, for which the assessment standard of EU law is unique. Similar to online sales restrictions, the potential of foreclosure effects associated with territorial exclusivity tends to be viewed rather critically in the EU. This may be related to the objective of the EU competition rules to reduce barriers between EU Member States and to contribute to the creation of an EU single market.[94] In the **U.S., no**

---

[92] Article 4 Reg. (EU) 2022/720; see also European Commission, Guidelines on vertical restraints (fn. 6), §§177 ff., for additional guidance on these restraints.

[93] Cooper *et al.*, A Comparative Study of United States and European Union Approaches to Vertical Policy, pp. 5 ff., available at: http://ssrn.com/abstract=699582; Sagers, "Coty, Amazon, and the Future of Vertical Restraints: Evolving Distribution Norms on Both Atlantic Shores" (2019). Law Faculty Articles and Essays, 988, 103 at 104.

[94] See ECJ, Judgment of 13 July 1966, *Consten and Grundig/Commission of the EEC* (56 and 58–64, ECR 1966 p. 299), ECLI:EU:C:1966:41: absolute territorial protection constitutes restriction "by object"; European Commission, Decision of 30 October 2002, AT.35706 — *PO/Nintendo distribution* on distribution; ECJ Judgment of 4 October 2011,

need is seen **to regulate individual categories of exclusivity** specifically, and cases falling in any such categories are consequently analyzed under the general rules. The different approaches are also reflected in the **enforcement**: Agencies in the EU intervene regularly against agreements stipulating exclusivity, whereas jurisprudence on exclusivity in the U.S. is scarce and agency enforcement appears to be virtually non-existent.

Japan stands in between. The JFTC has issued some guidance and issued cease-and-desist orders also in cases of vertical exclusivity arrangements. That said, the guidance does not go into details to the extent that is common in the EU. Thus, individual cases are analyzed based on broader principles.

(c) Resale price maintenance and similar restrictions of intra-brand competition

Suppliers may be **interested in having the reseller adhere to a certain price**. Thus, suppliers may recommend a resale price or even agree with the reseller on a binding resale price (resale price maintenance — RPM). Additionally, a supplier may allocate the territory among the resellers and prohibit them from promoting the products outside the territory (territorial restriction). Finally, a supplier may designate the way to sell products.

All these practices restrict intra-brand competition. In the above cases, **RPM directly restricts price competition** among retailers. **Territorial restrictions**, on the one hand, exclude other retailers from operating in the allocated territories and therefore are considered to be an **exclusionary practice** running counter to the objective of creating a single market in the EU. However, territorial restrictions **bear the risk of** dampening the retailers' promotional efforts, including price-cuts, and, thus, may also **have an indirect effect similar to RPM. Sales method restrictions** may likewise limit the **freedom of retailers** to introduce a cheaper way to resell products. The latter effects are particularly prominent for competition enforcement in Japan.

However, according to the economic theory, the general rule is that a supplier who has a monopoly power at one level of the distribution chain and sets the price maximizing its profit generally gains nothing by restricting competition in its downstream market (single **monopoly profit**

Football Association Premier League and others (C-403/08 and C-429/08, ECR 2011 p. I-9083) ECLI:EU:C:2011:631; Reg. 2018/302 on cross-border restraints on satellite emissions/online services & trade (so-called geo-blocking).

theorem). Rather, lessened competition in the downstream market facilitates the retailers to raise prices, resulting in double mark-ups both at upstream and downstream levels. Such a situation is called double marginalization, which harms both the downstream supplier by reducing its profit and consumers by raising the consumer price. Considering these, one may argue that, in the absence of foreclosure effects at the level of suppliers, any vertical restrictions are only to promote efficiency by, for instance, mitigating double marginalization or free-riding issues. For instance, RPM is used to lower mark-ups that retailers gain. Based on such a view, there is no reason for competition law to intervene with any vertical restraint except where foreclosure is concerned. The monopoly profit theorem is the background of trends in the jurisprudence to see RPM more favorably than it was seen originally.[95]

In addition, RPM and other restrictions of intra-brand competition with similar effects (e.g., territorial restrictions) can **facilitate collusion** among the suppliers or function to disguise the retailer's price fixing or market allocation cartels.

The EU, the U.S. and Japan each endorse **different views**, and their rules on practice to restrict intra-brand competition vary.

(1) EU law (RPM)

In EU law, it is necessary to distinguish **two questions** regarding RPM. The first question is whether the relevant measure is a unilateral action (by the supplier) or whether it constitutes an **agreement** (between the supplier and the resellers) because generally only the latter may give rise to competition concerns (Subsection a). The second question only comes to bear when an agreement can be established. This subsequent question is whether the agreement violates the rules on **price fixing** (Subsection b). As noted above, other restrictions of intra-brand competition are considered to (also) potentially come along with exclusionary (foreclosure) risks, which justifies treating them separately for the purposes of EU law.

---

[95]Note that while the monopoly profit theorem is certainly recognized in the EU literature, it has not had any impact on European jurisprudence (at least at ECJ level) at all to date. The jurisprudence also protects resellers' independence, irrespective of double marginalization (this may change, though; see comparison Section (4) in this chapter).

(a) Existence of an agreement?

In terms of **EU law**, an agreement on prices can be formed either between competitors or between undertakings active at different levels of the production or distribution chain. No agreement exists in case of price recommendations. However, whenever the supplier recommends a **minimum price** (or any other price that is not expressly labeled as a maximum price) **and, in parallel, exercises pressure** to make sure that the resellers do not go below the recommended price, any change of conduct on the resellers' side to avoid negative supplier reactions is indicative of an agreement.[96] The European Commission even considers a situation with high supplier market shares as increasing the risk that the resellers are forced into an agreement.[97] The national competition authorities may see market power less critically in this context.[98]

Where a supplier **unilaterally imposes maximum prices**, this unilateral behavior falls outside Article 101(1) TFEU. In fact, imposed maximum prices do not limit the freedom to go below a certain price and therefore may even be seen as an alternative to price recommendations. Moreover, when a supplier unilaterally decides to impose supply contingents and the resellers cannot influence the supplies by adhering to a certain policy, this is also not relevant under Article 101(1) TFEU.[99] However, it must be checked thoroughly whether the supplier truly acts unilaterally because an agreement may also come about if the unilateral behavior is embedded in a broader arrangement, depending on the context. Moreover, it should be noted that where the supplier is dominant, any unilateral decision to force the resellers to act in accordance with an imposed supplier policy may violate Article 102 TFEU.[100] This includes, but is not limited to, the imposition of a minimum resale price. In these instances, the supplier's refusal to deal would go beyond the normal

---

[96] See ECJ, Judgment of 18 September 2003, *Volkswagen/Commission* (C-338/00 P, ECR 2003 p. I-9189) ECLI:EU:C:2003:473, §§66–67.

[97] European Commission, Guidelines on vertical restraints (fn. 6), §200.

[98] FCO/BDB, Hinweispapier: Preisbindung im Lebensmitteleinzelhandel, 12 July 2017; Bauer u.a., WuW 2021, 606 (609).

[99] ECJ, Judgment of 6 January 2004, *BAI and Commission/Bayer* (C-2/01 P and C-3/01 P, ECR 2004 p. I-23) ECLI:EU:C:2004:2, §§98 ff., 101 ff.

[100] Article 102 TFEU is applicable beside Article 101 TFEU; see ECJ, Judgment of 21 February 1973, *Europemballage Corporation and Continental Can Company/Commission* (6/72, ECR 1973 p. 215) ECLI:EU:C:1973:22, §25.

course of business and effectively foreclose non-compliant resellers from the downstream market.[101]

(b) Evaluation under the rules on price fixing?

In EU law, agreements in which the supplier imposes a price on the reseller, i.e., RPM agreements, are considered to amount to **price restraints "by object"** under Article 101(1) TFEU.[102] This is also reflected in the Vertical BER, which considers RPM as a hardcore restraint.[103] That has not changed under the revised vertical rules, either.

However, despite this extremely critical legal approach to RPM, it is controversial whether it is economically justified to submit RPM agreements to the strict legal prohibitions of **price fixing** (because they are price-related agreements) or whether a more lenient treatment is justified because such agreements regularly do **not directly contribute to foreclosure** (although they may do so indirectly or contribute to collusion and the exploitation of consumers).[104] This question is of high practical relevance. In its sector inquiry into e-commerce, which preceded the current revision of the EU vertical rules, the European Commission in fact identified RPM as one of the most common restraints in online trade, at least in Europe.[105] That said, the question remains open.

The European Commission's enforcement practice was greatly reduced for a long time. The last European Commission vertical case for more than a decade was the *Yamaha* case decided in 2003.[106] This changed only in 2018 when the European Commission fined several companies, among other things, for using pricing algorithms to monitor RPM.[107] The national competition authorities have been more active over the years.

---

[101] Cf. ECJ, Judgment of 16 September 2008, *Sot. Lélos kai Sia* (C-468/06 to C-478/06, ECR 2008 p. I-7139) ECLI:EU:C:2008:504, §§34, 49, 70–71.

[102] See Chapter 1, Section V.1(a).

[103] Article 4 lit. a Reg. (EU) 2022/720; see also European Commission, Guidelines on vertical restraints (fn. 6), §§185 ff.

[104] See European Commission, Guidelines on vertical restraints (fn. 6), §§189, 196.

[105] European Commission, E-Commerce Sector Inquiry Final Report, 2017, §§28–29.

[106] European Commission, Decision of 16 July 2003, AT.37975 — *PO/Yamaha*.

[107] European Commission, Decisions of 24 July 2018, AT.40465, AT.40469, AT.40181, AT.40182 — *Pioneer et al.*

The German FCO also found that RPM may be used in hub-and-spoke cartel scenarios as well.[108]

The ECJ has not had to rule on RPM clauses for a long time.[109] The ECJ's *Pierre Fabre* judgment may potentially be read as also confirming the traditional hostile approach toward RPM.[110] However, the more recent *Coty* judgment indicates that the ECJ is open to making a **balanced assessment regarding quality-related competition restraints**.[111] It remains to be seen whether this openness may also extend to price-related restraints at some point.

(2) U.S. law

In relation to **restraints of intra-brand competition**, U.S. jurisprudence has shifted from *per se* violation to rule-of-reason analysis also regarding price-related restrictions. This shift must be seen in the context of the changes that first took place in relation to non-price restrictions.

The starting point was the Supreme Court's acknowledgment in *GTE Sylvania* that *the market impact of vertical restrictions is complex because of their potential for a simultaneous reduction of intra-brand competition and stimulation of inter-brand competition.*[112] The Supreme Court therefore held that the rule of reason is the right approach in relation to non-price vertical restrictions.[113]

With regard to **price restraints**, it took a while for the U.S. to depart from its *per se* approach, originally established in *Dr. Miles*.[114] However, in *Kahn*, the Supreme Court held that an imposed **maximum resale price** must be evaluated under the rule of reason.[115] In the reasoning, the Supreme Court insisted that *the primary purpose of the antitrust laws is*

---

[108]See FCO, Decision of 25 September 2009, B 3 – 123/08 – *Ciba Vision*, §§62–63.

[109]However, note the cases referred to in European Commission, Guidelines on vertical restraints (fn. 6), §195.

[110]ECJ Judgment of 13 October 2011, *Pierre Fabre Dermo-Cosmétique* (C-439/09, ECR 2011 p. I-9419) ECLI:EU:C:2011:649; see Section V.3.b(1)(c) in this chapter.

[111]ECJ, Judgment of 6 December 2017, *Coty Germany* (C-230/16) ECLI:EU:C:2017:941; see Section V.3.b(1)(c) in this chapter.

[112]*Continental T.V., Inc. v. GTE Sylvania, Inc.*, 433 U.S. 36, 51(1977).

[113]*Continental T.V., Inc. v. GTE Sylvania, Inc.*, 433 U.S. 36, 58–59 (1977).

[114]*Dr. Miles Medical Co. v. John D. Park & Sons Co.*, 220 U.S. 373 (1911).

[115] *State Oil Co. v. Khan*, 522 U.S. 3, 22 (1997).

to protect inter-brand competition[116] and also explained that *higher the price at which [product] is resold, the smaller the volume sold, and so the lower the profit to the supplier if the higher profit per [product] at the higher price is being snared by the dealer.*[117]

Finally, in **Leegin**, the Supreme Court overruled its earlier jurisprudence also with regard to imposed **minimum resale prices (RPM)** and held that, as a general rule, *vertical price restraints are to be judged by the rule of reason* and not under a *per se* standard.[118] The Supreme Court based its holding on the context-dependent economic appraisal and the procompetitive effects sometimes associated with vertical price restraints. Having said that, note that where horizontal price-fixing agreement exists among retailers, as in *Apple*, the practice may constitute a *per se* violation.[119]

(3) Japanese law

Under AMA Article 2(4), RPM **generally** constitutes an **AMA Article 19 violation** in Japan. RPM is viewed to be anticompetitive in general as it restricts the intra-brand price competition and lessens free competition. The JFTC views that such practice generally has the effect to maintain price at a higher level. It is also generally irrelevant whether the defendant has a leading market position, as the very fact that the supplier successfully implements the RPM indicates the substantial economic position of the defendant or its products.

The JFTC accepts that the RPM **may be justifiable** on the ground of double-marginalization or free-riding issues. However, the JFTC also insists that there should be no less-restrictive alternative (LRA) means to mitigate such a concern. Where an online retailer's free-riding of a brick-mortal retailer is the issue and the supplier wants the latter to continue to provide pre-purchase services, such as the explanation of the products, suppliers aiding the latter by treating them favorably would constitute more direct and less restrictive means. To date, there has been no case in

---

[116] *State Oil Co. v. Khan*, 522 U.S. 3, 15 (1997).

[117] *State Oil Co. v. Khan*, 522 U.S. 3, 16 (1997).

[118] *Leegin Creative Leather Products, Inc. v. PSKS, Inc.*, 551 U.S. 877 (2007).

[119] *U.S. v. Apple*, 952 F. Supp. 2d 638 (S.D.N.Y. 2013); 791 F.3d 290 (2d Cir. 2015); DOJ, Supreme Court Rejects Apple's Request to Review E-Books Antitrust Conspiracy Findings, press release No. 16–259 of 7 March 2016. The case basically concerned a hub-and-spoke cartel combined with an MFN restraint.

which either courts or the JFTC determine the RPM does not violate AMA Article 19 on such grounds.

Although **other price-related restraints** against downstream trading partners such as patentee's price restriction of licensee's products are assessed in light of GD para. 12, such practices generally fulfill the conditions of GD para. 12 and violate AMA Article 19 in the same way as RPM, as far as they restrict downstream price competition. Similar holds in relation to the restriction of advertising when it relates to pricing.

On the other hand, **vertical territorial restrictions** are assessed on a case-by-case basis. The JFTC may find that it restricts intra-brand competition and has the effect to maintain price at a high level and is, thus, anticompetitive. Alternatively, it may find it lawful as such restriction is necessary to promote retailers' investment in product promotional efforts. In assessing competitive effect, the JFTC takes into account the state of competition both at upstream and downstream, the manner of restriction and procompetitive justification. In general, it views passive-sales bans more skeptically. The JFTC considers that there is no competitive concern where the share of suppliers does not exceed 20%.

Vertical **restraints in relation to sales methods**, such as obliging the retailer in-person sales and other requirements relating to storage and presentation of the products, are generally lawful as far as such requirements are reasonable and imposed without discrimination. The selective distribution system, which has criteria relating only to the sales method, is assessed similarly and is generally lawful. Although the restriction of online distribution may still constitute a GD para. 12 violation, the position of the JFTC is not necessarily clear.

(4) The EU/U.S./Japanese approaches compared

RPM and similar restrictions of intra-brand competition are the area of the law on vertical agreements where the covered jurisdictions diverge the most. The theory of harm underlying RPM is the most controversial as RPM does not directly contribute to foreclosure. While, in the **EU**, the ECJ jurisprudence on non-price-related restraints shows increasing openness for a balancing of the effects of restraints on inter-brand and intra-brand competition (see Subsection 3.b(1)(c) on *Coty*), European case law and enforcement practice on price-related restraints continue to be rather dogmatic. This may again be due to the interest in preserving the pricing freedom of resellers and also to the simple fact that the ECJ has not had to rule on RPM for years.

The **U.S.** Supreme Court's jurisprudence aligns the assessment standard for non-price and price-related restraints under the rule of reason.[120] Thus, the U.S. jurisprudence is driven by the interest of consumers in the protection of inter-brand competition but excludes the pricing freedom of resellers from the assessment (as long as no collusion takes place at their level to the detriment of consumers).

The **Japanese** approach is to be situated again somewhat in between but in effect closer to the U.S. The JFTC's GD defines the categories of non-price and price-related restraints recognized equally in the EU and the U.S. However, when it comes to territorial restrictions or other restrictions of intra-brand competition, the focus is more on the contribution of these restraints on prices and not on any exclusionary effects (as would be the case in the EU). Thus, the JFTC's GD must be read as reflecting the U.S. Supreme Court's preference in protecting inter-brand competition even to the extent that intra-brand competition is being excluded from the market.

Good to know: What about statutory pricing obligations?

It is not only attractive for suppliers to interfere with the pricing decisions of resellers. The state may likewise have an interest in excluding price competition at the resellers' level. Regularly, the state will regulate resellers' prices where it considers a public interest to mandate the availability of products regardless of market prices (e.g., prescriptive drugs) or where it wants to ensure that resellers can generate a certain margin (e.g., booksellers in jurisdictions with book resale pricing rules).[121] Where the state imposes a pricing mechanism by law or administrative ordinance, it takes away the freedom to act of market participants, which excludes an assessment under the cartel prohibitions. In contrast, where it only authorizes suppliers to impose a price on resellers, these prohibitions may still apply.[122]

---

[120] It may be noteworthy in this context that Att'ny General Wahl explicitly referred to the *Leegin* judgment in its Opinion of 26 July 2017 in *Coty Germany* (C-230/16), ECLI:EU:C:2017:603, §41.

[121] See, e.g., §§3, 5 of the German *Buchpreisbindungsgesetz (BuchPrG)*.

[122] For the book pricing obligations, the suppliers actually do remain free to set a resale price. However, Article 101(1) TFEU here is still inapplicable because books are protected

(d) Price parity: Vertical restraints associated with various theories of harm

Price parity or **Most-Favored-Nation (MFN)** clauses are a type of competition restraint that is not specific to online trade but has become more widespread with the emergence of online platforms. MFN clauses have become an issue particularly with online booking portals for flights and hotel rooms, or other online marketplaces. Those platforms have been using price parity clauses (sometimes labeled **best-price** clauses) in the contracts with the commercial users of their platforms. These clauses require dealers using the platform to offer consumers (as platform users) the most favorable conditions on the platform, as compared to the dealers' own websites **(narrow MFN)**, or also other channels, including other platforms **(wide MFN)**.

The concerns associated with MFN clauses are **partly foreclosure-related and partly related to collusion**. This is for the following reasons: MFN clauses exclude pricing competition. Different firms may use MFN clauses for different reasons. However, when booking portals impose these clauses on their commercial users (e.g., hotel owners), they mainly do so to mitigate the risk that the commercial users free ride by using the portal as an information channel to consumers and then selling via other channels (meaning that the portal does not earn a commission). This is no problem when the booking portal has a small market share, but it can become a problem if the portal enjoys market power. In these cases, imposing an MFN clause may allow the portal to **neutralize the competitive threat of other portals** (because the commercial users are forced to charge the same price everywhere) and to **impose a uniform price level** to the detriment of consumers.

In **EU law, wide MFN clauses** are seen very critically because they restrain price competition between the platforms as well as between the platforms and the dealers.[123] Based on what was set out in the preceding

---

as a cultural value and the European Commission has not developed a competition policy taking into account this cultural value yet; see ECJ, 10 January 1985, 229/83 — Leclerc, Slg. 1985, 1, ECLI:EU:C:1985:1, §20.

[123] See at the level of the EC: Decision of 25 July 2013, 39.847 — *Ebooks (Apple)*; Decision of 3 August 2017, 40.153 — *E-book MFNs and related matters (Amazon)*; press releases of 19 and 29 July 2021 (flight booking systems: 40.618 — *Sabre*; 40617 — *Amadeus*); at national level, e.g.: FCO: Case Report of 9 December 2013 relating to a Decision of 26 November 2013, B6-46/12 — *Amazon* (hybrid platform); Decision of

paragraph, at platform level, the widespread use of such MFN clauses can effectively foreclose other platforms (e.g., another hotel booking portal) from entering the market. In addition, the widespread use means increased price transparency, which translates into a heightened risk of collusion. At the level of dealers, wide MFN clauses may contribute to an enhanced quality competition and allow to exclude free riders. However, wide MFN clauses may also increase the risk of dealer collusion (depending on other factors, e.g., hassle costs[124]).

Narrow MFN clauses likewise restrict price competition between the platforms and the dealers. However, the collusion risk is mitigated both at the platform and at the dealer level because the clauses do not limit platform competition. At the same time, they exclude dealer-free riding as well. A German court even considered narrow MFN clauses to be ancillary restraints, but this was not upheld on appeal.[125]

Under the **revised EU vertical rules**, the prices imposed outright by a platform operator should be considered to be price restraints "by object" whereas prohibitions to undercut the offer on the platform via offers made through other channels (wide MFN) could be exempted individually, and prohibitions to undercut the offer on the platform via offers on the dealers' own websites (narrow MFN) could even be block-exempted.[126]

Regarding MFN clauses, the competition issues examined in EU law have come up in the other covered jurisdictions in recent years as well. Before that, MFN clauses were discussed in a different context, at least in the U.S. In **U.S. law**, MFN clauses gained prominence in pricing agreements between **hospitals and physicians**, which were attacked by health insurers. In *Blue Cross & Blue Shield v. Marshfield Clinic*, the Court of

---

20 December 2013, B 9 — 66/10 — *HRS*; Decision of 22 December 2015, B 9-121/13 — *Booking*; press release of 20 December 2013 (HRS/Booking/Expedia); press release of 3 June 2015 (Verivox); UK CMA, press release of 24 September 2014 (car insurance; before Brexit); Decision of 19 November 2020, 50505 (home insurance).

[124]Hassle costs are the monetary and non-monetary costs that consumers bear when they invoke the best-price promise and want to be reimbursed the difference.

[125]Higher Reg. Ct. of Düsseldorf, Order of 4 June 2019, *Booking*, Kart 2/16 (V), ECLI:DE:OLGD:2019:0604.KART2.16V.00; reversed and remanded by Fed. Ct. of Justice, Order of 18 May 2021, *Booking*, Kart 2/16 (V), ECLI:DE:BGH:2021:180521B KVR54.20.0.

[126]Article 5(1) lit. d Reg. (EU) 2022/720; Guidelines on vertical restraints (fn. 6), §§359, 194.

Appeals for the Seventh Circuit held that MFN *"are standard devices [...]. It is not price fixing"*.[127] Thus, agreements of that type have been analyzed under a rule-of-reason standard. However, in *A US v. BCBSM,* the deciding court held that MFN clauses entitling health insurer BCBSM to the lowest price agreed with its competitors or even less than that ("MFN+") shielded BCBMS's <u>market power</u> against competitor advances.[128] In *United States v. Comcast,* the deciding court held that MFN clauses can protect the same incentives for the supplier as agreed exclusivity.[129] In this case, thus, market entrants had a right to not-less favorable terms (i.e., the entrants may themselves impose MFN).

Price parity clauses in an **online marketplace context** have been the subject of a U.S. court action against Amazon, which is discussed in Chapter 5 on digital ecosystems. Amazon is reported to have dropped the practice in the meantime.[130]

Amazon **Japan** was likewise suspected to have restricted business activities of the sellers in Amazon Marketplace by including the price parity clauses as well as selection parity clauses, i.e., clauses requiring sellers to offer via Amazon Marketplace all variations in color and size, etc. among all products they sell via other sales channels. The JFTC found such clauses to restrain competition by (i) limiting sellers' freedom to reduce prices and expand their lineups of goods that they sell via other sales channels, (ii) allowing the online shopping mall operator to achieve benefits for the shopping mall without making any competitive efforts and (iii) reducing the online shopping mall operators' incentives for innovation and hindering new entrants.[131] Since the JFTC accepted commitments offered by Amazon Japan to eliminate the suspected violation, it closed the case without finding a violation.

---

[127] *Blue Cross & Blue Shield v. Marshfield Clinic,* 65 F3d 1406 (1995), cert denied, 516 U.S. 1184 (1996).

[128] *AUS v. BCBSM,* 809 F.Supp 2d 665 (2011).

[129] *United States v. Comcast,* 808 F.Supp 2d 145 (D.D.C. 2011).

[130] Shu, Amazon reportedly nixes its price parity requirement for third-party sellers in the U.S., tech crunch, March 12, 2019.

[131] OECD, Global Forum on Competition, Economic Analysis and Evidence in Abuse Cases — Contribution from Japan — Session II, 7 December 2021, §§6–8.

Good to know: The European harmonization obligation of Article 3 Regulation 1/2003 in collaboration cases and national law in EU Member States

Article 3(2)(1) Regulation 1/2003 provides the following: *The application of national competition law may not lead to the prohibition of agreements, decisions by associations of undertakings or concerted practices which may affect trade between Member States but which do not restrict competition within the meaning of Article 81(1) of the Treaty [= Article 101(1) TFEU], or which fulfil the conditions of Article 81(3) of the Treaty [= Article 101(3) TFEU] or which are covered by a Regulation for the application of Article 81(3) of the Treaty.*

The purpose of this provision is to harmonize competition law in the EU and to make sure that it is not circumvented and undermined by national regulation. Nevertheless, national legislature sometimes includes rules in the national competition acts, e.g., to protect collaboration in an SME context or to carve out locally relevant sectors from the general cartel prohibition (e.g., §3 and §§28 ff. of the German Competition Act). Rules protecting SME collaboration are not problematic if they are interpreted in line with the objectives of EU competition law, i.e., allowing for rationalization but not for outright cartels. The sector-specific exceptions are usually more problematic, the more they deviate from the sectoral rules in the European Treaties. These exceptions risk violating the legal principles developed in ECJ 6/64 — *Costa/ENEL,* where the Court held the following:

The integration into the laws of each Member State of [Regulations] from the [EU], and more generally the terms and the spirit of the Treaty, make it impossible for the States [...] to accord precedence to a unilateral and subsequent measure over a legal system accepted by them on a basis of reciprocity.

Regarding price parity obligations, national legislature has tried to come to the aid of local hotel owners. For example, Article L. 311-5-1 of

(Continued)

(Continued)

the French LOI n° 2015-990 du 6 août 2015 pour la croissance, l'activité et l'égalité des chances économiques included a provision in the *code du tourisme* according to which *the hotelier remains free to grant the hotel customer any discount or tariff advantage, of whatever nature, any clause to the contrary being deemed unwritten* (informal translation; emphasis added). The Appendix to the Unfair Trade Practices Act (No. 32) and §7 of the Price Making Act in Austria include similar prohibitions of interference with the freedom of accommodation providers to set prices. It is unclear whether these rules are in line with Article 3(2)(1) Regulation 1/2003.[132]

---

[132]The same legal uncertainty exists with regard to Article 1(2) Reg. 1/2003: *Agreements, decisions and concerted practices caught by Article [101](1) of the Treaty which satisfy the conditions of Article [101](3) of the Treaty shall not be prohibited [...].*

Chapter 4

Single-Firm Conduct

I. The law

In all EU, U.S. and Japanese law, the assessment standard for coordinated behavior is **much stricter** and the legal consequences are more severe than for unilateral behavior. This is because unilateral independent action by individual firms is less likely to cause any competitive harm. Thus, market power is a central requirement for applying the rules on the abuse of dominance in Article 102 TFEU, on monopolization and attempts to monopolize in §2 Sherman Act[1] and on private monopolization under AMA Articles 2(5) and 3. Although Japanese law regulates unilateral conduct without market power under AMA Articles 2(9) and 19, sanctions imposed on the violation are significantly minor relative to horizontal collusion and private monopolization.

In this chapter, we focus on single-firm conduct, which may **include** scenarios where this conduct occurs in the **context of a contractual relationship** (e.g., in a tying or exclusive dealing context). The term "unilateral" conduct is reserved here for scenarios where there is no agreement. Further, note that single-firm conduct principally excludes oligopoly scenarios.[2]

---

[1]See ECJ, Judgment of 13 July 1966, *Consten and Grundig/Commission of the EEC* (56 and 58–64, ECR 1966 p. 299), ECLI:EU:C:1966:41, at p. 340; Judgment of 13 July 1966, Italy/Council of the EEC and Commission of the EEC (32/65, ECR 1966 p. 389), ECLI:EU:C:1966:42, at p. 408.

[2]But see Chapter 1, Section VI on these scenarios. Regarding the law in the EU Member States, see also the box in Section II.1 in this chapter.

1. Article 102 TFEU (abuse of dominance)

Any abuse by one or more undertakings of a dominant position within the internal market or in a substantial part of it shall be prohibited as incompatible with the internal market in so far as it may affect trade between Member States. Such abuse may, in particular, consist in:

(a) *directly or indirectly imposing unfair purchase or selling prices or other unfair trading conditions;*
(b) *limiting production, markets or technical development to the prejudice of consumers;*
(c) *applying dissimilar conditions to equivalent transactions with other trading parties, thereby placing them at a competitive disadvantage;*
(d) *making the conclusion of contracts subject to acceptance by the other parties of supplementary obligations which, by their nature or according to commercial usage, have no connection with the subject of such contracts.*

In addition, the following EU guidelines are important for the interpretation of this provision:

- On the relevant "market" within the meaning of Article 102 TFEU and generally within the meaning of EU competition law: Notice on the relevant market.[3]
- On the effect on "trade between Member States" in Article 102 TFEU: Guidelines on the effect on trade.[4]
- Regarding exclusionary abuses, see also European Commission Guidance on enforcement priorities (2009).[5]

---

[3] Commission Notice on the definition of relevant market for the purposes of Community competition law, OJ C 372, 9 December 1997, p. 5; accessible: https://eur-lex.europa.eu/legal-content/EN/ALL/?uri=CELEX:31997Y1209(01). This Notice is currently under review; see here: https://competition-policy.ec.europa.eu/public-consultations/2022-market-definition-notice_en.

[4] Commission Notice — Guidelines on the effect on trade concept contained in Articles 81 and 82 of the Treaty, OJ C 101, 27 April 2004, p. 81; accessible: https://eur-lex.europa.eu/legal-content/EN/ALL/?uri=CELEX:52004XC0427(06). See Chapter 1, Section III.2.

[5] European Commission, Communication from the Commission: Guidance on its enforcement priorities in applying Article 82 of the EC Treaty to abusive exclusionary conduct by dominant undertakings, OJ C 45, 24 February 2009, pp. 7–20, as amended by European Commission, Amendments Communication, OJ C 116, 31 March 2023, p. 1.

2. §2 Sherman Act (15 U.S.C. §2; monopolization)

Every person who shall monopolize, or attempt to monopolize, or combine or conspire with any other person or persons, to monopolize any part of the trade or commerce among the several States, or with foreign nations, shall be deemed guilty of a felony, and, on conviction thereof, shall be punished by fine not exceeding $100,000,000 if a corporation, or, if any other person, $1,000,000, or by imprisonment not exceeding 10 years, or by both said punishments, in the discretion of the court.

In the individual case, also the Robinson-Patman Act and §5 of the FTC Act may be relevant. See Chapter 1 on the former and Chapter 5 on the latter provision.

3. Articles 2(5) and 3 of the AMA (private monopolization) and Articles 2(9) and 19 of the AMA (unfair trade practices)

Articles 2(5) and 3
See Chapter 2 (Horizontal Collusion)

Article 19 *An enterprise must not employ unfair trade practices.*

Article 2(9) *The term "unfair trade practices" as used in this Act means an act falling under any of the following items:*

Article 2(9)(ii) [Discriminatory pricing]: *Unjustly and continually supplying goods or services at a price applied differentially between regions or between parties, thereby tending to cause difficulties to the business activities of other enterprise[s].*

Article 2(9)(iii) [Low price]: *Without justifiable grounds, continuously supplying goods or services at a price significantly below the cost incurred to supply them, thereby tending to cause difficulties to the business activities of other enterprises.*

Article 2(9)(v) [Abuse of superior dominant position]: *Engaging in any act specified in one of the following by making use of one's superior bargaining position over the counterparty unjustly, in light of normal business practices' is an unfair trade practice:*

a. *Causing said counterparty in continuous transactions (including a party with whom one newly intends to engage in continuous transactions; the same applies in (b) below) to purchase goods or services other than those to which said transactions pertain.*

b.   *Causing said counterparty in continuous transactions to provide money, services or other economic benefits.*

c.   *Refusing to receive goods in transactions with said counterparty, causing said counterparty to take back such goods after receiving them from said counterparty, delaying payment to said counterparty or reducing the amount of payment, or otherwise establishing or changing trade terms or executing transactions in a way disadvantageous to said counterparty.*

JFTC GP Para. 2 [Refusal to deal (including unilateral refusal to deal)]: *Unjustly refusing to trade or restricting the quantity or substance of goods or services pertaining to trade with a certain enterprise, or causing another enterprise to undertake any act that falls under one of these categories.*

JFTC GP Para. 3 [Discriminatory pricing]: *In addition to any act falling under the provisions of Article 2(9)(ii) of AMA, unjustly supplying or accepting goods or services for a consideration which discriminates between regions or between parties.*

JFTC GP Para. 4 [Discriminatory treatment]: *Unjustly affording favorable or unfavorable treatment to a certain enterprise in regard to the terms or execution of a trade.*

JFTC GP Para. 10 [Tie-in Sales, etc.]: *Unjustly causing another party to purchase goods or services from oneself or from an entrepreneur designated by oneself by tying it to the supply of other goods or services, or otherwise coercing the said party to trade with oneself or with an entrepreneur designated by oneself.*

JFTC GP Para. 14 [Unfair interference to competitors' trade]: *Unjustly interfering with a transaction between another enterprise who is in a domestic competitive relationship with oneself or with the corporation of which one is a stockholder or an officer, and its transacting party, by preventing the effecting of a contract, or by inducing the breach of a contract, or by any other means whatsoever.*

II. The liable actors and anticompetitive effect

A **conceptual divergence** exists between EU law on the one hand and U.S. law and Japanese law on the other hand as to what triggers the analysis of behavior that may run counter to the rules on single-firm conduct. In the EU, Article 102 TFEU addresses companies in a certain market position specifically. In the U.S. and Japan, the analysis starts rather with a finding of monopoly and similar harm in the market.

However, looking more closely, the **likelihood of a violation increases under all relevant provisions if the relevant company enjoys a particular market position**. This justifies starting this chapter (like Chapter 2) with a section on the liable actors and anticompetitive effect.

1. EU

Under Article 102 TFEU, only undertakings in a dominant position are subject to the prohibition of abusive behavior. The ECJ has defined the dominant position in its constant jurisprudence as a

> *[p]osition of economic strength enjoyed by an undertaking which enables it to **prevent effective competition being maintained** on the relevant market **by giving it the power to behave to an appreciable extent independently** of its competitors, customers and ultimately of its consumers.*[6]

Thus, two conditions must be fulfilled to find "dominance":

- the power to behave *"to an appreciable extent"* independently of other market participants,
- the potential of preventing maintenance of effective competition.

Undertakings meeting these criteria are considered to have a "special responsibility" for the maintenance of competition.[7] This means that although being dominant is not prohibited, a dominant undertaking is exposed to increased liability risks under the European competition rules.

A question of debate has been whether Article 102 TFEU also covers dominant positions on the demand side (monopsony power). This was

---

[6]ECJ, Judgment of 14 February 1978, *United Brands/Commission* (27/76, ECR 1978 p. 207) ECLI:EU:C:1978:22, §65 (highlighting only here); Judgment of 13 February 1979, *Hoffmann-La Roche/Commission* (85/76, ECR 1979 p. 461) ECLI:EU:C:1979:36, §38.
[7]ECJ, Judgment of 9 November 1983, *Michelin/Commission* (322/81, ECR 1983 p. 3461) ECLI:EU:C:1983:313, §57.

because the above ECJ definition does not address the power of an undertaking to act independently of other suppliers.[8] Nevertheless, the GC and the European Commission have examined monopsony power already in several cases.[9] However, note that even so, Article 102 TFEU applies only to a limited extent to state-owned enterprises if they act as purchasers. This is because, according to the ECJ, *[t]he nature of the **purchasing activity** must be determined according to whether or not the **subsequent use of the purchased goods** amounts to an economic activity.*[10] Moreover, the competition rules apply to purchases of input materials for services of general economic interest only subject to further conditions (Article 106(2) TFEU).

The European Commission applies the following criteria in order to establish a dominant position within the meaning of the ECJ jurisprudence. According to the European Commission, the *power to act independently* is basically the **power to raise prices** without competitive constraints.[11] To establish whether an undertaking has the power to raise prices, the European Commission examines the market position of the relevant undertaking (market share and its stability, access to supply or sales markets), other factors that are relevant for the likely, timely and sufficient market entry of competitors and the existence of countervailing buyer power. In that context, the test for determining whether market entry is likely is whether entry is profitable taking into account factors such as the barriers to expansion or entry, reactions of the (dominant) undertaking and others, and the risks and costs of failure.

Moreover, according to the European Commission, the *potential of preventing the maintenance of effective competition,* at least on principle, requires a delineation of the **relevant market** where the dominant position is capable of producing anticompetitive effects. The market is defined mainly from the buyers' perspective and with a focus on the homogeneousness of market characteristics. The sellers' perspective is used to complete the picture. Thus, the market definition requires a test to determine which products are substitutable against each other (demand/supply

---

[8]Open: ECJ, Judgment of 28 March 1985, *CICCE/Commission* (298/83, ECR 1985 p. 1105) ECLI:EU:C:1985:150, §§22–30.

[9]See, e.g., GC, Judgment of 17 December 2003, *British Airways/Commission* (T-219/99, ECR 2003 p. II-5917) ECLI:EU:T:2003:343, §§101–109.

[10]See ECJ, Judgment of 11 July 2006, *FENIN/Commission* (C-205/03 P, ECR 2006 p. I-6295) ECLI:EU:C:2006:453, §26 (highlighting only here).

[11]EC Guidance on enforcement priorities (fn. 5), §§9 ff.

substitution) and in which geographic area the supply and demand structure is homogeneous. In rare cases, differences in time can become relevant as well (e.g., for cultural or sports events and trade fairs). The demand substitutability of products can generally be tested by considering a "hypothetical small (in the range of 5% to 10%) but permanent relative price increase in the products and areas".[12] This test is also called the SSNIP test.[13] Product substitutability is additionally relevant if "suppliers are able to switch production to the relevant products and market them in the short term without incurring significant additional costs or risks" in response to a relevant price change.[14]

Once the relevant market has been defined, it is necessary to assess whether the undertaking concerned is able to prevent *"the maintenance of effective* competition". In this context, also competitive forces from outside that market may be taken into account to **assess the market power** of the undertaking concerned as well as other existing structural **barriers to entry**. So-called **"potential competition"** by firms entering the market in the foreseeable future (i.e., typically within 2–3 years) is not part of the market but may constitute a relevant competitive constraint.

Finding a dominant position is typically challenging. Hence, according to the ECJ, single-firm dominance may be **presumed** if the relevant undertaking has a market share of 50%.[15] In contrast, the European Commission considers such dominance "not likely" below a market share of 40%.[16]

Good to know: Dominance and other relevant positions in EU Member State law

In the EU, the Member States may apply their own rules on abuses as long as they do not neglect to also apply Article 102 TFEU, where

(Continued)

---

[12] European Commission, Notice on the relevant market (fn. 3), §17.
[13] "SSNIP" = "Small but significant and non-transitory increase in price".
[14] European Commission, Notice on the relevant market (fn. 3), §20.
[15] ECJ, Judgment of 3 July 1991, *AKZO/Commission* (62/86, ECR 1991 p. I-3359), §60.
[16] European Commission, Guidance on enforcement priorities (fn. 5), §14.

(Continued)

applicable.[17] Thus, e.g., German law still includes several provisions that lower the bar for applying the abuse rules or simply diverge from Article 102 TFEU to a certain extent. For example, the German rules also allow one to find abuses where the undertaking concerned only possesses "relative market power" or "superior market power".[18] In addition, Germany recently introduced a special provision for abuses of undertakings of "paramount cross-market significance".[19] Moreover, §18(3) of the German Competition Act defines its own general criteria for finding dominance but focuses less on price and also considers financial strength beside market shares.

Furthermore, it is pointed out already in Chapter 1, Section VI that Article 102 TFEU — unlike §2 Sherman Act and Japanese law — also applies in case of joint dominant positions (oligopoly). The same is actually true for abuse provisions in EU Member State law. Some national competition acts, e.g., those of Austria and Germany, even include statutory rules on which criteria allow a finding of joint dominance and when joint dominance may be presumed. In Germany, for instance, three undertakings (or fewer) are presumed to be jointly dominant if they have a market share of at least 50% and five undertakings (or fewer) are presumed to be jointly dominant if they have a market share of at least 66%.[20]

---

[17]Article 3(1)(2) Reg. 1/2003. See also Renda *et al.*, Study on the Legal Framework Covering Business-to-Business Unfair Trading Practices in the Retail Supply Chain, Prepared for the European Commission, DG Internal Market, Final Report, 26 February 2014, on the applicable national rules in this context.

[18]§18(1), (3) GWB. Relative market power: other undertakings as suppliers or purchasers depend on the undertaking concerned in such a way that sufficient and reasonable possibilities for switching to third parties do not exist and there is a significant imbalance in power; superior market power: power in relation to small and medium-sized competitors.

[19]§19a GWB.

[20]§18(5) and (6) GWB. Pursuant to §18(7) GWB, the presumption in §18(6) can be rebutted if the relevant undertakings demonstrate that (i) the conditions of competition are such that substantial competition between them can be expected or (ii) the body of undertakings has no paramount market position in relation to the remaining competitors. Similar: §4(2), (2a) of the Austrian KartG.

2. U.S. law

§2 Sherman Act separates unilateral conduct (which is not based on a conspiracy) into two categories: monopolization and attempt to monopolize. The U.S. Supreme Court has held that **monopolization** within the meaning of §2 has two elements: *(1) the possession of monopoly power in the relevant market, and (2) the willful acquisition or maintenance of that power as distinguished from growth or development as a consequence of a superior product, business acumen, or historic accident.*[21] Meanwhile, the Supreme Court held that three elements must be fulfilled with regard to **attempts to monopolize**, which do not require any defined market power: *(1) defendant has engaged in predatory or anticompetitive conduct with (2) a specific intent to monopolize and (3) a dangerous probability of achieving monopoly power.*[22]

Therefore, §2 Sherman Act requires either a finding of existing monopoly power at the time of litigation or prosecution[23] or at least a **high probability** that the practice at issue would create such power. Note, though, that in U.S. law, the power element relates to the anticompetitive effects, rather than to the liable entities.

Like in the EU, establishing monopoly power on principle requires defining the **relevant market** and an analysis of the conditions on the relevant market.[24] However, **presumptions** may help in the assessment also under §2. Although U.S. courts have been reluctant to use a general market share threshold, it is fair to say that monopoly power is typically only found if the company's share of relevant market exceeds 70%.[25] For the "attempt to monopolize" (or "conspiracies to monopolize"),[26] the

---

[21] *United States v. Grinnell Corp.*, 384 U.S. 563, 570–71 (1966); *Verizon Communications Inc. v. Law Offices of Curtis v. Trinko, LLP* 540 U.S. 398, 407 (2004).
[22] *Spectrum Sports v. McQuillan*, 506 U.S. 447 (1993).
[23] *United States v. Aluminum Co. of America (Alcoa)*, 148 F.2d 416 (2d. Cir. 1945).
[24] *Spectrum Sports v. McQuillan*, 506 U.S. 447, 448 (1993) [establishing that *"the dangerous probability [...] requires inquiry into the relevant product and geographic market and the defendant's economic power in that market"*].
[25] *Exxon Corp. v. Berwick Bay Real Estates Partners*, 748 F.2d 937, 940 (5th Cir. 1984); *Colo. Interstate Gas Co. v. Natural Gas Pipeline Co. of Am.*, 885 F.2d 683, 694 n.18 (10th Cir. 1989); *United States v. Dentsply Int'l, Inc.*, 399 F.3d 181, 187, 188 (3d Cir. 2005).
[26] See Chapter 1, Section VI.

threshold would be lower, by definition[27]: Concerning the "dangerous probability", it is in any case necessary to consider *"the relevant market and the defendant's ability to lessen or destroy competition in that market"*.[28] Whether a company can be found to be liable depends additionally on its anticompetitive intent and its conduct.[29]

3. Japanese law

The AMA allows finding violations in cases of both exclusionary practices and exploitation. However, the rules on private monopolization can only be applied to exclusionary practices. Exploitation in the form of an imposition of unfair conditions can only be addressed as an unfair trade practice, which requires that the relevant entity holds a superior bargaining position to be liable.

Private monopolization, which is defined by AMA Article 2(5) and prohibited by AMA Article 3, is the main provision regulating unilateral exclusionary conduct. To find a violation, the relevant market, termed "particular field of trade", must be defined and the practice at issue must have established, maintained or strengthened market power in that market. Note that although the law only requires market power rather than monopoly power or a dominant position, in practice the enterprise found liable typically holds an extensively large market share.

Article 19 (prohibition of unfair trade practices) supplements the private monopolization regulation by enabling the JFTC and the court to stop a practice likely to cause competitive harm in its incipiency if it will lessen free competition in general. Although this normally requires defining the relevant market and assessing the state of competition, it adopts a low standard to find a violation. If the enterprise at issue has **less than 20% market share**, it is unlikely to be found liable. However, where the method to exclude competitors is clearly unfair, a GP para 14

---

[27]The 4th Circuit has articulated market share thresholds for this element as well: <30% presumptively no dangerous probability; 30–50% usually no dangerous probability; >50% potential dangerous probability; *M & M Medical Suppliers and Service v. Pleasant Valley Hospital*, 981 F.2d 160, 168 (4th Cir. 1992). See also Chapter 2, Section VI.1.b for conspiracies and Section III.2 in this chapter for attempted monopolization.

[28]*Spectrum Sports, Inc. v. McQuillan*, 506 U.S. 447, 456 (1993).

[29] See Section III.2 in this chapter.

violation (unfair interference in a competitor's trade) may be found, without defining the relevant market, regardless of the relevant entity's market share. Reflecting its preventive nature, however, penalties based on AMA Article 19 violation are minor in relation to the exclusionary practices.

On the other hand, AMA Article 2(9)(v), which is prohibited as unfair trade practice under AMA Article 19, encompasses exploitative abuse. To find a violation, the business entity must have a **superior bargaining position**. For this, the business entity does not have to have superior economic power in general: It suffices if it has superior bargaining power relative to its trading partners. Superiority exists where its trading partners have no option but to accept disadvantageous trading conditions or requirements imposed due to the fact that termination of the transaction with that entity would cause serious disruption to their businesses. An entity's position is evaluated not by defining its market power but rather by the degree of dependency, position in the market, presence or non-existence of alternative trading partners and relational-specific investment. On the other hand, actual competitive harm is not required; it is sufficient that such abuse undermines the foundation of free competition by negating weaker trading partners' independent and free business judgments. The JFTC also notes that abusers benefit from advantages while weaker market participants incur disadvantages, which distorts the competitive conditions. However, note that the JFTC does not specifically concretize either the effect to undermine the foundation of free competition or the competitive advantages and disadvantages. The assessment of the JFTC and the courts focuses on the issue of whether the defendant has caused its counterparties unreasonable disadvantages.

III. The prohibited anticompetitive conduct

All Article 102 TFEU, §2 Sherman Act and the AMA prohibit companies enjoying the requisite market power or economic position to engage in **unilateral conduct-harming competition**. Thus, all statutes prohibit **exclusionary** conduct to the detriment of competitors. In addition, Article 102 TFEU and AMA Articles 2(9)(5) and 19 may also apply to **exploitative** conduct to the detriment of consumers.

1. EU law

(a) General notes

Article 102 TFEU prohibits undertakings to abuse their dominant position. The ECJ, in its constant jurisprudence, defines abusive conduct as follows:

> *behaviour [...] which is such as to influence the structure of a market where, as a result of the very presence of the undertaking in question, the degree of competition is weakened and which, through recourse to methods different from those which condition normal competition in products or services on the basis of the transactions of commercial operators, has the effect of hindering the maintenance of the degree of competition still existing in the market or the growth of that competition.*[30]

This definition of abusive conduct is related to the definition of a dominant position and is, again, composed of two elements:

- The market structure must already have been weakened because of the presence of the undertaking in question (consequence of market dominance).
- The undertaking must engage in conduct which differs from normal competition and additionally restricts competition.

The legal standard for assessing whether conduct differs from normal competition is included in the first half of the general abuse definition, as set out in the ECJ's *Hoffmann-La Roche* judgment: that is, it must be examined whether the relevant undertaking engages in *behaviour [...] which [is marked by a] recourse to methods different from those which condition normal competition in products or services on the basis of the*

---

[30] ECJ, Judgment of 13 February 1979, *Hoffmann-La Roche/Commission* (85/76, ECR 1979 p. 461) ECLI:EU:C:1979:36, §91. Divergent: ECJ, Judgment of 11 December 1980, *L'Oréal/De Nieuwe AMCK* (31/80, ECR 1980 p. 3775) ECLI:EU:C:1980:289, §30, which combines the definitions of dominance and abuse but also requires an "appreciably" independent behavior. However, this definition has not been taken up again in the ECJ's case law.

transactions of commercial operators.[31] Over time, the ECJ slightly rephrased the assessment standard and alternatively referred to *methods other than those that are part of competition <u>on the merits</u>.*[32] (Emphasis added.)

As stated above, such conduct may either be exclusionary to the detriment of competitors or exploitative to the detriment of consumers.

(b) Exclusionary conduct

Regarding exclusionary conduct, the ECJ has held that *any practice the implementation of which holds no economic interest for a dominant undertaking, except that of eliminating competitors so as to enable it subsequently to raise its prices by taking advantage of its monopolistic position, must be regarded as a means other than those which come within the scope of competition on the merits.* (Emphasis added.)[33]

Thus, when it comes to exclusionary abuses, it is essentially necessary to examine whether the relevant practice **excludes competitors** by using **other means than a better product**, thus reducing choice and leading to consumer harm ("foreclosure"). In fact, most abuses fall into this category, which covers behavior such as exclusive dealing (exclusive purchasing and conditional rebates), tying/bundling, predation, or refusal to supply and margin squeeze.[34] Some abuses may be considered to be particularly harmful because they even have an immediate structural impact on the market, for example, abusive company takeovers.[35]

Article 102 TFEU does not distinguish between competition violations "by object" or "by effect". Originally, the provision was interpreted strictly legally, i.e., it was not required to consider the actual effects of the conduct (so-called **form-based approach**). That being said, starting in the

---

[31]ECJ, Judgment of 13 February 1979, *Hoffmann-La Roche/Commission* (85/76, ECR 1979 p. 461) ECLI:EU:C:1979:36, §91.

[32]ECJ, Judgment of 27 March 2012, *Post Danmark* (C-209/10, Publié au Recueil numérique) ECLI:EU:C:2012:172, §25.

[33]ECJ, Judgment of 12 May 2022, *Servizio Elettrico Nazionale and others* (C-377/20) ECLI:EU:C:2022:379, §77.

[34]See: European Commission Guidance on enforcement priorities (fn. 5).

[35]See ECJ, Judgment of 21 February 1973, *Europemballage Corporation and Continental Can Company/Commission* (6/72, ECR 1973 p. 215) ECLI:EU:C:1973:22, end of §26, §29.

late 1990s, the European Commission advocated a different approach to competition law which was oriented at finding consumer harm (and at allowing company behavior absent such harm).[36] This approach was called a "more economic approach" or an "effects-based approach". The European Commission favored this approach in order to focus on particularly harmful cases and to free up resources to that end. The **more economic approach** led to various changes in the handling of cases under Article 101 and Article 102 TFEU. In particular, regarding Article 101(3) TFEU, the European Commission persuaded the EU legislature to (generally) switch to a self-assessment system instead of the former system requiring administrative exceptions or so-called "comfort letters".[37] The European Commission did not give up BERs and Guidelines, but it acknowledged efficiency defenses expressly in the Vertical BER and the related Guidelines and it withdrew (though not officially) from an enforcement of the vertical rules for several years. Regarding Article 102 TFEU, the European Commission published an ambitious **Staff discussion paper** on exclusionary abuses in 2005, which again included an efficiency defense.[38] Finally, the merger control rules were reformed and also included an efficiency defense.[39]

However, in the following years, the ECJ dealt several blows to this approach, especially with regard to Article 101 TFEU. In that regard, the ECJ first made clear that it rejected a **rule of reason** assessment as is standard in U.S. law.[40] The ECJ likewise rejected the **consumer welfare standard** developed by the Chicago school.[41]

In contrast to the ECJ's rigid stance concerning Article 101 TFEU, the case law on Article 102 TFEU was more ambiguous for years and became clearer only gradually. In *Tomra*, a case concerning a rebate scheme, the ECJ clarified that an abuse only requires showing that the conduct *tends*

---

[36] See White Paper, OJ 1999 C 132/1.

[37] Article 1(2) Reg. 1/2003.

[38] European Commission, Staff discussion paper on exclusionary abuses, 2005; available at: https://ec.europa.eu/competition/antitrust/art82/discpaper2005.pdf.

[39] Recital 29 of Reg. 139/2004.

[40] ECJ, Judgment of 30 January 2020, *Generics (UK) and others* (C-307/18) ECLI: EU:C:2020:52, §104.

[41] ECJ, Judgment of 6 October 2009, *GlaxoSmithKline Services and others/Commission and others* (C-501/06 P, C-513/06 P, C-515/06 P and C-519/06 P, ECR 2009 p. I-9291) ECLI:EU:C:2009:610, §63.

to restrict competition or that the conduct is **_capable of having that effect_**.[42] In *TeliaSonera Sverige*, a margin squeeze case, however, the ECJ held — more ambiguously in the eyes of some — that the *practice must have an anticompetitive effect on the market, but the effect does not necessarily have to be concrete, and it is sufficient to demonstrate that there is an anticompetitive effect which may potentially exclude competitors who are at least as efficient as the dominant undertaking.* (Emphasis added.)[43] In *Post Danmark*, a case involving selective discounts, the ECJ then refined its jurisprudence for finding exclusionary abuses and acknowledged the **As-Efficient-Competitor (AEC)** test as the benchmark test for the "marginalization" (potential exclusion) of competitors.[44] However, in a *Post Danmark II* judgment, the ECJ withdrew this acknowledgment again at least partly, for it held that no AEC test was required for **super-dominant undertakings**. Moreover, it made clear that no abuse exists if the relevant conduct is justified by efficiencies.[45]

The current understanding of Article 102 TFEU was set out in 2017 in the ECJ's ***Intel*** judgment: In that case, the Court accepted (or at least did not reject) the European Commission's approach to differentiate between abusive practices based on their seriousness, similar to the distinction between restraints "by object" and "by effect" in Article 101 TFEU. Accordingly, a form-based approach may apply for certain abuses even beyond the ones listed in Article 102 TFEU **(by-nature abuses)**. In these instances, the conduct is presumptively unlawful, i.e., without an AEC test being necessary. An assessment of all relevant circumstances is necessary only if the undertaking concerned presents evidence that its conduct is not capable of restricting competition.[46] Examples of conduct potentially falling into the category of abuses "by nature" include predatory pricing (at least if it is likely to eliminate competition), margin squeeze (similar

---

[42]ECJ, Judgment of 19 April 2012, *Tomra and others/Commission* (C-549/10 P) ECLI:EU:C:2012:221, §68.

[43]ECJ, Judgment of 17 February 2011, *TeliaSonera Sverige* (C-52/09, ECR 2011 p. I-527) ECLI:EU:C:2011:83, §64 (margin squeeze).

[44]ECJ, Judgment of 27 March 2012, *Post Danmark* (C-209/10) ECLI:EU:C:2012:172, §§20–22 (selective discounts).

[45]ECJ Judgment of 6 October 2015, *Post Danmark* (C-23/14) ECLI:EU:C:2015:651, §§47, 57, 59.

[46]ECJ, Judgment of 6 September 2017, *Intel/Commission* (C-413/14 P) ECLI:EU:C: 2017:632, §142.

standard), exclusive dealing (including loyalty-inducing rebates and also exclusive purchasing?), tying of two separate products (including bundled discounts pushing the price below the cost for the tied product) and refusal to deal (at least for indispensable input products if competition down-stream is eliminated).

For behavior not falling into one of these categories, it is necessary to **analyze all (potential) effects** in order to show that the behavior is capable of restricting competition. However, the European Commission's burden of proof is again relieved because it is the responsibility of the relevant undertaking to come forward with evidence that might justify its behavior (Article 2 Reg. 1/2003). The "more economic approach" is reflected only to a limited extent in the justification grounds recognized by the courts: the "objective necessity" defense, the "meeting competition" defense and the "efficiency defense".

Good to know: Abusive conduct in EU Member State law

In the EU, Member States may also regulate conduct under their own abuse rules as long as they do not neglect to also apply Article 102 TFEU, where applicable.[47] In this context, national abuse rules may indeed deviate from EU law to a larger extent than the national cartel prohibitions. Again, Germany is an example: In the most recent reform of the Competition Act, the German legislature banned certain conduct as abusive which is not necessarily considered to violate Article 102 TFEU.[48] However, where Article 102 TFEU is applicable, national agencies and courts must enforce Article 102 TFEU in the relevant cases in parallel as well.[49]

(c) Exploitative conduct

Exploiting customers, e.g., through excessive prices or deteriorated quality, is rarely a strategy that can be maintained over longer periods. This is because such conduct provides incentives for other suppliers to enter the market with a better offer. The EU concept of exploitative abuses, thus, is

---

[47] Article 3(1)(2) Reg. 1/2003.

[48] However, in most cases, the definitions of abusive conduct are in line with the case law; see esp. §19(2), §19a(2) GWB.

[49] Article 3(1)(2) Reg. 1/2003.

only relevant in particularly cemented markets where the market position of the dominant undertaking is barely contestable (e.g., because it controls a network infrastructure, enjoying a natural monopoly).

The assessment for finding an abuse here starts, again, with the concept of competition on the merits. However, no competition exists in the relevant market, which might serve as a benchmark for finding *methods different from those which condition normal competition* if the position of the dominant undertaking cannot be challenged by competitors in the long term (e.g., by undercutting prices). In *United Brands*, an early case, the ECJ acknowledged this and ruled that it may also constitute a deviation from competition on the merits where *the dominant undertaking has made use of the opportunities arising out of its dominant position in such a way as to reap <u>trading benefits which it would not have reaped if there had been normal and sufficiently effective competition</u>.*[50] (Emphasis added.)

Two conclusions may be drawn from that ruling: First, while the general test for abuses is whether the abusive behavior has had a detrimental effect on competition (*"effect of hindering"* = "effects causality"), finding a deviation from competition on the merits in exploitation cases requires that (also) a causal link be established between the undertaking's dominant position and its conduct ("strict causality"). Second, a deviation from competition on the merits does not necessarily equal an exploitation of consumers. However, according to the ECJ, the dominant undertaking **exploits consumers** particularly by *charging a price which is excessive because it has <u>no reasonable relation to the economic value</u> of the product supplied.* (Emphasis added.)[51]

The ECJ went on to explain in this context when the price charged has no reasonable relation to the economic value of the product:

> *This excess could, inter alia, be determined objectively if it were possible for it to be calculated by making a comparison between the selling price of the product in question and its cost of production, which would disclose the amount of the profit margin [...] The questions therefore to be determined are <u>whether the difference between the costs</u>*

---

[50]ECJ, Judgment of 14 February 1978, *United Brands/Commission* (27/76, ECR 1978 p. 207) ECLI:EU:C:1978:22, §249; see also §§250–253.
[51]ECJ, Judgment of 14 February 1978, *United Brands/Commission* (27/76, ECR 1978 p. 207) ECLI:EU:C:1978:22, §250.

actually incurred and the price actually charged is excessive, and, if the answer to this question is in the affirmative, whether a price has been imposed which is either unfair in itself or when compared to competing products. [O]ther ways may be devised [as well]. (Emphasis added.)[52]

Thus, the usual test requires an economic comparison of the costs of the product and its price and a normative judgment ("unfairness"). But also in this context, it is a problem that usually no competition is left that might serve as a benchmark in exploitation cases. In practice, the courts and authorities therefore examine the prices on comparable markets to find an "excessive" difference between the costs and the price.

2. U.S. law

In 1945, the U.S. Court of Appeals for the Second Circuit held in *U.S. v. Aluminum Co. of America (Alcoa)* that monopolization prohibited by §2 of the Sherman Act generally requires a finding of exclusionary conduct, but that it is irrelevant if *the monopoly has not been used to extract from the consumer more than a "fair" profit* (exploitation).[53]

As stated above, "monopolization" encompasses any *willful acquisition or maintenance* of monopoly power, and it is necessary to distinguish from that any *growth or development as a consequence of a superior product, business acumen, or historic accident.*[54] For "attempted monopolization", anticompetitive conduct with a specific intent to monopolize is necessary.

Under §2 Sherman Act, exploitative abuse, namely the practice of charging high prices or imposing unfair terms, is not prohibited. A single practice, such as setting high prices, does not bring about a monopoly or the high likelihood of achieving a monopoly. That being said, the prospect of achieving a monopoly position provides important incentives to engage in competition, either with a better product offer or with lower prices. Hence, the Supreme Court has held that the very *opportunity to charge*

---

[52]ECJ, Judgment of 14 February 1978, *United Brands/Commission* (27/76, ECR 1978 p. 207) ECLI:EU:C:1978:22, §251–253; see also ECJ, Judgment of 14 September 2017, *AKKA/LAA*, C-177/16, EU:C:2017:689), §§37–38 (comparison between prices in different Member States).

[53]*United States v. Aluminum Co. of America (Alcoa)*, 148 F.2d 416 (2d. Cir. 1945).

[54]*United States v. Grinnell Corp.*, 384 U.S. 563, 570–71 (1966).

monopoly prices — at least for a short period — is what attracts 'business acumen' in the first place; it induces risk taking that produces innovation and economic growth. The Court went on to say that *to safeguard the incentive to innovate, the possession of monopoly power will not be found unlawful unless it is accompanied by an element of anticompetitive conduct.*[55]

Moreover, from the definition and the elements of "monopolization" and the "attempt to monopolize", it should be clear that only possession of monopoly power and exercising such power to raise prices would not constitute a §2 violation on their own. It should be also clear that the conduct must have the effect to acquire or maintain monopoly power or a dangerous probability to bring about such power. Additionally, the DOJ specified in a report in 2008 under which circumstances it considers that §2 Sherman Act may be violated. The DOJ withdrew the entire report in 2009 to allow for a more rigorous enforcement standard.[56] That said, the report lists a number of general principles that still appear valid today, as is likewise reflected in the case law:

> *Acquiring or maintaining monopoly power through assaults on the competitive process <u>harms consumers</u> and is to be condemned.*
>
> *<u>Mere harm to competitors</u> — without harm to the competitive process — does <u>not</u> violate §2.*
>
> *Competitive and exclusionary conduct <u>can look alike</u> — indeed, the same conduct can have both beneficial and exclusionary effects — [...].*
>
> *Because competitive and exclusionary conduct often look alike, courts and enforcers need to be <u>concerned</u> with both <u>underdeterrence and overdeterrence</u>.*
>
> *Standards for applying §2 should <u>take into account</u> the [associated] <u>costs</u>, including error and administrative costs [...].*

Lower courts and commentators have been trying to establish more general concepts or principles to capture all or a large part of anticompetitive practices, which include leverage, predation and raising a rival's cost. Although none of these categories explains the possible varieties of

---

[55] *Verizon Communications v. Law Offices of Courts Trinko, LLP*, 540 U.S. 398, 407 (2004).
[56] DOJ, press release of 11 May 2009.

§2 cases comprehensively, they help readers to understand the applicable theories of harm or why a particular conduct is or is not banned.

3. Japanese law

(a) Exclusionary conduct

Private monopolization has essentially two elements: an exclusionary practice and an anticompetitive effect. To find exclusion under AMA Article 2(5), the anticompetitive effect must be caused by a practice which is going beyond a normal competitive method.[57] It is understood that there is no private monopolization as long as an enterprise competes on its own merits, be it competition on low cost, innovative products or good customer service. In relation to unilateral conducts, the courts and JFTC found exclusion in cases of coercive practices or practices of a predatory nature in the sense that the conduct cannot be explained by efficiency. This implies that there is always room for the defendant to argue that the practice at issue is aiming at lower cost/prices and improvement of quality and, thus, the practice at issue does not constitute an unlawful exclusion. In any case, the provision prohibiting private monopolization is rarely enforced and both the JFTC and private parties tend to have recourse to AMA Article 19, under which the JFTC does not need to establish market power.

Unfair trade practices within the meaning of Article 19 more specifically comprise violations which include unilateral refusals to deal, predatory pricing, discriminatory pricing and interference with a competitor's trade. In general JFTC practice, the conduct of single firms is carefully compared with other practices brought about by horizontal and vertical agreements so as not to intervene excessively with a business entity's day-to-day practice. An exception to that cautious approach may be JFTC GP 10 (tie-in sales) and 14 (unfair interference with a competitor's transaction). For these, the unlawful nature lies not only in lessening free competition but also in using unfair methods of competition. In the case of tying, the buyer's free choice is impeded. Meanwhile, the JFTC and courts find GP 14 violations only where clearly oppressive practices and clear breach

---

[57] Supreme Court, 17 December 2010, 57-II Shinketsu-shu 215 (NTT East); Supreme Court, 28 April 2015, 69-III Minshu 518 (Japanese Society for Rights of Authors, Composers and Publishers [JASRAC]).

of the norm of merit-based competition exist.[58] For all types of practice, a justification based on procompetitive effect, efficiency or the broader public interest may be taken into account.[59]

(b) Exploitative conduct

AMA 2(9)5 lists the abusive practices that constitute an AMA 19 violation if undertaken by a business entity with a **superior bargaining position**.[60] Abusive practices are found where they disadvantage the trading partner and typically entail retrospective changes to contractual terms, an imbalance in duties and obligations, or both. Such abuses include late payments, reduction of price, return or rejection of acceptance of products and services contrary to what is once promised, requiring payments and services and coerced payment of purchases of unnecessary products. The defendant may submit justifications for all types of conduct. For instance, the defendant may have found defects in products and thus returned them or requested a price reduction.[61] If such justification exists, there is no abuse to begin with.

4. The standards for finding prohibited conduct compared

The legal standards for finding prohibited conduct under Article 102 TFEU, §2 Sherman Act and AMA **differ** not only because of the way the relevant provisions are written and interpreted but also in view of the **legal principles underpinning the law**. This becomes apparent when examining individual categories of prohibited unilateral conduct.

In general, in the EU, case law exists under Article 102 TFEU for unilaterally imposed discrimination, predatory pricing, refusals to deal, margin squeeze/raising rivals' costs, rebates, prevention of parallel trade,

---

[58] Dokusen kinshi ho kenkyu kai, Hokokusho: Fukosei na torihiki hoho ni kansuru kihon teki na kangae kata, 8 July 1972 (1972 AMA Study Group Report), 382 Kosei torihiki 34–35; 383 Kosei torihiki 56–61(1982); JFTC Hearing Decision, 16 February 2009, 55 Shinketsu-shu 500 (Daiichi Kosho Karaoke Systems).

[59] Supreme Court, 14 December 1989, 43-XII Minshu 2078 (Tokyo Slaughterhouse); Osaka High Court, 30 July 1993, 1479 Hanrei Jiho 21 (Toshiba Elevator).

[60] Tokyo High Court, 3 March 2021, _ Shinketsu-shu _ (*Ralse*).

[61] JFTC, Guidelines Concerning Abuse of Superior Bargaining Position under the Antimonopoly Act (2010) IV.3.

protection of ancillary markets and leveraging practices, IP-related abuses, capacity reductions and less often abusive takeovers and abuses of regulatory procedures.[62] While in the U.S., exclusivity or exclusive contract and tying[63] are categorized as vertical restraints and conventionally assessed under §1 Sherman Act, these tend to be considered a unilateral conduct in the EU and assessed under Article 102 TFEU. Meanwhile, in the U.S., although §2 Sherman Act may be relevant for most of these practices as long as they create or maintain monopoly power, conduct captured by §2 includes mainly predatory pricing, refusals to deal and abuse of regulatory processes including IP-related practices. In contrast to these, in Japan, different sets of provisions deal with varieties of unilateral conducts as unfair trade practices, while private monopolization broadly covers exclusionary abuses with substantial competitive harm.

Imposed **exclusivity and tying** are special cases. In EU law, at least tying is typically assessed under Article 102 TFEU as a unilateral exercise of dominant market power (even though Article 101 TFEU may apply in parallel if the dominant company uses, e.g., a supply agreement). In U.S. and Japanese law, the dominance concept is not relevant to these practices, which means that both anticompetitive exclusivity and tying can only be assessed under §1 Sherman Act (unless §2 kicks in) and in light of AMA Articles 2(5) (private monopolization) or 2(9) (unfair trade practice).

In the following, we focus on predatory pricing **(Subsection a)**, unilateral refusal to deal **(Subsection b)** and tying **(Subsection c)**, which are most relevant in practice and where the case law in the relevant jurisdictions has developed most.

(a) Predatory pricing

Predatory pricing — pricing below cost — is a sub-category of predation, which covers predatory innovation, predatory bidding and other types of conduct which sacrifice short-term profits to obtain anticompetitive gain in the long run. As noted in Subsection (b) below, the U.S. law relating to unilateral refusal to deal may appear to be predation as it now emphasizes

---

[62] See Jones/Van der Woude, Competition Law Handbook, 2020 Edition, pp. 169 ff.
[63] See Hovenkamp, Federal Antitrust Policy, 6th ed., 2020, Chapters 7–8, 10. However, regarding tying, see also the discussion of §2 aspects in §7.6a (pp. 391–392) and §7.6c (p. 397).

short-term sacrifice for an anticompetitive outcome in the long run. In this section, we deal with a strategy to exclude rivals with low prices.

(1) EU law and U.S. law

In the EU, any pricing below the Average Avoidable Cost (AVC) is presumed illegal, as is pricing below Average Total Cost (ATC) when used with a plan to eliminate competitors.[64] In the U.S., in contrast, below-cost prices ("predation") principally benefit consumers. By way of exception, a monopolist is considered to act anticompetitively when it lowers prices below cost to drive out its (remaining) competitors from the market and raises prices afterward again. Therefore, predation may constitute monopolization at least where a "dangerous probability" of recoupment exists.[65] This reasoning is in line with the Chicago School and its consumer welfare standard. However, no consensus has emerged yet as to what the most "appropriate" measures of cost are in predatory pricing case.[66]

(2) Japanese law

AMA Article 2(9)(iii) sets out four elements to find unlawful low prices: (i) setting a price significantly below the cost, (ii) continuity, (iii) likelihood to cause difficulties to other business operations and (iv) lacking justifiable grounds. "Significantly below cost" is understood to mean that the price is below average valuable cost or below the cost which would not be incurred if the entity at issue had not been involved in the relevant practice.[67] The second element, continuity, is assessed on a case-by-case basis. To satisfy the third element, the low price needs to cause detriment to other business entities, typically rivals. The continuity element is met where the time length is long enough to damage the prospect of the other entity's sustainability.[68] The last element, lacking justifiable grounds, is

---

[64] See ECJ Judgment of 3 July 1991, *AKZO/Commission* (62/86, ECR 1991 p. I-3359), ECLI:EU:C:1991:286, §72.

[65] *Brooke Group Ltd. v. Brown & Williamson Tobacco Corp.*, 509 U.S. 209 (1993). See also Hovenkamp (5th, 2016) pp. 478–80 regarding the required intent in this context.

[66] *United States v. AMR Corp.*, 335 F.3d 1109 (10th Cir. 2003).

[67] JFTC, Guidelines Concerning Unjust Low Price Sales under the Antimonopoly Act (1984, last revised 2017) 3(1)A.

[68] JFTC, Guidelines Concerning Unjust Low Price Sales under the Antimonopoly Act (1984, last revised 2017) 3(1)B.

interpreted to mean lessening free competition.[69] This is presumed when the other three elements have been established. The defendant must submit evidence that justifiable grounds that would negate anticompetitive effect exist and substantiate the claim. Such justification exists in cases of, e.g., promotional discounts when the defendant launches new products.

Low price not satisfying all the elements above falls under JFTC GP 6, which requires (i) below-cost low price, (ii) likelihood to cause difficulties to another's business operation and (iii) being unfair. For this, the cost benchmark is average total cost (ATC), rather than average variable cost (AVC).[70] If the price is above AVC, unfair exclusion is unlikely, although it is possible as long as the price is below ATC; thus the JFTC and the court further examine the likely effect under the third element.[71] The third element, unfairness, is interpreted to mean lessening free competition.[72] Such effect is not presumed and the JFTC or a plaintiff must demonstrate such effect based on specific circumstances existent in the relevant market. Lessening free competition does not require market power: Still, it would be difficult to argue such effect is caused where the entity has no economic power.

Both AMA 2(9)(iii) and JFTC GP para. 6 relate to AMA Article 19 (unfair trade practice), for which the penalty is minor. Where an enterprise has substantial economic power and the effect of low price is serious, the JFTC or a plaintiff may opt for a private monopolization claim under AMA Articles 2(5) and 3.[73] For a private party, this does not provide any additional remedies, while the JFTC can impose an administrative fine if it chooses this avenue. Private monopolization has three elements in relation to exclusionary practices: (i) exclusion by way of a method falling outside normal competition method, (ii) substantial restraints of competition in a particular field of trade and (iii) contrary to the public interest.

---

[69]Dokusen kinshi ho kenkyu kai, Hokokusho: Fukosei na torihiki hoho ni kansuru kihon teki na kangae kata (8 July 1972) (1972 AMA Study Group Report).

[70]Tokyo High Court, 28 November 2007, 54 Shinketsu-shu 699 (Japan Post Yu-Pack).

[71] This makes contrast to AMA Article 2(5)(iii), for which continuity and inhibition to another company's business activities generally suffices to find a violation. The penalty also differs. Article 2(5)(iii) violation may result in administrative fines when repeated. In contrast, an administrative fine is not imposed for GD 6 violation, even if repeated.

[72]Dokusen kinshi ho kenkyu kai, Hokokusho: Fukosei na torihiki hoho ni kansuru kihon teki na kangae kata (8 July 1972) (1972 AMA Study Group Report).

[73]JFTC, The Guidelines for Exclusionary Private Monopolization under the Antimonopoly Act (2009, last revised 2020) II.2.

As long as the price exceeds the cost that is incurred to provide the products or services at issue, it would not be deemed outside the normal competition method. The second element means that a low price resulted in the establishment, maintenance or enhancement of market power in a relevant market. Once the first and second elements are met, the third element would be easily met. Although, in theory, justification is always possible, either on the ground of procompetitive effect or based on broader public interest, there has been no case in which the JFTC or the Court has accepted such justification.

(b) Unilateral refusal to deal

A unilateral refusal to deal means that there is neither agreement, either horizontally or vertically, nor coercion involved. Rather, a firm refuses to enter into a transaction based on its own business judgment. This kind of practice is known for its potential to raise competitive issues, but it may do so only in very particular circumstances. The assessment standard for unilateral refusal to deal has evolved over time in all of the EU, the U.S. and Japan.

(1) EU law

In the EU, the general standard is that a dominant supplier of an input product in an **existing supply relationship** acts abusively if (i) it refuses continued supplies on the relevant upstream market and if (ii) this refusal leads to an "elimination" of competition downstream (without any objective justification).[74]

A more elaborate standard applies for so-called **essential facilities**, where other companies claim access upstream even outside an existing business relationship. The ECJ has recognized the essential facility doctrine at least for IP-protected goods.[75] Under this doctrine, a dominant

---

[74]ECJ, Judgment of 6 March 1974, *Istituto Chemioterapico Italiano and Commercial Solvents/Commission* (6 and 7–73, ECR 1974 p. 223) ECLI:EU:C:1974:18, §§25–26. It is unclear whether efficiencies may outbalance the negative impact on market structure in these cases.

[75]Note that the relevant case law concerns product competition, not R&D or technology competition. In those types of competition, the rules of IP law define to what extent third parties may gain access to IP-protected technologies.

supplier acts abusively if (i) it refuses to supply an indispensable (not duplicable) input product and if (ii) this results in consumer harm. The input product must not have been marketed yet, i.e., it is sufficient that there is demand on a "hypothetical market" for that product.[76] Moreover, the finding of consumer harm where the essential facility consists of IP-protected goods presupposes that the IP protection is taken into account. Thus, consumer harm not only requires that competition be eliminated downstream without any objective justification but that the supplier also prevents the development of a new product.[77]

The GC and the European Commission have applied the essential facility doctrine also in other scenarios, e.g., to claims for access to **infrastructures**. The ECJ recently clarified that this is indeed possible unless *the infrastructure in question was financed by means not of investments specific to the dominant undertaking, but by means of public funds and that undertaking is not the owner of that infrastructure.*[78] Infrastructure operators frequently have a "natural monopoly" because they control an infrastructure, e.g., a harbor or a fixed-line telecommunications network.[79] Thus, it makes sense to consider the infrastructure to be an essential (i.e., non-duplicable) input. In this context, the European Commission does not deem it to be necessary that the behavior of the supplier prevented the development of a new product. Moreover, the legislature may facilitate access to an essential infrastructure by regulation and thereby remove the need to resort to the essential facility doctrine.[80] However, the ECJ recently also clarified that the "essential facility" doctrine does not apply anyway where the (regulated) entity **destroys an infrastructure** previously reserved to itself, whereby *the infrastructure inevitably becomes unusable by competitors but also by the dominant undertaking itself.* (Emphasis added.)[81]

---

[76]ECJ, Judgment of 29 April 2004, *IMS Health* (C-418/01, ECR 2004 p. I-5039) ECLI:EU:C:2004:257, §44.

[77]ECJ, Judgment of 29 April 2004, *IMS Health* (C-418/01, ECR 2004 p. I-5039) ECLI:EU:C:2004:257, §§37, 48 ff.

[78] ECJ, Judgment of 12 January 2023, *Lietuvos geležinkeliai/Commission* (C-42/21 P) ECLI:EU:C:2023:12, §87.

[79]See Chapter 1 regarding the elements of a natural monopoly.

[80]GC, Judgment of 18 November 2020, *Lietuvos geležinkeliai/Commission* (T-814/17) ECLI:EU:T:2020:545, §92.

[81]ECJ, Judgment of 12 January 2023, *Lietuvos geležinkeliai/Commission* (C-42/21 P) ECLI:EU:C:2023:12, §§83–84.

Some uncertainty continues to exist due to the GC's interpretation of the "essential facilities" doctrine in its *Microsoft* judgment of 2004. Whereas the ECJ had held that the refusal at issue must "eliminate all competition", the GC found it to be sufficient that the refusal would "eliminate all effective competition".[82] And while the ECJ had held that the refusal must prevent the marketing of "new goods or services", the GC found it sufficient that undertakings downstream were "deterred" from marketing products "of better quality".[83] It has been an issue of debate since then whether the GC's interpretation was consistent with or exceeding the bounds of ECJ case law.

(2) U.S. law

In U.S. law, unilateral refusal to deal is assessed in light of general monopolization and attempt to monopolize elements explained earlier. In general, the courts tend to emphasize that *there is no duty to aid competitors*[84] and consequently focus on *a willingness to forsake short-term profits to achieve anticompetitive end*.[85] Regarding refusals to deal, the Supreme Court originally set out a general standard in *Aspen Skiing*.[86] Pursuant to that judgment, §2 Sherman Act is violated where a monopolist has marketed input before and then (i) willfully denies competitor access, (ii) despite consumer demand and (iii) without justification. However, the Supreme Court later appears to have moved away from finding a violation in simple refusals to deal. This conclusion imposes itself because, in *Verizon v. Trinko*, the focus shifted from the rule established in *Aspen Skiing* to the (demanding) requirement of proving exclusionary harm (aligning the *Aspen* doctrine with the predation standard of *Trinko*): *The jury may well have concluded that Ski Co. elected to forgo these short-run*

---

[82] ECJ, Judgment of 26 November 1998, *Bronner* (C-7/97, ECR 1998 p. I-7791) ECLI:EU:C:1998:569, §41; GC, Judgment of 17 September 2007, *Microsoft/Commission* (T-201/04, ECR 2007 p. II-3601) ECLI:EU:T:2007:289, §563.

[83] ECJ, Judgment of 29 April 2004, *IMS Health* (C-418/01, ECR 2004 p. I-5039) ECLI:EU:C:2004:257, §49; GC, Judgment of 17 September 2007, *Microsoft/Commission* (T-201/04, ECR 2007 p. II-3601) ECLI:EU:T:2007:289, §971.

[84] *Verizon Communications v. Law Offices of Curtis v. Trinko, LLP*, 540 U.S. 398 (2004).

[85] *Ibid.*; see also *Aspen Skiing Co. v. Aspen Highlands Skiing Crop.*, 472 U.S. 585, 610–611 (1985) ("willing to sacrifice short-term benefits […] in exchange for a perceived long-run impact on its small rival").

[86] *Aspen Skiing Co. v. Aspen Highlands Skiing Corp.*, 472 U.S. 585 (1985).

benefits because it was more interested in reducing competition in the Aspen market over the long-run by harming its smaller competitor.[87]

The ***essential facilities doctrine*** was recognized in the lower courts in the past. For example, the Court of Appeals for the Second Circuit applied the doctrine in *MCI Communications v. AT&T* under virtually the same conditions as is recognized in the GC and European Commission practice in Europe.[88] However, the Supreme Court has not expressly endorsed the essential facility doctrine to date and instead made clear in *Verizon v. Trinko* that an essential facility-type claim could not be made successfully. It is often said that mandating access under antitrust law is *beyond the practical ability of a judicial tribunal to control,* as it would require *the court to assume the day-to-day controls characteristic of regulatory agency.*[89] An essential facility claim could anyway not be made successfully where a regulator could compel access to the facility.[90]

(3) Japanese law

Unilateral refusals to deal may constitute an **unfair trade practice** and private monopolization. First, JFTC GD para. 2 designates any type of refusal to deal as an Article 19 violation, as long as it is deemed "unfair". In this context, unfairness is interpreted to equal a lessening of free competition,[91] which is further understood as meaning that anticompetitive effects exist in incipiency. Here, the refusal to deal needs to contribute to the creation or enhancement of economic power in a relevant market. Proving effects is easier than establishing market power, yet it is still difficult. Furthermore, respecting the respective business entity's freedom to choose its trading partners, the JFTC and the court have held that

---

[87] *Aspen Skiing Co. v. Aspen Highlands Skiing Corp.*, 472 U.S. 585, 608 (1985), requoted in *Verizon Communications v. Law Offices of Curtis v. Trinko*, LLP, 540 U.S. 398. On this, see also, e.g., Hovenkamp, The Antitrust Duty to Deal in the Age of Big Tech, 131 Yale L.J. 1483, 1496 ff. and critically 1508 ff. (2022); Fox, Is There Life in Aspen After Trinko? The Silent Revolution of Section 2 of the Sherman Act, 73 Antitrust L.J. 153, 155 ff. (2005).

[88] *MCI Communications Corp. v. AT&T Co.*, 708 F.2d 1081 (7th Cir. 1983).

[89] *Verizon Communications v. Law Offices of Curtis v. Trinko, LLP*, 540 U.S. 398 (2004).

[90] *Verizon Communications v. Law Offices of Curtis v. Trinko, LLP*, 540 U.S. 398 (2004): essential facility doctrine "never recognized".

[91] Dokusen kinshi ho kenkyu kai, Hokokusho: Fukosei na torihiki hoho ni kansuru kihon teki na kangae kata, 8 July 1972 (1972 AMA Study Group Report).

unilateral refusals to deal are deemed to be unfair in only two cases.[92] The first is where the defendant has engaged in other AMA violations, such as resale price maintenance, and refused to deal to effectuate such violations. This situation is uncontroversial as this is not a "pure" unilateral refusal to deal: It is only a method used to enforce different restrictive conditions. The second is where the defendant refused to deal based solely on a motivation contrary to the AMA, such as excluding rivals to maintain its economic power. The second scenario may relate to a pure unilateral refusal to deal. There has been no case in which unilateral refusals to deal falling under the second category have been found to date.

Unilateral refusal to deal may also constitute a **private monopolization** when it causes serious competitive harm to the extent it creates, or enhances, market power.[93] The elements for private monopolization are noted above and are the same as in the case of predatory pricing. A refusal must have an exclusionary effect, implying mere possession of the essential facility and subsequent denial of access to it is insufficient; the practice must be deemed beyond the normal method of competition. Clearly, refusing to deal due to lack of capacity or IP protection (like in the EU/U.S.) does not constitute a private monopolization as such action is a normal competitive business practice.

(c) Exclusivity and tying

Regarding exclusivity and tying, it is already pointed out above in relation to Article 101 TFEU and §1 Sherman Act that the assessment standard differs considerably in the EU, the U.S. and Japan.

(1) EU law

As noted above, in the EU, exclusivity and tying may be assessed under both Articles 101 and 102 TFEU.[94] However, in practice, exclusivity is

---

[92] JFTC, Guidelines Concerning Distribution Systems and Business Practices (1991, revised 2017); Tokyo District Court, 28 July 2011, 58-II Shinketsu-shu 227 (*Tokyo Star Bank*).

[93] JFTC, The Guidelines for Exclusionary Private Monopolization under the Antimonopoly Act (2009, last revised 2020) II.5.

[94] ECJ, Judgment of 21 February 1973, *Europemballage Corporation and Continental Can Company/Commission* (6/72, ECR 1973 p. 215) ECLI:EU:C:1973:22, §25.

mostly assessed under Article 101 TFEU although particularly exclusive purchasing is also addressed in the guidelines under Article 102 TFEU. Tying is dealt with in the guidelines under both Articles 101 and 102 TFEU. In practice, still, tying is mainly dealt with under Article 102 TFEU as the scope of Article 101 TFEU has remained somewhat unclear for tying.

Under Article 102 lit. d TFEU, tying may be considered abusive if (i) the tying and tied products are two separate products, (ii) the undertaking concerned is dominant in the market for the tying product, (iii) the undertaking allows customers to obtain the tying product only together with the tied product and (iv) the practice forecloses competition. In its *Microsoft* judgment, the GC held that the question of whether two products are separate must be assessed based on the actual customer demand.[95] In line with the ECJ's jurisprudence, it also held that it was sufficient if the tying behavior is capable of restricting competition.[96] In addition, it held that an abuse finding presupposed (v) the absence of an objective and proportionate justification.[97]

The *Microsoft* judgment shows another important characteristic of which it is unclear whether it is of general relevance for EU law: In the assessment of whether the tying was capable of restraining competition, the focus was on both existing competitors and innovation incentives for competitors. The GC certainly also considered Microsoft's own innovation efforts, raised as a defense, but found Microsoft's claims not to be substantiated enough.[98] Microsoft consequently lost its case on tying.

(2) U.S. law

In the U.S., exclusivity and tying may violate both §1 (through the contractual arrangement) and §3 Clayton Act as well as §2 Sherman Act (due to monopolization if rivals are harmed unnecessarily).[99] Tying involving

---

[95] GC, Judgment of 17 September 2007, *Microsoft/Commission* (T-201/04, ECR 2007 p. II-3601) ECLI:EU:T:2007:289, §§842, 852 and §§917–918.

[96] GC, Judgment of 17 September 2007, *Microsoft/Commission* (T-201/04, ECR 2007 p. II-3601) ECLI:EU:T:2007:289, §867.

[97] GC, Judgment of 17 September 2007, *Microsoft/Commission* (T-201/04, ECR 2007 p. II-3601) ECLI:EU:T:2007:289, §§1144 ff.

[98] GC, Judgment of 17 September 2007, *Microsoft/Commission* (T-201/04, ECR 2007 p. II-3601) ECLI:EU:T:2007:289, §§655, 692 ff.

[99] See Hovenkamp, Federal Antitrust Policy, 6th ed., 2020, p. 397.

market power may be subject to a modified *per se* prohibition under §1 Sherman Act. The requirements are as follows: (i) the defendant has appreciable economic power in the tying market, (ii) the tying concerns two separate products, (iii) the defendant affords consumers no choice between products and (iv) the practice has the effect of foreclosing a substantial amount of commerce.[100]

In *U.S. v. Microsoft*, the Court of Appeals reached a similar result for technical tying by applying a tightened rule-of-reason test under §1 Sherman Act. However, it made clear that competitors must actually be foreclosed in this case due to the novelty of technical tying.[101] Thus, unlike in the EU, the court required a finding of actual foreclosure effects. Moreover, unlike in the EU, the focus was on existing competitors (static competition) and innovation incentives for Microsoft only (i.e., not on dynamic competition!). In that context, since tying was assessed under §1 Sherman Act, Microsoft only had to make a reasonable claim of innovation efforts and had the benefit of the doubt.[102]

(3) Japanese law

GD Paragraph 10 designates **tying** as an **unfair trade practice** prohibited under AMA Article 19. To find a GD 10 violation, the factfinder must establish (i) two separate products, (ii) coercion to buy a tied product and (iii) unjustness. Coercion is found when a substantial number of customers are forced to buy a tied product.[103] Such coercion is generally found where the defendant has the economic power in the market for the tying product.

In relation to tying, unjustness means either foreclosure effect resulting in lessening free competition or employing unfair methods of competition. For the **foreclosure effect**, the focus is the effect on the state of competition in tied-product market and defendant's market share and

---

[100] *Eastman Kodak Co. v. Image Technical Services, Inc.*, 504 U.S. 451 (1992).

[101] *U.S. v. Microsoft Corp.*, 253 F.3d 34 (D.C. Cir. 2001) at IV.B.

[102] *U.S. v. Microsoft Corp.*, 253 F.3d 34 (D.C. Cir. 2001): *Moreover, because innovation can increase an already dominant market share and further delay the emergence of competition, even monopolists have reason to invest in R&D; Applying per se analysis to such an amalgamation creates undue risks of error and of deterring welfare-enhancing innovation.*

[103] JFTC Hearing Decision, 28 February 1992, 38 Shinketsu-shu 41 (*Fujitaya*).

other facts indicating foreclosure is assessed.[104] In relation to the **unfairness of the competition method**, the ground for condemnation is in the fact that the defendant takes advantage of strong demand for the tying product and inhibits buyer's free selection.[105]

Tying may also constitute a **private monopolization** when its foreclosure effect is serious and results in establishment or enhancement of market power. The elements for this are noted above (see Section III.3.a) or are the same as in the case of predatory pricing.[106]

(d) Comparison

In comparison, the EU dominance rules and the U.S. and Japanese monopolization rules diverge given their theoretical underpinning when it comes to the application in individual cases. Notably the U.S. standard for finding anticompetitive **below-cost pricing** is more demanding than the EU standard, which reflects the market-effects-based concept of monopolization. The predation concept of Article 102 TFEU, in contrast, benefits enforcers as it relieves them from dealing with the difficult issue of recoupment. On unilateral **refusals to deal**, the law in all covered jurisdictions shows remarkable convergence. In all three jurisdictions, companies are generally allowed not to deal with others, based on their freedom of contract. It is only under particular circumstances that a refusal to deal may raise concerns from a competition perspective. Even then, the stopping of business relations is more easily frowned upon than the refusal to grant access to an essential facility. The U.S. Supreme Court has provided a reason for this reservation of the courts: Judicial courts are not well placed to handle the monitoring of access under the essential facility doctrine.

Regarding **exclusivity and tying**, Article 102 TFEU sets a lower bar for the evaluation of unilateral conduct than the monopolization rules in the U.S. and Japan. This has had the consequence that especially tying is typically assessed as a unilateral behavior in the EU, whereas it is dealt with under the cartel prohibition in the U.S. and under the prohibition of

---

[104]JFTC, Guidelines Concerning Distribution Systems and Business Practices (1991, last revised 2017) I.2.7.

[105]Osaka High Court, 30 July 1993, 1479 Hanrei Jiho 21 (*Toshiba Elevator*).

[106]JFTC, The Guidelines for Exclusionary Private Monopolization under the Antimonopoly Act (2009, last revised 2020) II.4.

unfair trade practices in Japan. In this regard, the EU and the Japanese approaches appear more convincing than the U.S. approach because exclusivity and tying usually do not raise competitive concerns if the parties freely conclude an agreement. The situation is different when one party has a dominant position, which may allow it to force exclusivity or tied products on the other party.

IV. The remedies

1. EU and U.S. law

In cases of exclusionary abuses of dominance and monopolization, the design of remedies is of particular importance. This is because the relevant laws require dominance or monopoly power. Thus, they **only kick in once the market is close to tipping** in favor of one particular firm or has tipped in its favor already.[107] The prohibited conduct exacerbates the market conditions further. Thus, it is insufficient to counter exclusionary abuses and monopolization with fines and criminal penalties (i.e., the sanctions for horizontal collusion) or to simply prohibit the relevant conduct (as is done in cases of other collaboration — if agencies intervene at all).

Moreover, it should be noted that the nature of the considered remedies in a competition or antitrust case provides an **indication** of whether the **underlying theory of harm is robust**. Thus, the authorities and the courts are held to ensure that imposed remedies are suitable to neutralize the anticompetitive behavior. However, what this implies can be seen differently with, this time, the standard for §2 Sherman Act being the more stringent one.

According to the Supreme Court, antitrust remedies in **U.S. law** must generally seek to *unfetter a market of anticompetitive conduct.*[108] Thus, in monopolization cases, they must *terminate the illegal monopoly, deny to the defendant the fruits of its statutory violation, and ensure that there*

---

[107] See again Judgment of 14 February 1978, *United Brands/Commission* (27/76, ECR 1978, p. 207) ECLI:EU:C:1978:22, §65 (highlighting only here); Judgment of 13 February 1979, *Hoffmann-La Roche/Commission* (85/76, ECR 1979 p. 461) ECLI:EU:C:1979:36, §38: dominance as the *power "to prevent effective competition being maintained".*

[108] *Ford Motor Co. v. United States*, 405 U.S. 562, 577 (1972); *United States v. Microsoft Corp.*, 253 F.3d 34 (D.C. Cir. 2001).

remain no practices likely to result in monopolization in the future.[109] Unsuitable or insufficient measures are not accepted.[110] The courts do not hold the agencies accountable for allowing the relevant companies to participate in the design of the remedies, although it is certainly possible to settle a case based on company commitments (as happened, e.g., in *U.S. v. Microsoft*).[111]

With regard to **EU law**, the ECJ has ruled that it is for the European Commission to *impose on the undertakings concerned any behavioral or structural remedies which are proportionate to the infringement committed and necessary to bring the infringement effectively to an end.*[112] Similar to the U.S. Supreme Court, the ECJ has held that the European Commission *is required to assess in each case how serious the alleged interferences with competition are and how persistent their consequences are. That obligation means in particular that it must take into account the duration and extent of the infringements complained of and their effect on the competition situation in the Community. If anti-competitive effects continue after the practices which caused them have ceased, the Commission thus remains competent [...] to act with a view to eliminating or neutralising them.*[113]

However, whereas the U.S. courts have stressed the importance that the remedies imposed are suitable and, in terms of their necessity, are justified by some **minimum effectiveness**, the EU GC and the European Commission have put an emphasis on the **outer limits** of what may be considered necessary. Thus, the GC took the position that it is *not for the Commission to impose on the parties its choice from among all the various potential courses of action which were in conformity with*

---

[109] *United States v. United Shoe Mach. Corp.*, 391 U.S. 244, 250 (1968); *United States v. Microsoft Corp.*, 253 F.3d 34 (D.C. Cir. 2001).

[110] Cf. *United States v. Grinnell Corp.*, 384 U.S. 563 (1966): *The mere dissolution of the combination by Grinnell's divestiture of its affiliates will not reach the root of the evil; there must be some divestiture on the part of ADT [= one particularly relevant affiliate], with 73% of the market, to be determined by the District Court.*

[111] See Chapter 5, Section II.2.e.

[112] ECJ, Judgment of 29 June 2010, *Commission/Alrosa* (C-441/07 P, ECR 2010 p. I-5949) ECLI:EU:C:2010:377, §39.

[113] ECJ, Judgment of 4 March 1999, *Ufex and others/Commission* (C-119/97 P, ECR 1999 p. I-1341) ECLI:EU:C:1999:116, §§93–94.

the Treaty.[114] In its practice, the European Commission consequently focuses on ending the abusive behavior through the imposed remedies but not necessarily on restoring a competitive market structure. Moreover, it involves the undertakings concerned in the design of the remedies to avoid going beyond what is necessary. In particular, with regard to the remedies imposed on digital platform companies, the European Commission's approach has given rise to ongoing complaints in practice that the remedies imposed do not improve the competitive situation.[115]

It is **not clear** what the **reason is for those differences** in practice. It cannot be ruled out that the GC and the European Commission have simply misinterpreted the ECJ's jurisprudence. However, it may also be relevant in the present context that the U.S. courts decide themselves on what the remedies must achieve, whereas the EU Courts (and especially the GC, which decides on questions of law and facts) restrain themselves in order not to interfere with the role of the European Commission as an administrative enforcer of the EU rules.

2. Japanese law

Under the AMA, the JFTC issues a cease-and-desist **order** that the entity take all measures "necessary to eliminate the act in violation of the provisions".[116] In case of private monopolization, the JFTC also imposes an administrative fine.

The JFTC has great **discretion** in deciding what is necessary to eliminate the violations in terms of **stopping the anticompetitive conduct** (not restore competition). It has been understood that such measures may include orders to *transfer a part of the relevant enterprise's business* or

---

[114]GC, Judgment of 18 November 2020, *Lietuvos geležinkeliai/Commission* (T-814/17) ECLI:EU:T:2020:545, para. 312.

[115]Lomas, Google rivals call on EU to set rules for search engine preference menus, techcrunch.com, 7 October 2021; Lomas, Google's EU Android choice screen isn't working say search rivals, calling for a joint process to devise a fair remedy, techcrunch.com, 27 October 2020; Chee, Exclusive: Group of 165 Google critics calls for swift EU antitrust action — letter, Reuters, 12 November 2020; Lambert u. a., Letter of 22 November 2018, RE: AT.39.740 — Google Search (Comparison Shopping), available on MLex; Gambrell, Google's Top Search Results Spotlight a Narrowing of the Open Web, Bloomberg Businessweek, 23 October 2019.

[116] AMA Articles 7 and 20.

other divestitures if necessary (AMA Article 7). However, in practice, it will be difficult to find that divestiture is necessary to ensure that unlawful action has been ceased, and the JFTC has never ordered divestiture in cases other than share acquisitions.

AMA Article 8–4 has a separate provision to **restore competition** in cases of persevering monopoly power. This provision has not been used in practice to date. However, the JFTC has used its competences under Article 8–4 to generate a deterrent effect and to influence future behavior (e.g., in cases involving exploitation).

Generally, the **JFTC** does not order payment of **damages to the aggrieved parties** because it is unclear whether it has the formal competence. However, the JFTC accepts commitments in informal procedures to that end.

V. Summary: The prohibitions and remedies compared

When we compare Article 102 TFEU and §2 Sherman Act, it becomes apparent that **the bar for finding a violation of Article 102 TFEU is much lower than** the bar for finding a **violation of §2 Sherman Act**. The Japanese **AMA comes in the middle**: It may be harder to find private monopolization than an abuse under Article 102 TFEU, but it is easier to find unfair trade practices under AMA Article 19, which is likewise prohibited under this statute. In the following, we summarize the key parallels and differences first as regards the prohibitions and then as regards the remedies in case the relevant prohibitions have been violated. In each case, for easier reading, we first contrast the EU and the U.S. rules and then discuss the Japanese rules in comparison.

1. The prohibitions compared

1. **Dominant undertakings** in EU law have a *"special responsibility not to allow [their] conduct to impair genuine undistorted competition"*, meaning, among others, that the relevant conduct may be prohibited simply because it is "capable of" restricting competition. This concept of "special responsibility" does not exist in U.S. law, meaning that it is necessary to positively establish monopolization (or, at least, a "dangerous probability" of success). Further, EU law allows one to

apply the dominance rules also to companies in a joint dominant (oligopoly) position, whereas "shared monopolies" are not recognized in U.S. law.

2. Both EU law and U.S. law recognize **exclusionary abuses**. However, in this context, several differences must be noted:

   - First, harm to **individual competitors** is only relevant in both EU and U.S. law if it deteriorates the market structure (competitive process) further. However, the legal standard in EU law allows one to assume this condition to be fulfilled more easily (see first point above).

   - Second, while both jurisdictions intend to protect consumers and allow justification on the ground of efficiencies for the benefit of consumers, they differ in whether exclusionary abuses require **consumer harm**. Although consumer harm (or at least an absence of consumer benefits) is necessary under both EU and U.S. law, EU law allows one to simply presume such harm in cases of abuses "by nature".

   - Third, another important difference lies in the allocation of the **burden of proof**: In the EU, certain practices are presumed to be abusive by their nature. Regarding other practices, the European Commission has to bring a *prima facie* case. Then, only to the extent that the defendant submits evidence on pro-competitive effects has the European Commission to prove that these benefits do not outweigh the anticompetitive effects.[117] In the U.S., it is always for the plaintiff to prove monopolization and for the defendant to bring forward a pro-competitive justification in all cases.

3. There are **no exploitative abuses** in U.S. law.

Japanese law, different from EU and similar to U.S. law, does not require dominance but is triggered when there is competitive harm in the form of creation or strengthening of market power giving rise to private monopolization (or such effect to a lesser extent in cases of unfair trade practices). Like EU and U.S. law, it recognizes exclusionary abuses and, like EU law and unlike U.S. law, also exploitative abuses.

However, concerning **exclusionary abuses**, Japanese law has some **specific features** of its own. Hence, where a method to exclude competitors is clearly oppressive and contrary to merit-based competition norms,

---

[117] See Article 2 Reg. 1/2003.

the practice may constitute an AMA violation regardless of other factors. Further, while no practices are presumed to be abusive by their nature (different from EU law), a presumption may apply in predatory pricing cases based on the price level relative to cost (different from U.S. law). Otherwise, it is for the competition authorities and plaintiffs to establish that the practice at issue is anticompetitive in the sense that the conduct at issue leads to the acquisition or maintenance of monopoly power, or such probability, as distinguished from the normal competitive process. Proving these is not easy. In such context, the defendant's pro-competitive justification is only one of the factors to deny such anticompetitive conduct.

2. The remedies compared

If a violation is established, then the remedies under §2 Sherman Act imposed tend to go much farther than under Article 102 TFEU in an exclusionary case. In particular, **U.S. courts** seem to favor unilaterally imposed **structural measures** (including company break-ups) as suitable remedies. In contrast, based on the GC's jurisprudence, the European Commission ordinarily only imposes **behavioral remedies** and allows participation of the undertakings concerned in order to ensure that its remedy orders are limited to what is necessary and proportionate.

Similar to the rules on remedies in EU law, private monopolization under **Japanese law** may likewise give rise to behavioral measures and — at least theoretically — to structural measures. However, also in Japan, a **strong preference** exists **for behavioral remedies.**[118]

The regulation of **superior bargaining position** in Japan is typically meant to address retrospective changes and the JFTC never intends to be a price regulator. Yet, parties may negotiate with a dominant company having recourse to these laws. In the U.S., this would be impossible — unless a sector-specific regulation applies or the state antitrust law provides otherwise.

---

[118]Regarding structural measures, see AMA Article 8–4 on monopolistic situations. Further, see Wakui, Antimonopoly Law, 2nd ed., 2019, pp. 73–74 for the details.

Chapter 5

Digital Ecosystems and Exclusion/Exploitation at Platform Level

I. Introduction

Particularly large online platforms and digital ecosystems merit a closer look. Digital ecosystems may consist of several economic platforms (e.g., Google with the Android operating system, the Play Store and the search applications). Alternatively, they may include a combination of economic platforms and non-platform services (e.g., Amazon with its own sales and its Market Place platform). Over time, the operators of large online platforms and digital ecosystems in the World (excluding China) (i.e., Google, Amazon, Apple, Facebook and Microsoft — GAFAM) and likewise in the China (e.g., Alibaba, Bytedance, JD.com, Tencent, Weibo and Xiaomi) have revealed the limitations of traditional competition/antitrust law enforcement.

To understand why there have been more and more calls for regulating the relevant companies in recent years, it is necessary to understand how large platforms and digital ecosystems can profit from the inherent tendencies of platform markets to concentrate and how platform operators can build up market power (Section 1). In addition, however, it is necessary to also consider the specific characteristics of digital ecosystems, which allow ecosystem operators to achieve economic power even across markets (Section 2).

1. How can digital platforms build up market power?

Platforms (in the economic sense) act as **intermediaries** between user groups. This means that they offer services to different user groups, with the service consisting of interaction between these user groups. The service offer can consist of the platform drawing the attention of one user group to an offer of the other user group (attention platform). Alternatively, the platform may also allow transactions to be carried out directly (transaction platform).

An **example** of a transaction platform may be a communication service or a social network for end users, or a search engine standing between people offering online content or products, and people searching for such content or products. An attention platform exists where a platform is financed by business users displaying ads via the platform. Of course, both types of platforms can be combined into one business model.

In any event, the platform operator may economically be most accurately described as a supplier of a **parallel service to the different user groups** via the platform, meaning that the platform would itself be a "platform market" or "multi-sided market". Alternatively, the platform operator may also be considered to be an **intermediary standing between users potentially belonging to separate relevant markets**. The latter view makes it easier to apply the competition law tools to define markets, but it reaches its limits in social networks, i.e. one-sided transaction platforms, where the platform users cannot be considered to belong to separate markets (e.g., men/women on a dating portal).

In *Ohio v. Amex*, a case concerning credit cards, the U.S. Supreme Court considered the market offer of the card organization, which stands as a platform between banks (card "issuers") and merchants accepting the cards ("acquirers"). It held that "the **key feature of transaction platforms** is that they **cannot make a sale to one side** of the platform **without simultaneously making a sale to the other**".[1] This, however, does not mean that all platform users necessarily pay the same price. Indeed, the platform operator may even decide to offer the platform service to **one side for free**, i.e., in the digital world typically to the consumers using an online platform. In that case, another side may have to pay the price,

---

[1] *Ohio v. American Express Co.*, 585 U.S. ___ (2018).

e.g., the merchants on an online marketplace or advertisers on a search platform or in a social network.

The **markets** in the economic sense on which platforms operate (platform markets) may **tend toward concentration**. Whether this is the case is determined, in particular, by the extent of the network effects that make platform use attractive. Having more users can make the platform more attractive for users of the same group (direct network effect) or users of a different group (indirect network effect). The extent to which network effects contribute to concentration depends on additional factors, such as platform size and differentiation, parallel use and switching options, and the characteristics of the groups of platform users. In this context, network effects and platform size (because of the associated economies of scale) promote concentration, while platform differentiation and the extent to which users use different platforms or differ from one another reduce concentration. However, access to transaction-relevant data and the development of a combined service offering (economies of scope) can further reinforce existing concentration tendencies.

Concentration is only problematic if the platform position cannot be challenged permanently. From an economic perspective, we may hence say that the **market has "tipped"** in favor of the relevant platform. And in terms of EU competition law, the company operating the platform is in a "dominant" position (but it need not have reached monopoly power in terms of U.S. law). The **decisive factor** in determining whether dominance exists is the **intermediary position of the platform**. The build-up of market power in platforms is influenced by the following two factors: (i) the bilateral dependency of users on platform services, which results from the fact that users can only establish contact with users on the other side of the platform through the platform, (ii) the fact that (potential) competitors are not able to make any effective competitive advances.

The **extent** to which the platform operator **enjoys market power** must be determined primarily on the basis of the extent of network effects and the other factors influencing the strength of network effects. Another relevant aspect is the extent to which the platform operator has exclusive access to user-relevant data. Further, the significance of all the relevant elements can be influenced by any innovation-driven competitive pressure, as both disruptive and merely incremental innovations can relativize any market power over time.

2. How can digital ecosystems build up cross-market power?

As stated in the introductory paragraph, so-called digital ecosystems have emerged in the platform economy over time. Digital ecosystems combine several product and service offerings beyond the operation of a single platform. In this respect, they **operate across markets (conglomerates)**. At the same time, hardware, software and/or services are in a compatible and complementary relationship with one another in their activities and are also linked with one another via — possibly exclusively managed — data inventories.

In digital ecosystems as well, the operators benefit from certain advantages in competition. More precisely, the ecosystem operators are able to combine their platform power on individual markets as well as their exclusive data access and the possibility to use data across markets. These advantages enable ecosystem operators to **restrain competition**. They may first do so **by raising entry barriers** in the markets for their core services. This makes it harder for market entrants, thus weakening the contestability of these markets, and once the barriers have become insurmountable, the ecosystem operators may be able to limit unfairly the access of commercial users to their services or data and to exploit commercial users and consumers. The second competition restraint may come about if the platform ecosystem operators **leverage their market power into other markets**, in order to exclude competition there.

II. Exclusionary practices

1. The relevant legal standards

The efficiencies associated with network effects in the **platform economy** are welcome under EU, U.S. and Japanese law alike. However, where platform operators use anticompetitive agreements to make markets tip (e.g., by imposing price parity), these agreements may violate their competition laws relating to vertical restriction, namely Article 101 TFEU and national cartel prohibitions in the EU, §1 Sherman Act in the U.S. and the AMA Article 19. Where they act unilaterally to this end, this may constitute an abuse of dominant position or superior market power in the EU, its Member States (e.g., §20(1), (3a) of the German Competition Act) and in Japan. In Japan, such conduct may also constitute a private monopolization under AMA Articles 2(5) and 3. In the U.S., the relevant behavior may constitute monopolization or an attempt to monopolize under §2 Sherman Act.

Similarly, the fact that **digital ecosystem operators** benefit from economies of scale and scope is of no concern under the competition and antitrust rules. Agreements concluded by ecosystem operators to raise entry barriers (e.g., by limiting interoperability and locking in consumers) may, however, fall foul of Article 101 TFEU and its equivalents in the Member States or §1 Sherman Act. Where an ecosystem operator is dominant, Article 102 TFEU may be violated through unilateral practices to foreclose competitors (upstream foreclosure, e.g., again through price parity) or commercial users (downstream foreclosure).[2] Aggressive unilateral practices capable of lessening or destroying competition such that monopoly power ensues may also constitute attempted monopolization and violate §2 Sherman Act. In Japan, the relevant provisions are Articles 2(5) and 3 (private monopolization) and AMA Articles 2(9) and 19 (unfair trade practices).

Moreover, in EU law, where **entry barriers** have become **insurmountable**, refusing commercial users access to the ecosystem operator's services or data at so-called FRAND[3] conditions may contravene Article 102 TFEU as a refusal to deal.[4] Moreover, according to the ECJ, a dominant undertaking may also violate Article 102 TFEU by **leveraging** its market power at least under *special circumstances*, for example, when the undertaking concerned has a quasi-monopolistic position in a market, also making it *a favoured supplier* in another market.[5] On this basis, the GC held that abusive tying is possible for dominant platform operators whose abusive behavior has cross-market effects.[6]

Monopolization or an attempt to monopolize under §2 Sherman Act as well as the AMA Article 19 (GD para. 2) is more difficult to

---

[2] See again European Commission Guidelines on non-horizontal mergers (Ch. 3 fn. 62), §§31 ff., 58 ff. on the differentiation between "customer" (upstream) and "input" (downstream) foreclosure.

[3] FRAND = Fair, reasonable, and non-discriminatory.

[4] ECJ, Judgment of 16 July 2015, *Huawei Technologies* (C-170/13) ECLI:EU:C:2015:477, §§42 ff.

[5] ECJ, Judgment of 14 November 1996, *Tetra Pak/Commission* (C-333/94 P, ECR 1996 p. I-5951) ECLI:EU:C:1996:436, 27–29.

[6] GC, Judgment of 17 September 2007, *Microsoft/Commission* (T-201/04, ECR 2007 p. II-3601) ECLI:EU:T:2007:289, §§901, 920 ff., 1339.

establish in relation to **unilateral refusal to deal**. This is not only because of the more demanding standard for finding monopoly power or the necessary factors[7] but also because unilateral refusal to deal is largely untouched in the U.S. and Japan. Regarding unilateral practices to **leverage** existing monopoly power into other markets, the Court of Appeals for the 2nd Circuit held in *Berkey Photo, Inc. v. Eastman Kodak* that *[T]he use of monopoly power attained in one market to gain a competitive advantage in another is a violation of §2, even if there has not been an attempt to monopolize the second market. It is the use of economic power that creates the liability.*[8] However, the Supreme Court clarified in *Trinko* that there has to be indeed a *dangerous probability of success* in monopolizing the second market.[9] In any case, the leveraging theory of harm under §2 Sherman Act applies not only where a firm operates in different markets but also where it uses vertical integration to foreclose competition upstream or downstream.[10]

Finally, the rules on unilateral conduct cover behavior that **harms the market structure**. This is certainly true for the U.S. and Japan and also for the EU. According to the ECJ, particularly stringent conduct requirements under **Article 102 TFEU** apply if the *the degree of dominance reached [so] substantially fetters competition [...] that only undertakings remain in the market whose behaviour depends on the dominant one.* For then it may be seen as abusive if the dominant undertaking (e.g., a dominant ecosystem operator) *by an alteration to the supply structure [= structure-related conduct] which seriously endangers the consumer's freedom of action in the market [...] practically [eliminates] all competition.*[11] This jurisprudence rests specifically on the **integration of supply alternatives**, regardless of any subsequent exclusionary behavior and

---

[7] See Chapter 4, Section II.2 and 3.

[8] *Berkey Photo, Inc. v. Eastman Kodak Co.*, 603 F.2d 263, 276 (2d Cir. 1979), cert. denied, 444 U.S. 1093 (1980).

[9] *Verizon Commc'ns, Inc. v. Law Offices of Curtis V. Trinko, LLP*, 540 U.S. 398, 415 n. 4 (2004): *"To the extent the Court of Appeals dispensed with a requirement that there be a 'dangerous probability of success' in monopolizing a second market, it erred."*

[10] *United States v. Paramount Pictures*, 334 U.S. 131, 173–175 (1948).

[11] ECJ, Judgment of 21 February 1973, *Europemballage Corporation and Continental Can Company / Commission* (6/72, ECR 1973 p. 215) ECLI:EU:C:1973:22, 26 and 29; see also ECJ, Judgment of 3 October 1985, CBEM / CLT and IPB (311/84, ECR 1985 p. 3261), end of §26.

regardless of reactions of other market participants. In that respect, its closest parallel in **U.S. and Japanese law** is merger control, i.e., §7 Clayton Act[12] and Chapter 4 of the AMA. In addition, it is recognized there that a **merger to monopoly** may violate §1 or §2 Sherman Act as well as the rules on private monopolization in Japan.[13]

2. The enforcement practice in the EU, the U.S. and Japan

The **European Commission** and the national competition authorities in Europe have conducted numerous **investigations** into the large ecosystem operators under Article 101 and Article 102 TFEU. In several instances, agencies, States and private plaintiffs have initiated proceedings or brought **suits** respectively in the **U.S.** based on the suspicion that the same practice was also violating §1 or §2 Sherman Act. In some instances, plaintiffs have lodged cases that preceded the investigations in the EU or that go beyond them. In **Japan**, the JFTC took some measures in 16 digital-related cases already, although it places more emphasis on speedy resolution by means of commitment decisions and does not impose formal (hard) measures in those cases. In addition, it has monitored **self-preferencing** practices of large platform operators, among others, in a number of surveys.

In the relevant cases, the alleged competition (or antitrust) violations **typically combined several exclusionary practices** that raised barriers to market entry. In some cases, the alleged violations would affect the core markets of the respective ecosystem operators (e.g., the markets for online search and intermediation services, social network services or online advertising services).[14] In most cases, however, the allegations of competition (or antitrust) violations **presupposed that the ecosystem operators already enjoyed an entrenched position in its core markets** and did not specifically address the potential of violations to further raise entry barriers there. Rather, they focused on the ecosystem operator's use of its

---

[12] 15 U.S.C. §18.

[13] See, e.g., *United States v. First Nat'l Bank of Lexington*, 376 U.S. 665, 669–673 (1964). It is unclear yet whether this rule also extends to systematic take-overs of nascent competitors; see Hovenkamp, Federal Antitrust Policy, 6th ed., 2020, pp. 377–378.

[14] See, e.g., European Commission, Decision of 20 March 2019, AT.40.411 — *Google Search (AdSense)*; appeal pending: GC, *Google and Alphabet/Commission (Google AdSense for Search)* (T-334/19).

entrenched position to raise barriers to entry in markets conquered at a later date or to leverage its market power through tying or by favoring its own services (so-called self-preferencing) into additional markets.

In some instances, it was also alleged that ecosystem operators **refused to deal** with providers of downstream services or degraded their services (e.g., in the display of web search results). A number of examples from the case practice regarding the GAFAM companies are provided in the following.

(a) **Google**

In its *Google Android* decision, the European Commission found that online search giant Google had violated Article 102 TFEU by offering a free package consisting of the Android operating system and the Play Store, as well as some essential apps such as the Google search app and YouTube. In the European Commission's view, this package — which was very attractive to original equipment manufacturers (OEMs) — served to raise barriers to entry on the mobile operating systems and app store markets, as other companies could not compete with Google's offering (thereby protecting Google's position on the search and search advertising markets). At the same time, Google was able to use the no-cost package offering to prevent app vendors, for example, from offering better apps to OEMs, such as smartphone manufacturers. In this way, Google was also able to leverage its market power in areas where it was not yet dominant.[15] The European Commission imposed conduct-related remedies, but no structural remedies, to undo the materialized harm to competition. The GC mostly upheld the decision, with the exception of the European Commission's allegation that Google had made revenue share agreements conditional on the exclusive pre-installation of Google Search on a predefined portfolio of devices.[16]

A partly related U.S. case was brought by the **DOJ and 11 States**, which largely centers on the role of the Android mobile operating system as well. Plaintiffs here allege that Google has monopolized the markets for general search services, search advertising and general search text ads

---

[15] European Commission, Decision of 18 July 2018, AT.40099 — Google Android.

[16] GC, Judgment of 14 September 2022, *Google and Alphabet/Commission (Google Android)* (T-604/18) ECLI:EU:T:2022:541; further appeal pending: Google and Alphabet/ Commission (C-738/22 P).

through exclusivity agreements (including agreements with tying elements) with companies for the distribution of its software (including device manufacturers) and unilateral conduct to block distribution channels and competitors.[17] Another lawsuit filed by another 38 States for various practices concerning the search and search advertising market has partly been joined.[18]

In another partly related U.S. case — though again based on a different theory of harm — 37 States alleged the creation of artificial barriers around the Google Play Store and the prevention of app pre-installation through exclusivity agreements. In addition, plaintiffs here complain that Google forces in-app payments via the Play Store and engages in unfair conduct.[19] The case was settled with most plaintiffs in September 2023.

In *Google Shopping*, the European Commission found that Google violated Article 102 TFEU by displaying the results of price comparison searches (vertical search) alongside the results of the general search (horizontal search) in such a way that it placed its own price comparison service at the top of the search results and downgraded competing comparison services. In this case, the European Commission's theory of harm was not based on the accusation of anticompetitive bundling, but rather on self-preferencing in the presentation of search results.[20] The decision was largely confirmed by the GC in this respect; a further appeal is pending.[21] Like in the *Google Android* case, the European Commission imposed conduct-related remedies but no structural remedies to undo the materialized harm to competition. In both cases, market participants later complained that the remedies were not sufficient to improve the competitive situation.[22] The European *Google Shopping* proceedings have no direct equivalent in the U.S. The FTC had closed its case there prior to the European Commission's decision and also did not reopen the investigation at a later point in time.[23]

---

[17] *United States of America v. Google LLC*, 1:20-cv-03010 (D.C. Cir.).

[18] *State of Colorado v. Google LLC*, 1:20-cv-03715, (D.C. Cir.).

[19] *State of Utah v. Google LLC*, 3:21-cv-05227 (N.D. Cal. 2021).

[20] European Commission, Decision of 27 June 2017, AT.39740 — *Google Search (Shopping)*.

[21] GC, Judgment of 10 November 2021, *Google and Alphabet/Commission (Google Shopping)* (T-612/17) ECLI:EU:T:2021:763; further appeal pending: ECJ, *Google und Alphabet/Commission (Google Shopping)* (C-48/22 P).

[22] See the references in fn. 115 in Chapter 4.

[23] FTC, press release of 3 January 2013, *In the Matter of Google Inc.*

In its ongoing ***Google Adtech*** investigation, the European Commission is examining under Articles 101 and 102 TFEU whether Google is using its presence at "almost all levels of the supply chain for online display advertising"[24] to reserve user data for advertising on websites and in apps for its own use (self-preferencing) and restricting third parties' access to those data.[25] This case is largely mirrored by an action which the DOJ and 17 U.S. states brought in April 2023.[26] In March 2021, the European Commission and the UK CMA moreover opened investigations against Google and Facebook for **colluding and preventing advertising auctions**.[27] The cases mirror an earlier and related U.S. lawsuit, which was filed by 10 States.[28] However, the European Commission dropped its investigation in late 2022, stating that its initial concerns — that the two Big Tech firms agreed to weaken and exclude a competing technology — had not been confirmed.

A related action was nevertheless brought by the DOJ and eight States in the U.S. in 2023 in Virginia. Plaintiffs based their complaint on §2 Sherman Act. They allege that Google used **serial acquisitions** and anticompetitive **auction manipulation** to subvert competition in Internet advertising technologies.[29]

It also should be noted that the European Commission had provided **merger clearance** to Google's acquisition of online ad company DoubleClick before, which has drawn much criticism.[30] However, the FTC did not raise objections against the acquisition either.[31]

---

[24] European Commission, press release IP/21/3143, 22 June 2021.

[25] European Commission, AT.40670 — *Google* — *Adtech and Data-related practices.*

[26] *United States v. Google LLC*, 1:23-cv-00108-LMB-JFA, filed 17 April 2023.

[27] European Commission, AT.40774 — *Google-Facebook (Open Bidding) agreement*; CMA, press release of 11 March 2022.

[28] *The State of Texas v. Google, LLC*, 4:20-cv-00957 (E.D. Texas), and *The State of Texas v. Google, LLC*, 4:20-cv-00957 (MDL).

[29] DOJ, press release of 24 January 2023.

[30] European Commission, Decision of 11 March 2008, M.4731 — *Google/DoubleClick*. On this case, see Helberger *et al.* (BEUC), EU Consumer Protection 2.0, Structural asymmetries in digital consumer markets, A joint report from research conducted under the EUCP2.0 project, March 2021, §23; The American Antitrust Institute, Google Acquisition of DoubleClick: Antitrust Implications, 6 November 2007, available at: https://www.europarl.europa.eu/cmsdata/183974/20080130ATT20155EN.pdf.

[31] FTC, *Google/DoubleClick*, File No. 071-0170; Early Termination Notice of 20 December 2007; FTC press release of 20 December 2007.

(b) Amazon

The European Commission had been investigating, concerning the *Amazon Marketplace*, whether Amazon is using non-public business data of independent merchants selling through its Marketplace for its own retail business in direct competition with those merchants, in a case opened in July 2019. The allegation was based on Amazon having a hybrid platform business model (dual role) in that it operates a market-place and has its own retail business.[32] In another investigation, among other things, on *Amazon's Buy Box*, the European Commission had been investigating suspicions under Article 101 or Article 102 TFEU that Amazon gives anticompetitive preferential treatment to its own offers and offers from sellers who use Amazon's logistics and shipping services ("shipping-by-Amazon") in the shopping cart field (Buy box) and as part of "Prime".[33] While both cases in the EU were closed in late 2022, the FTC filed a complaint against Amazon in September 2023.[34]

An **Italian** agency investigation **related to** the European Commission's *Buy Box* case resulted in a record fine at national level in 2021.[35] Moreover, the **German** FCO investigated, among other things, potentially abusive terms and conditions imposed by enforced by Amazon and Apple on the sale of branded products by third-party retail-ers and controls on third-party retailers' prices.[36] An investigation on price control mechanisms and brand-gating is continuing under national law (§19a GWB).[37] These cases have no equivalent in U.S. law.

At EU Member State level, the German FCO and the UK CMA had investigated Amazon's **price parity clauses** earlier, alleging that Amazon had used its dual role as online merchant and marketplace operator to collude under Article 101 TFEU with other merchants by use of a price

---

[32] European Commission, AT.40462 — *Amazon Marketplace*.

[33] European Commission, AT.40703 — *Amazon — Buy Box* (ongoing).

[34] European Commission, press release IP/22/7777 of 20 December 2022; FTC complaint 2:23-cv-01495, filed 26 September 2023. The European cases were closed after Amazon had made commitments to address the Commission's concerns.

[35] AGCM, press release of 9 December 2021.

[36] See, e.g., Mundt, "Den Amazon-Marktplatz haben wir genau im Blick", interview in F.A.Z., 16 September 2021.

[37] FCO, press release of 14 November 2022.

parity clause.[38] Amazon's use of price parity clauses was also the subject of a U.S. lawsuit which was, however, dismissed after less than one year in 2022.[39] This suit additionally concerned a margin maintenance agreement (MMA), whereby wholesalers guarantee Amazon's margin when Amazon purchases a product wholesale and resells it at a price determined by Amazon. The U.S. suit was based on a collusion and a monopolization theory of harm. An appeal is pending.[40]

In Japan as well, serious problems have emerged **between platform operators and commercial platform users**, particularly in relation to online shopping malls and app stores. A large number of businesses were increasingly dependent on certain platforms, specifically the online shopping malls of Amazon and Rakuten, among others, and the app stores of Google and Apple.

The JFTC concluded one investigation against Amazon by commitments (abuse of superior bargaining position with regard to inventory compensation and forced sponsorships) and a few informally (regarding MFN and abuse of superior bargaining position).[41] In addition, the JFTC also conducted investigations against Rakuten and online booking portals and accepted commitments in several cases (regarding exclusive dealing and abuse of superior bargaining position with shipping fees).[42]

(c) Facebook

The European Commission launched proceedings against Facebook in June 2021, investigating whether Facebook is violating Article 101 or

---

[38] FCO, Case report of 9 December 2013 on Decision of 26 November 2013, B6-46/1 — *Amazon Price Parity clause*; CMA, OFT press release of 1 October 2013, CE/9692/12.

[39] *District of Columbia v. Amazon.com, Inc.*, 2021-CA-001775-B (D.C. Super. 2021); *re* the dismissal: https://www.thewellnews.com/law/antitrust/d-c-attorney-general-loses-again-in-antitrust-claims-against-amazon/.

[40] https://www.law360.com/articles/1524464/dc-ag-appealing-toss-of-amazon-antitrust-suit.

[41] See JFTC, press releases of 10 September 2020 (inventory compensation); 1 June 2017 (MFN), 15 August 2017 (e-book MFN); 11 April 2019 (abuse of superior bargaining position regarding point service).

[42] See, e.g., JFTC, press releases of 25 October 2019 (Rakuten MFN regarding online travel agencies); 6 December 2021 (Rakuten shipping fees); 16 March 2022 (Booking.com MFN), 2 June 2022 (Expedia MFN).

Article 102 TFEU by **tying its online classified ads service** "Facebook Marketplace" to its social network. The European Commission is also investigating allegations that Facebook has used advertising data in competition with advertisers in other markets, such as classified ad services.[43]

Two **U.S. civil lawsuits** brought by the FTC and 48 U.S. States and territories are partly related. In these cases, plaintiffs allege that Facebook violated §2 Sherman Act and §7 Clayton Act respectively with the **acquisition of Instagram (2012) and WhatsApp (2014)** as well as the imposition of anticompetitive conditions on software developers. The lawsuits were provisionally dismissed in January and June 2021, respectively, and admitted after amended re-filing in January 2022.[44]

In this context, it should be noted that the European Commission had provided **merger clearance** to Facebook's acquisition of WhatsApp before, whereas the Instagram acquisition was subject only to national review in the EU, which has been heavily criticized in the meantime.[45] The FTC had not objected against both acquisitions before, either.[46] However, the European Commission later fined Facebook for submitting misleading information.[47]

(d) Apple

The European Commission initiated three parallel proceedings against Apple in June 2020 for abusive practices under Article 101 or Article 102 TFEU in connection with the operation of the *Apple App Store*.[48] The investigations focus on Apple's mandatory use of its in-house system for in-app purchases and contractual restrictions on developers' ability to

---

[43]European Commission, AT.40684 — *Facebook leveraging*.

[44]*State of New York v. Facebook, Inc.*, 1:20-cv-03589, and *Federal Trade Commission v. Meta Platforms, Inc.* 1:20-cv-03590 (D.D.C. 2020).

[45]European Commission, Decision of 3 October 2014, M.7217 — *Facebook/WhatsApp*.

[46]FTC, File No. 121–0121 — *Facebook/Instagram*, press release of 22 August 2012; File No. [...] — *Facebook/WhatsApp*, press release of 10 April 2014.

[47]European Commission, Decision of 26 July 2017, M.8228 — *Facebook/WhatsApp* (Article 14.1 proc.).

[48]European Commission, AT.40716 — *Apple — App Store Practices*; AT.40652 — *Apple — App Store Practices (e-books/audiobooks)*; AT.40437 — *Apple — App Store Practices (music streaming)*.

inform iPhone and iPad users of cheaper alternative in-app purchase options. The alleged practices protect Apple's position regarding the app store and regarding app-related transactions. They may also allow Apple to leverage its market power into the payments market.

In the U.S., *Epic Games* sued Apple Inc. based on §1 and §2 Sherman Act with regard to Apple's use of its app store monopoly (as Apple mandates the use of Apple Pay for in-app purchases) and the enforcement of commissions of 15–30% for in-app purchases *vis-à-vis* app developers.[49] The case was mostly dismissed in 2021, but Epic appealed and its appeal is supported by 35 States and the DOJ.

In another case opened against Apple in June 2020, the European Commission is investigating the integration of *Apple Pay* into commercial apps and websites on iPhones and iPads, the restriction of access to the NFC (near field communication) "tap and go" feature on iPhones to payments in online stores and retail stores and alleged denials of access to Apple Pay.[50] This investigation goes beyond the action brought by Epic in the U.S. inasmuch as it rests on a "refusal to deal" theory of harm.

The JFTC has investigated **Apple's in-app payment** system as well but closed the case after Apple agreed to change its practice worldwide.[51]

(e) Microsoft

In its ongoing cases, the European Commission has been relying repeatedly on an earlier investigation into Microsoft in 2004, where it had found that Microsoft had abused its market power by deliberately **restricting interoperability** between Windows PCs and non-Microsoft work group servers **and** by **tying its Windows Media Player (WMP)**, a product where it faced competition, with its ubiquitous Windows operating system, thereby leveraging its near monopoly in the market for PC operating systems (OS) onto the markets for work group server operating systems and for media players.[52]

A preceding judgment of the Court of Appeals for the Federal District had partly affirmed the finding that Microsoft violated §2 of the Sherman

---

[49] *Epic Games, Inc. v. Apple Inc.*, 4:20-cv-05640 (N.D. California).
[50] European Commission, AT.40452 — *Apple — Mobile payments*.
[51] JFTC, press release of 2 September 2021.
[52] European Commission, Decision of 24 March 2004, AT.37792 — *Microsoft*; upheld on appeal: GC, Judgment of 17 September 2007, *Microsoft/Commission* (T-201/04, ECR 2007, p. II-3601) ECLI:EU:T:2007:289.

Act by **illegally maintaining a monopoly in the operating system market**. The court, however, remanded the case for the illegal **tying of Windows and Internet Explorer** under §1 Sherman Act. It found that the empirical evidence regarding the alleged foreclosure effects was insufficient.[53] The case was settled afterward.

In July 2020, **Slack** filed a complaint against Microsoft about the **bundling of the Teams chat and video collaboration platform** with Office 365.[54] It was reported that Microsoft, in order to avert the formal opening of proceedings, sought to settle the case, but the European Commision still launched a formal investigation in July 2023.[55]

III. Platform-to-consumer exploitative practices

As stated above, companies with substantial market power may use that power not only to the detriment of competitors but also to the detriment of consumers. Article 102 TFEU also applies to such exploitative practices. In the context of digital ecosystems, the provision has gained some prominence for exploitation used to (also) exclude competitors. In contrast, §2 Sherman Act only captures exclusionary conduct. The application of exploitative practices used to exclude competitors is controversial at best. Such practices can, however, be captured by §5 FTC Act. In Japanese law, AMA Article 19 may apply.

1. EU law

In the context of digital ecosystems, exploitation has been relevant in a number of cases already. The reason is that it is **easy to exploit users where platform markets have tipped permanently** in a way causing entry barriers to become insurmountable. However, in the cases decided so far, the authorities and courts did not examine exploitation under the above test in an isolated fashion but rather examined whether the ecosystem operator was exploiting consumers and at the same time excluding competitors ("exploitation to exclude").

---

[53] *U.S. v. Microsoft*, 253 F.3d 34 (2001).

[54] Slack press release of 22 July 2020.

[55] Chee, Exclusive: Microsoft seeks to settle EU antitrust concerns over Teams — Sources, Reuters of 13 December 2022; EU Commission, AT.40721 – Microsoft Teams, Decision of 27 July 2023.

An important example is the German ***Facebook*** case (although this case has been examined, not under Article 102 TFEU but under national law). The German **Federal Court of Justice** held provisionally in an interim decision that Facebook collects and combines user **data from external sources** (also labeled "off data") in a way that **makes it more difficult** for other social networks and online advertising providers **to compete**. In doing so, Facebook also raises barriers to market entry. At the same time, Facebook's data collection **also** represents **consumer exploitation**. This is because Facebook siphons off consumers' data to improve all of its services, regardless of whether consumers themselves are only interested in using individual Facebook services and not others. **The fact that Facebook's behavior may also violate data protection rules is irrelevant** in this context. By raising the barriers to entry in the social networking space, Facebook can also indirectly gain control of the online advertising market and thus expand its market power.[56]

The **FCO** had tried to argue before that Facebook **exploited consumers by violating data protection rules** as to "off data".[57] However, statements from FCO officials indicate this theory of harm has meanwhile been abandoned, although an appeal is pending.[58] It is noteworthy that a U.S. class action was brought based on a similar theory of harm in late summer 2023.[59]

Good to know: The European harmonization obligation of Article 3 Regulation 1/2003 and abuse law in the EU Member States

Article 3(1)(2) Regulation 1/2003 provides the following: *Where the competition authorities of the Member States or national courts apply national competition law to any abuse prohibited by Article 82 of the Treaty, they*

---

[56]Fed. Ct. of Justice, Order of 23 June 2020, *Facebook*, KVR 69/19, ECLI:DE:BGH:2020:230620BKVR69.19.0.

[57]FCO, Order of 6 February 2019, B6-22/16 — *Facebook*. An English translation of the order is available at: https://www.bundeskartellamt.de/SharedDocs/Entscheidung/EN/Entscheidungen/Missbrauchsaufsicht/2019/B6-22-16.pdf?__blob=publicationFile&v=5.

[58]Higher Reg. Ct. of Düsseldorf, Order of 24 March 2021, Kart 2/19 (V); see also ECJ, Judgment of 4 July 2023, C-252/21 - Meta Platforms and others (Conditions générales d'utilisation d'un réseau social) ECLI:EU:C:2023:537 on the data-protection related aspects of this case. *Meta Platforms and others* (C-252/21) (pending).

[59]*Maximilian Klein v. Meta*, 3:20-cv-08570-JD, filed 15 September 2023.

(Continued)

shall also apply Article 82 of the Treaty [= Article 102 TFEU]. Article 3(2)(2) adds to this: *Member States shall not under this Regulation be precluded from adopting and applying on their territory stricter national laws which prohibit or sanction unilateral conduct engaged in by undertakings.*

In its Facebook decision, the FCO argued that it need not apply Article 102 TFEU because "the concept of protection developed by German case law on the general clause of Section 19(1) GWB, which relies heavily on decisions about values based on both fundamental rights and ordinary law in order to determine abusive conduct, has so far found no equivalent in European case law or application practice".[60] This is, however, not the standard of the law as Article 3(1)(2) simply requires an (examination and) application of Article 102 TFEU where it is applicable.

The German legal literature sometimes tries to justify the non-application of Article 102 TFEU with the argument that even if Article 3 Regulation 1/2003 were infringed, the application of national rules would be sufficient to reach the objectives of Article 102 TFEU. This is again not correct, for two reasons: In substance, national rules cannot account for the Union interests pursued by Article 102 TFEU. And in terms of interpreting Article 102 TFEU and Article 3 Regulation 1/2003, only the ECJ is competent under Article 267(1) and (3) TFEU to provide a final and binding interpretation of the rules.

The European Commission has meanwhile initiated proceedings, or at least considered such initiation, in several other cases which rest on a theory of harm potentially combining exploitative and exclusionary elements. Notably, the European Commission has been investigating whether ***Amazon*** is using ***non-public business data*** of independent merchants selling through Amazon Marketplace for its own retail business in direct competition with those merchants, in a case opened in July 2019.[61] The allegation was based on Amazon having a hybrid platform business

---

[60]FCO, Order of 6 February 2019, B6-22/16 — *Facebook* §914.
[61]European Commission, AT.40462 — *Amazon Marketplace* (ongoing). The German FCO had actually launched an investigation into Amazon's terms of use for merchant users of its marketplace shortly before the European Commission. This case has been closed in the

model (dual role) in that it operates a marketplace and has its own retail business. However, as noted above, the case was settled in late 2022.

2. U.S. law

---

§5 FTC Act (15 U.S.C. §45(a)(1))

Unfair methods of competition in or affecting commerce, and unfair or deceptive acts or practices in or affecting commerce, are hereby declared unlawful.

In U.S. law, §5 FTC Act allows one to examine scenarios where firms with market power treat other market participants unfairly or deceive them. According to FTC, an act or practice is **unfair** where it (i) causes or is likely to cause substantial injury to consumers, (ii) cannot be reasonably avoided by consumers and (iii) is not outweighed by countervailing benefits to consumers or to competition. Thus, the "unfairness prong" of §5 FTC Act protects consumers against exploitation of their dependency, regardless of the reasons for that dependency.

An act or practice is **deceptive** where (i) a representation, omission or practice misleads or is likely to mislead the consumer, (ii) a consumer's interpretation of the representation, omission or practice is considered reasonable under the circumstances and (iii) the misleading representation, omission or practice is material. Thus, the "deception prong" of §5 FTC Act addresses exploitations of information asymmetries existing between a firm and the consumers.

The FTC is cautious not to stretch the boundaries of §5 FTC Act as this would compromise legal certainty and might deter investment. Thus, the FTC brings data **privacy cases mostly under the "deception" branch** of §5 FTC Act. Relevant FTC cases potentially relevant also have concerns, e.g., data anonymity,[62] confidentiality[63] and the disclosure of

---

meantime after Amazon committed to amend its terms of use; see FCO, release of 17 July 2019.

[62] FTC, *In the Matter of Compete, Inc.*, Docket C-4384, 102 3155 (2013).

[63] FTC, *In the matter of Eli Lilly and Company*, Docket C-4047; File No. 0123214, 133 FTC 763, 766 (2002).

information.[64] In these cases, though, the FTC did not deal with ecosystems specifically. That being said, the FTC has investigated ecosystems under §5 FTC Act as well. In these investigations, the FTC has strived to limit the ecosystem operators' collection of data.[65]

In sum, the application of §5 FTC Act typically rests on theories of harm that are unrelated to the idea of protecting (generally) functioning markets against conduct restraining competition. Instead, §5 FTC Act is applied in cases of **perceived market failures** which inhibit consumers from being able to take advantage of the choices created by competitive markets.[66] Thus, FTC investigations may be triggered by companies abusing the imbalance of power in the bilateral relationship to disregard the need for consumer notice/consent. But they may also be initiated with a view to protecting consumers' reasonable expectations of privacy as such.

Good to know: Algorithmic collusion as exploitation?

It has already been mentioned that a debate exists on whether the use of pricing algorithms contributes to explicit or tacit (implicit) collusion. A related question is whether dealers possess enough market power to jointly exploit consumers. It is conceivable that the presence of platforms is key in this context. This is for the following reasons:

1. <u>Data</u> can have a competitive impact on the digital economy. The strategic value of data depends on the market structure (e.g., high market concentration and homogeneous goods), the quality of the relevant data and surrounding information, and the quantity of information flows.
2. <u>Algorithms</u> are tools to analyze big amounts of data faster.

(Continued)

---

[64]*FTC v. Toysmart.com, LLC*, 00-11341-RGS, 2000 WL 34016406 (D. Mass. July 21, 2000).

[65]FTC, *In the matter of Microsoft Corporation*, Docket C-4069; File No. 0123240, 134 FTC 709, 715; *United States v. Facebook*, 1:19-cv-02184 — part of FTC settlement re Cambridge Analytica.

[66]OECD, Country Studies, U.S. Updated Report 2004, DAF/COMP(2005)13, 20 January 2005, §10; available at: https://www.oecd.org/unitedstates/34427452.pdf.

(Continued)

3. Platforms such as online marketplaces (e.g., hotel or flight booking portals) are not only market players, but they also centralize the market organization for others. This increases transparency for the commercial platform users and may allow them to identify relevant data and to react faster.

These factors allow commercial platform users to differentiate their prices to address more customers. However, the consumers may have to pay more than in the case of uniform prices. At the same time, less information is readily available to consumers as these use no or less sophisticated algorithms on the platform, i.e., information asymmetries exist.

Thus, in terms of competition law, it may be necessary to define markets fragmented by the use of pricing algorithms more narrowly than other markets to account for the possibility to price-discriminate. In that regard, the U.S. Horizontal Merger Guidelines provide valuable guidance — the European Commission's Notice on the relevant market does not address the issue so far (but is under review).[67]

Alternatively, regulation may be necessary to counter-balance the information asymmetries. This may be justified because information asymmetries constitute a market failure, i.e., the competition on the market is not functioning properly anymore for structural reasons.

---

3. Japanese law

Article 19 of the AMA applies to three categories of cases. One category is formed by **practices lessening free competition**. This category requires a low level of economic power and covers behavior producing fewer clear-cut effects than monopolization in the US. The second category includes the **use of unfair methods** and can be considered an "unfair competition" or business tort category abroad. The third category relates to **abuses of a superior bargaining position**. It was originally applied only to exploitations in a business-to-business context. However, the

---

[67] DOJ/FTC, Horizontal Merger Guidelines, 19 August 2010, §3; European Commission, Notice on the relevant market (Ch. 4 fn. 3); *re* the review, see also European Commission, press release IP/21/3585, 12 July 2021.

JFTC published guidelines on Transactions between Digital Platform Operators and Consumers that Provide Personal Information.[68] These guidelines clarify that an abuse of a superior bargaining position can also take place in a business-to-consumer context. Articles 2(9)(v) and 19 may capture exploitative practices if the relevant behavior falls into one of the categories.

IV. The reform debate

The competition law investigations conducted against the operators of large online platforms and digital ecosystems have met with **complaints** in all three covered jurisdictions. The **investigations in the EU** usually have been launched so far when markets had tipped already. They take **too long** and the imposed remedies are **too weak** to be effective. One reason for these shortcomings may be that ecosystem operators have exclusive access to relevant data while the competition agencies lack these data and still bear the burden of proof. Regarding the EU internal market, an additional risk emerged when some EU Member States, particularly Germany, started regulating competition in digital markets on their own. In **Japan**, the situation is similar. The JFTC has conducted investigations but has not been able to restore competition once markets had tipped in favor of one company. And on top of various limitations of the JFTC's AMA law enforcement activities, the AMA is not a law that imposes disclosure obligations in a comprehensive manner.

In the **U.S., the antitrust agencies completely refrained** from interfering with the digital markets based on the antitrust rules for a long time. Behind this may have been the idea that markets correct themselves and that agencies should not deter innovation through the enforcement of rules that had not been designed for the digital world.

This situation has evolved. The **EU** started to develop a **comprehensive set of regulations** for the digital world around 2019, with the "Digital Markets Act" (DMA) being the most relevant piece of regulation in a competition-related context. In the **U.S.**, a **number of bills** were introduced in Congress which resemble the DMA in substance or sharpen the

---

[68] JFTC, Guidelines Concerning Abuse of a Superior Bargaining Position in Transactions between Digital Platform Operators and Consumers that Provide Personal Information (17 December 2019).

tools for intervention and sanctions to counter anticompetitive conduct. Although most of these bills have failed, regulating digital platform operators remains high on the agenda. In Japan, rather conservative transparency legislation seems to produce sizeable effects. In addition, further legislation may be on its way.

1. EU: The Digital Markets Act and other reform proposals

When it comes to changes in EU competition law, it must be taken into consideration that it is very **difficult to change the substance** of the law (Articles 101 and 102 TFEU).[69] It is much easier to modify the procedural rules (EU secondary legislation). The **European Commission opened the discussion** at EU level formally with the proposal of a so-called New Competition Tool (NCT) in June 2020. This NCT would have allowed the European Commission to intervene before competition violations occurred in individual markets. In addition, the European Commission also proposed a Digital Services Act, which would subject all kinds of platforms to certain obligations, with more stringent obligations potentially for "large" platforms. These obligations would not necessarily be competition related. They would also apply irrespective of the competitive situation in individual markets.

A **shift from platforms to digital ecosystems** took place when the European Commission presented its proposal for a **Digital Markets Act** in December 2020, which entered into force **as Regulation (EU) 2022/1925** on 1 November 2022.[70] The DMA incorporates the competition-related aspects

---

[69]This was initially considered to alleviate the European Commission's burden of proof; see Crémer/de Montjoie/Schweitzer, Competition Policy for the digital era, Final Report, 2019, pp. 61–62, and in the following Espinoza/Fleming, Margrethe Vestager eyes toughening "burden of proof" for Big Tech, Financial Times of 30 October 2019; Crofts/Hirst, Vestager pledges to tame tech's "dark side" in second EU mandate, MLex of 27 November 2019; Madero Villarejo, Antitrust in times of upheaval, speech of 10 December 2019, S. 5; https://ec.europa.eu/competition/speeches/text/sp2019_13_en.pdf.

[70]Regulation (EU) 2022/1925 of the European Parliament and of the Council of 14 September 2022 on contestable and fair markets in the digital sector and amending Directives (EU) 2019/1937 and (EU) 2020/1828 (Digital Markets Act), OJ L 265, 12 October 2022, p. 1 See also Commission Implementing Regulation (EU) 2023/814 of 14 April 2023 on detailed arrangements for the conduct of certain proceedings by the Commission pursuant to Regulation (EU) 2022/1925 of the European Parliament and of the Council, OJ L 102, 17 April 2023, p. 6.

of the Commission's earlier ideas. However, it follows a new philosophy in that it is not intended to protect functioning markets (like EU competition law) but rather to deal with the failure of markets where large digital ecosystems are present. In order to protect the contestability and fairness of such markets (Article 1(1) DMA), the European Commission proposed a very formal regulatory instrument, apparently to allow the new rules to apply easily, and in order to regain regulatory control.

One feature of the DMA is that its Article 3 foresees a **formal designation of** addressees (so-called **gatekeepers**) typically without much individual assessment. A review may take place only upon application. This is different from the approach under competition law where it must first be assessed whether the relevant company is indeed the right addressee under the rules. In principle, the DMA should only apply to the largest platform operators (GAFAM/GAMMA),[71] even though industry representatives have warned that the quantitative thresholds (especially the number of users) would also cover smaller competitors (e.g., Microsoft's Bing and Snapchat).[72]

The DMA submits its addressees to **conduct obligations in relation to** defined **core platform services** (e.g., search intermediation, social networking or cloud services)[73] in Articles 5–7 **and to transparency obligations** in Articles 14–15. Pursuant to its Article 8(1), the addressees must be able to **prove complete and ongoing compliance**. This would relieve the Commission of its burden of proof to a large extent. Moreover, any applicable **obligations apply across markets and in parallel**. This means that

---

[71] European Commission, Proposal for a Regulation of the European Parliament and of the Council on contestable and fair markets in the digital sector (Digital Markets Act), COM/2020/842 final, 15 December 2020, p. 1; Impact Assessment, SWD(2020) 363 final, 15 December 2020, §§14 ff.

[72] See Consultation contribution by Microsoft, 3 May 2021, available at: https://ec.europa.eu/info/law/better-regulation/have-your-say/initiatives/12418-Legislativpaket-uber-digitale-Dienste-Instrument-zur-Vorabregulierung-sehr-gro%C3%9Fer-Online-Plattformen-die-als-Torwachter-fungieren/F2256709_de, p. 6 ff. *While precise EU MAU [= Million Active Users] numbers are not publicly available, based on global MAU estimates it is likely that several will exceed the thresholds set forth in the DMA. More than 17 social networks have more than 250 million MAU, e.g., Pinterest (459 million), Snapchat (433 million), Reddit (430 million), and Twitter (330 million). Yet none are a must have for advertisers seeking to reach end users. Separately, looking at a different platform category, Microsoft Bing, our search engine, has more than 45 million MAU too.*

[73] See Article 2 No. 2 of the DMA for the complete list.

the situation in individual markets is irrelevant and that no balancing of pro- and anticompetitive market effects takes place. Instead, the DMA takes a holistic view and obliges ecosystem operators to abide by a rule set barring many types of behavior that, through their interplay, helped create the unassailable ecosystems that are dominating the digital economy today.

The **conduct obligations** defined in Article 5 are based on the previous case practice of the European Commission and Member State agencies and should be interpreted against that background. In contrast, Article 6 DMA foresees obligations "susceptible of being further specified", which address conduct that may contribute to the tipping of markets or the protect market participants in permanently tipped markets (access rights and prohibition of self-preferencing). During the legislative process, it was an issue of discussion whether especially the data access obligations should be moved from Article 6 to Article 5 (which would have limited the scope for DMA addressees to argue in favor of specification). It was also an issue of **discussion whether the DMA should include a general prohibition** of takeovers in case of systematic non-compliance. This rule would have aimed at preventing the *buying up of potential competitors*, especially in nascent markets (i.e., start-ups). However, the institutions participating in the legislative process ultimately refrained from far-reaching changes of such type.[74]

Good to know: The Korean regulation of in-app payments[75]

In 2021, the Korean legislature revised the Monopoly Regulation and Fair Trade Act, and also the Telecommunication Business Act was amended regarding app stores and billing systems. The latter amendment garnered a significant amount of attention. It included an article which proscribes the operators of app stores from "unfairly using their bargaining position" to

---

[74]Note that the 11th amdt. to the German Competition Act instead empowers the FCO to divest companies as a preventive measure following a market investigation revealing structural disruptions of competition (§32f of the Competition act, as amended).

[75]See Lee, Main Developments in Competition Law and Policy 2021 — Korea, 14 February 2022 for a detailed account of the developments in Korea in 2021; available at: http://competitionlawblog.kluwercompetitionlaw.com/2022/02/14/main-developments-in-competition-law-and-policy-2021-korea/.

(Continued)

force the providers of apps distributed through their app stores to use specific payment systems for transactions made in their apps. The amendment entered into force in September 2021. However, the targeted U.S. app store operators Apple and Google made no effective changes in their practices and many commercial users continued to complain about the commission rates charged on the app stores. Hence, the Korean Communications Commission (KCC) announced that it will revise its rules to clarify the scope and meaning of the newly introduced provision by providing examples of an unfair use of the asymmetric bargaining position. It remains to be seen which impact these revisions will have on the market.

The **European Commission** is the **sole enforcer** of the DMA and is entrusted with considerable discretion in its task. The European Commission is empowered to supplement the obligations if necessary and to conduct market investigations in order to define additional addressees, to identify systematic non-compliance and to amend the conduct obligations. In addition, the European Commission may levy fines and penalty payments in cases of non-compliance. The provisions of the DMA for non-compliance (Articles 18, 29 et seq.) are based on the Cartel Procedure Regulation 1/2003. Just as there, the European Commission proposal provides in principle for the priority of conduct-related remedial measures. However, where a gatekeeper has *systematically infringed one or more of the obligations,* the European Commission may impose both behavioral or structural remedies (including a temporary precautionary prohibition on future mergers).[76]

For its part, the European Commission has indicated that it might make **greater use of structural remedies** also **in complex abuse proceedings** under Regulation 1/2003 in the future.[77] This would probably be justified, taking into account that remedies and sanctions under the DMA would be imposed to rectify non-compliant behavior (regardless of its market effects), whereas remedies and sanctions would also need to address the harm to competition associated with the behavior.

An important characteristic of the DMA is that it foresees a **role for the national agencies only in non-compliance cases** and there only at a

---

[76]Article 18(2) DMA.
[77]European Parliament, E-000133/2022, Answer given by Executive Vice-President Vestager on behalf of the European Commission (22 February 2022); EU Commission press release IP/23/3207, 14 June 2023 (re Google Adtech).

preparatory stage, and it barely addresses **private enforcement**. Moreover, the role of national agencies is reduced further because under the ECJ jurisprudence on the priority of application for directly applicable provisions of European law, the directly applicable conduct obligations of the DMA will mean that discretionary intervention rules at national level (e.g., the German §19a of the German Competition Act) will probably lose their practical relevance to a large extent.[78] It must be noted, though, that **stricter national rules** (e.g., §20(3a) of the German Competition Act) **and rules servicing a different purpose** than the DMA may continue to apply.

Good to know: The DMA and Germany's prohibition of abuses of "paramount cross-market significance" (§19a of the German Competition Act) compared

DMA	§19a of the German Competition Act
• Objectives: preserving "contestability and fairness" in case of market failures due to emergence of large platforms (incl. digital ecosystems).	• Objective: protection of undistorted competition.
• Application to "gatekeepers" meeting statutory criteria.	• Discretionary agency intervention to define addressee (§19a(1)) and to impose conduct obligations (§19a(2)).
• Conduct and transparency obligations apply automatically and in parallel across markets.	• Conduct obligations resemble DMA but apply not in relation to "core platform services" and are partially defined more broadly.
• Situation on individual markets irrelevant, i.e., no balancing of pro- and anticompetitive effects; no efficiency defense.	• Consumer harm required, i.e., efficiency defense possible (burden of proof: norm addressee).
• Early administrative intervention to avoid competition remedies; remedies to neutralize violation of obligations but not to address harm to competition.	• Remedies to neutralize abusive behavior and to address harm to competition.[79]

---

[78]See ECJ, Judgment of 15 July 1964, *Costa / E.N.E.L.* (6–64, ECR 1964 p. 585), ECLI:EU:C:1964:66 (as quoted in the box in Chapter 3, Section V.3.d).

[79]But not necessarily to restore competition; see Chapter 4, Section IV, on unilateral behavior.

The DMA must be seen in the context of other EU regulations (including legislative proposals), which complement it with a view to non-competition-related objectives. These include, in particular, the following:

- the **Digital Services Act** (Reg. No. 2022/2065 — DSA),[80] in conjunction with the EU Copyright Directive (Dir. No. 2019/790),[81] which together regulate the liability of platform operators for content accessible via the platform,
- the **P2B Regulation** (Reg. No. 2019/1150), which governs the relationship between platform operators and commercial users and regulates the terms of use of the platform,
- the **Regulation on a framework for the free flow of non-personal data** (Reg. No. 2018/1807 — FFDR),[82] the **Data Governance Act** (Reg. No. 2022/868 — DGA)[83] and the proposed **Data Act**, which together create a new regulatory regime for accessing data as an economic resource, excluding gatekeepers in terms of the DMA as beneficiaries,[84]
- the **General Data Protection Regulation** (Reg. No. 2016/679 — GDPR), which governs the processing of personal data and the protection of privacy,

---

[80] Regulation (EU) 2022/2065 of the European Parliament and of the Council of 19 October 2022 on a Single Market For Digital Services and amending Directive 2000/31/EC (Digital Services Act), OJ L 277 of 27 October 2022, p. 1.

[81] Directive (EU) 2019/790 of the European Parliament and of the Council of 17 April 2019 on copyright and related rights in the Digital Single Market and amending Directives 96/9/EC and 2001/29/European Commission, OJ L 130, 17 May 2019, p. 92.

[82] Regulation (EU) 2018/1807 of the European Parliament and of the Council of 14 November 2018 on a framework for the free flow of non-personal data in the European Union, OJ L 303 of 28 November 2018, p. 59.

[83] Regulation (EU) 2022/868 of the European Parliament and of the Council of 30 May 2022 on European data governance and amending Regulation (EU) 2018/1724 (Data Governance Act), OJ L 152 of 3 June 2022, p. 1. See in conjunction also Directive (EU) 2019/1024 of the European Parliament and of the Council of 20 June 2019 on open data and the re-use of public sector information (recast), OJ L 172 of 26 June 2019, p. 56.

[84] Data Act: Proposal for a Regulation on harmonised rules on fair access to and use of data, COM(2022) 68 final, 23 February 2022; accessible: https://ec.europa.eu/newsroom/dae/redirection/document/83521.

- the proposed **AI Regulation**, which aims to ensure the protection of fundamental rights when processing data by means of AI,[85]
- the **Regulation on electronic identification and trust services for electronic transactions** (Reg. No. 910/2014 — eIDAS) and the **Regulation on Digital Operational Resiliency** (Reg. No. 2022/2554 — DORA), which regulate risk aspects of ID services and financial services, including interoperability aspects.[86,87]

A problem not conclusively solved by the DMA (and the additional regulations) is that they take the existence of digital ecosystems as a given and only include **a few rules to open up markets again** (e.g., through data access/portability and interoperability requirements). Furthermore, the conduct obligations of the DMA are fraught with the burden that, in the case of infringements, only the conduct relating to individual core platform services and relating to individual platform sites is stopped. In this case, the **gatekeeper would retain the economic benefits** of its infringing conduct to the extent that the conduct generates such benefits for the gatekeeper's business otherwise (especially on other platform sites of

---

[85] European Commission, Proposal for a Regulation of the European Parliament and of the Council laying down harmonised rules on Artificial Intelligence (Artificial Intelligence Act) and amending certain Union legislative acts, COM(2021) 206 final, 21 April 2021.

[86] Regulation (EU) No. 910/2014 of the European Parliament and of the Council of 23 July 2014 on electronic identification and trust services for electronic transactions in the internal market and repealing Directive 1999/93/European Commission, OJ L 257 of 28 August 2014, p. 73; Regulation (EU) 2022/2554 of the European Parliament and of the Council of 14 December 2022 on digital operational resilience for the financial sector and amending Regulations (EC) No. 1060/2009, (EU) No. 648/2012, (EU) No. 600/2014, (EU) No. 909/2014 and (EU) 2016/1011, OJ L 333 of 27 December 2022, p. 1.

[87] Other potentially relevant rules, depending on the context, can be found in various additional EU directives; e.g., the Data Base Directive (Dir. No. 96/9/EC); the Directive on electronic commerce (Dir. No. 2000/31/EC) whose provisions on platform liability were transferred to the DSA; the Audiovisual Media Services Directive (Dir. No. 2010/13/EU — AVMD); the Directive (EU) 2019/1024 on open data and the re-use of public sector information (recast); the Directives on certain aspects concerning contracts for the supply of digital content and digital service, and the sale of goods (Dir. No. 2019/770 and 2019/771); and the Directives on unfair trade (Dir. No. 2006/114/EC concerning misleading and comparative advertising) and on consumer protection law (esp. Dir. No. 93/13/EEC on unfair terms in consumer contracts, Dir. No. 2005/29/EC concerning unfair business-to-consumer commercial practices); as well as the Directive on cybersecurity (Dir. No. 2022/2555).

affected multilateral markets). Thus, incentives may remain for "gate-keepers" to purposefully violate the DMA.

2. U.S.

In the U.S., a **Congressional inquiry** into competition in the digital markets identified significant market power problems in the platform economy in 2020.[88] This quickly triggered a political discussion on whether the regulatory toolbox should be expanded beyond the existing antitrust rules. In this context, there was less concern about the substance of the law than in the EU because it is similarly possible to tighten the substantive standard of review for platforms and digital ecosystems as are procedural amendments. In the course of 2021, the following five legislative proposals addressing the major platform operators were introduced in the House of Representatives and the Senate, respectively.[89] Most of these proposals, however, died a silent death in the course of 2022, and despite a presidential statement calling for action.[90] The first bill listed below was reintroduced in summer 2023.[91] Apart from that, it is unclear whether and when U.S. legislature will make a new effort to pass these laws or similar laws[92]:

- H.R. 3816/S.2992 — **American Innovation and Choice Online Act**, which would prohibit discrimination and self-preferencing,
- H.R. 3825 — **Ending Platform Monopolies Act**, which would facilitate the enforcement of structural separation in case of intra-ecosystem conflicts of interest,

---

[88] Nadler *et al.*, Investigation of Competition in Digital Markets, Majority Staff Report, U.S. House of Representatives, 2020; accessible: https://democrats-judiciary.house.gov/issues/issue/?IssueID=14921.

[89] Sykes, The Big Tech Antitrust Bills, CRS Report, R46875, 13 August 2021 (only on the first 4 bills).

[90] US President Biden calls for bipartisan Big Tech legislation, MLex, 11 January 2023.

[91] See, Klobuchar, Grassley, Colleagues Introduce Bipartisan Legislation to Boost Competition and Rein in Big Tech, press release of 15 June 2023; accessible: https://www.klobuchar.senate.gov/public/index.cfm/2023/6/klobuchar-grassley-colleagues-introduce-bipartisan-legislation-to-boost-competition-and-rein-in-big-tech.

[92] Regarding the stalling of legislative proceedings, see Wheeler, Big Tech giving European consumers what they deny Americans, Brookings, 28 December 2022 (on H.R. 3816, H.R. 3825, H.R. 3826 H.R. 3849, and S.2710 — The Open App Markets Act).

- H.R. 3826 — **Platform Competition and Opportunity Act**, which would prohibit acquisitions of current and potential competitors and shift the burden of proof of negative impact to central platform markets,
- H.R. 3849 — **Augmenting Compatibility and Competition by Enabling Service Switching (ACCESS) Act**, which would enforce interoperability and data portability,
- H.R. 3843 — **Merger Filing Fee Modernization Act**, which would contain regulations on the calculation of merger control thresholds and with a view to resources. This Act became law in December 2022.[93]

In addition, several **bills were proposed by the Senate**, for which, however, legislative support has equally mostly waned away.[94] The only proposal for which the prospects have remained open to this date appears to be the following:

- S.2039 — **Tougher Enforcement Against Monopolists (TEAM) Act**, which would codify the consumer welfare standard and add a market share-based presumption of anticompetitive conduct (Substantial Lessening of Competition — **SLC**) in the Clayton Act with respect to large corporations, tighten merger thresholds in Hart-Scott-Rodino Act and revise Supreme Court jurisprudence to the extent that it makes antitrust damage actions more difficult (Illinois Brick, Hanover Shoe)[95]; otherwise, it overlaps with the Merger Filing Fee Modernization Act.

The House bills were **more in line with existing U.S. antitrust law** and less geared toward constant monitoring and regulation than the DMA in the EU. They tended to include higher application thresholds. They also focused less on the platform-to-consumer relationship than the DMA.

---

[93] https://www.natlawreview.com/article/merger-filing-fee-modernization-act-2022.

[94] S.225 — Competition and Antitrust Law Enforcement Act (overlapping: S.3267 — Consolidation Prevention and Competition Promotion Act); S.1074 — Trust-Busting for the Twenty-First Century Act; S.2710 — Open App Markets Act. *Re* S.2039, S.225 and S.1074 with further details: JDSupra (no author), New Antitrust Bills Highlight Continued Big Tech Scrutiny, 23 June 2021; accessible: https://www.jdsupra.com/legalnews/new-antitrust-bills-highlight-continued-9434161/. On the slim prospects of S.1074, see https://govtrackinsider.com/josh-hawleys-trust-busting-for-the-twenty-first-century-act-would-ban-mergers-or-acquisitions-by-a-e173b244bf97; on S.2710, see the reference in fn. 89 above.

[95] *Illinois Brick Co. v. Illinois*, 431 U.S. 720 (1977); *Hanover Shoe, Inc. v. United Shoe Machinery Corp.*, 392 U.S. 481 (1968).

Moreover, the legislative proposals would not have barred the combination of data and formation of data silos (in contrast to Article 5 lit. a DMA). In contrast, they put strong emphasis on interoperability and portability, even more so than the DMA. On the other hand, however, they would have gone so far as to propose the break-up of large platform companies. This is an option not so readily available in the EU as the large operators of digital ecosystems all have their seats in the U.S.

3. Japan

In 2020, the Japanese Legislature passed Act No. 38 on Improving Transparency and Fairness of Digital Platforms **(Transparency Act)**. The Act was considered to complement the AMA although it is enforced by the Ministry of Economy, Trade and Industry (METI), rather than the JFTC. It must be seen also in conjunction with the Act on the Protection of Personal Information (enforced by the Personal Information Protection Commission) and the Act for the Protection of Consumers on Digital Platforms, etc. (enforced by the Consumer Affairs Agency).

In the interest of fair and free competition (Article 1), the Transparency Act submits Specified Digital Platform Providers (SDPP) to obligations to **inform users** (commercial users and end users, as the case may be) **of the terms and conditions of online transactions** in a specified way.[96] It also empowers METI to issue recommendations and orders and to make public announcements to enforce these obligations.

As a legislative novelty, the Transparency Act includes **agile governance features**. Agile governance emphasizes a process of implementation, evaluation and improvement, and a dialog with stakeholders. The government is no longer a unilateral rule-setter but rather a facilitator of that process. To this end, the Transparency Act empowers METI to develop principles and obliges SDPP to establish procedures and systems on that basis (co-regulation). This is accompanied by reporting and monitoring obligations.

After the entry into force of the Transparency Act, METI pursued its **implementation** actively, and after the first year, a remarkable 70–80% of business users felt that SDPPs' disclosure and support for business users had improved since the Transparency Act came into force.[97] Improvements

---

[96] In that regard, the Transparency Act resembles to some extent the P2B Regulation in the EU.

[97] METI, Evaluation on Transparency and Fairness of Specified Digital Platforms, 22 December 2022; accessible: https://www.meti.go.jp/english/press/2022/1222_003.html.

also appear to have materialized in the procedure and communications relating to returning goods, suspending accounts and resolving complaints. Indications exist that the Transparency Act also has had positive effects regarding self-preferencing practices and data-related issues.

It is to be expected that the Japanese legislature will consider further legislation on online platforms in the near future, notably on mobile ecosystems.[98]

Good to know: The Chinese stance toward digital ecosystems

A number of the large digital ecosystems operating today are based in China. The Chinese state had subjected the operators of those ecosystems only to light-touch monitoring under the competition rules for a long time. This started to change with the formation of SAMR in 2018. In the following, the **AML was revised**, and the amendments came into effect on 1 August 2022. Moreover, the SAMR published **draft implementing provisions to the AML** (September 2022) and **draft revisions to the Anti-Unfair Competition Law** (November 2022).[99] The Supreme People's Court issued an **Interpretation on Several Issues Concerning the Application of the People's Republic of China Anti-Unfair Competition Law** in September 2021. Moreover, based on Article 9 No. 3 AML, the **Anti-Monopoly Guidelines of the Anti-Monopoly Commission of the State Council on the Platform Economy** were released in February 2021, which include detailed guidance on how SAMR will address issues in the platform economy. The structure of the Guidelines is the following:

Chapter I General provisions (Articles 1–4)
Chapter II Monopoly agreements (Articles 5–10)
Chapter III Abuse of dominant position (Articles 18–21)
Chapter IV Concentration of undertakings (Articles 18–21)
Chapter V Abuse of administrative power (Articles 22–23)
Chapter VI Supplementary provisions (Article 24)

---

[98] See Sakamaki, New *ex ante* rules proposed to regulate Google, Apple in Japan's mobile ecosystem report, MLex, 26 April 2022.
[99] See: https://www.china-briefing.com/news/what-has-changed-in-chinas-amended-anti-monopoly-law/ concerning the AML draft implementing provisions.

(Continued)

Important aspects are that a market definition is generally considered necessary for the competition assessment in the platform economy (different from what was stated in an earlier draft). A platform is defined as a business organization form that enables interdependent bilateral or multilateral entities to interact under the rules provided by a particular carrier through Internet information technologies, so as to jointly create value. If cross-platform network effects inside such a platform impose sufficient competition constraints on platform users, however, then the agency can define the whole business of the platform enterprise (consisting of many platforms, in other words, of many industries) as a single relevant product market. In the context of the platform economy, the Guidelines indicate moreover that SAMR intends to also investigate monopoly agreements in hub and spoke structures despite the lack of precedent cases. Regarding dominant positions, the Guidelines acknowledge the essential facility doctrine in relation to platforms but exclude data collected by platforms from the ambit of assessment. Moreover, the rules on discriminatory treatment exclude users' privacy information, transaction history, individual preferences and consumption habits.

The SAMR had started test cases in the digital economy already before the publication of the final Guidelines. These cases included an investigation against Alibaba, which ended with a record fine (USD 2.8 bln.) for "exclusive dealing agreements" preventing merchants from selling products on rival e-commerce platforms ("choosing one from two"). In addition, SAMR also pursued a "softer" approach with guidance letters and invitation to interviews at SAMR (e.g., with 34 online firms on 13 April 2021).[100]

V. Conclusions

The development of the rules and practices regarding digital ecosystems is in flux. Nevertheless, there appears to be a **consensus that additional**

---

[100]Zhang, Agility Over Stability: China's Great Reversal in Regulating the Platform Economy, 28 July 2021, Forthcoming in Harvard International Law Journal, Vol. 63(2) (2022), at 35; accessible: https://awards.concurrences.com/IMG/pdf/the_great_reversal_nov._4.pdf.

rules are needed. This is because the operations of large digital ecosystems can have a structural effect on the market, which contributes to **permanent market failures**.

The associated potential **competition issues** are as follows:

- tipping of platform markets,
- raise of structural barriers to entry into platform markets (with an associated risk of access refusals and exploitation),
- potential that operators enlarge their ecosystems by leveraging the power acquired on their core markets into additional markets.

The **experience with the agency enforcement** of the competition rules in the EU is that investigations under Articles 101 and 102 TFEU have been launched when markets had tipped in an almost irreversible fashion. They have taken too long, and the imposed remedies have been too weak to be effective. In the U.S., the agencies have kept their hands off the digital markets for too long, although tougher remedies would have been available under the Clayton and Sherman Acts.

Hence, the **EU** has chosen to subject digital ecosystems to **comprehensive regulation**, at the heart of which is the DMA with the objective to protect the contestability of markets and the fairness of bilateral relations between the platforms and their users. However, a more robust approach may additionally be needed to restore competition since the DMA focuses on behavior on individual platform sides to an extent that incentives may remain to violate its conduct obligations purposefully. Moreover, the DMA continues to impose conduct obligations (like the agency interventions before) but does not undo any harm to competition that has materialized following a violation.

In addition, exploitation based on data (platforms) and information asymmetries between commercial platform users (merchants) and consumers pose problems not yet addressed conclusively in the EU.

In the **U.S.**, ambitious legislative projects were put on track, out of which the American Innovation and Choice Online Act and the Open App Markets Act appeared at first to have the best prospects of becoming law. However, the process stalled for most of the U.S. bills at a later point. The only exceptions are the Merger Filing Fee Modernization Act, which became law, and the TEAM Act, for which the prospects still appear to be open. However, these two bills focused the least on the issue of digital ecosystems. Thus, it remains to be seen whether U.S. legislature will make further efforts to rein in big tech in the years to come.

In **Japan**, legislation is more moderate at present but may be stepped up in the future.

In all covered jurisdictions, new legislation of digital businesses may mean **avoiding more draconic measures** such as breaking up or nationalizing large online platforms or digital ecosystems (which would also prove difficult for businesses operated from abroad). At the same time, however, particularly the EU approach appears to be fraught with the risk of over-regulation. Thus, it remains to be seen which approach will be the most effective without excessive detrimental effects in the long run.

Chapter 6

Remedies and Appeals, Private Actions

I. General notes

Whereas the substantive prohibitions in competition/antitrust law reflect to a large extent the economic understanding, the legal effects of violations differ. The same holds for the rules on the procedure, which are rooted in the legal traditions of the relevant jurisdictions. In this context, another important difference between the jurisdictions covered in this book becomes relevant.

At **EU** level and in many continental legal systems of EU Member States, competition enforcement is **inquisitorial** and, thus, falls under the responsibility of agencies. The European Commission and national agencies conduct administrative investigations which require them to uncover elements proving an infringement or relieving the relevant undertakings (and individuals, where applicable) of the charges. The undertakings concerned have to submit to the investigation and are not an opponent with equal standing *vis-à-vis* the relevant agency. In some continental jurisdictions, however, it is not the agency itself but a court (upon agency application) which adopts the decision.[1] In addition, private parties may bring civil lawsuits either based on an agency decision (follow-on action) or standalone. These actions may be brought to obtain injunctions or to claim damages. However, stand-alone actions are difficult to bring as parties cannot rely on agency findings, and no discovery procedure exists.

---

[1] See, e.g., §26 ff. of the Austrian Cartel Law (*Kartellgesetz*).

In contrast, **U.S.** competition enforcement takes place in an **adversarial system** in which the parties generally present their case as opponents in court. Agencies are not required to conduct a separate and formal administrative investigation before going to court. This is the reason why also U.S. agencies generally pursue their cases in civil or criminal actions. A peculiarity is the FTC, which is equipped with an administrative system under which it first attempts to issue a consent decree and then launches Administrative Law Judge (ALJ) proceedings leading to the FTC's final determination and orders. However, also the FTC has increasingly opted for bringing its cases to civil court recently. Moreover, the FTC ALJ proceeding actually takes place in an adversarial setting.[2]

The **Japanese** enforcement system falls somewhere in the middle. Civil suits on a standalone basis are possible both for damages and injunctions. Criminal sanctions also play an important role for which the JFTC first files an accusation with the public prosecutor and the case is decided by the court. However, they are relatively rare, and the JFTC's administrative orders play a critical role in ensuring compliance with the AMA. Recent AMA amendments are making the Japanese enforcement system more akin to the EU system.[3]

The covered jurisdictions all combine public and civil enforcement. For this reason, we first take a holistic view in the following (Section II). After that, we discuss public enforcement through agencies (both in administrative and court proceedings; Section III) and then turn to damage actions by private parties (Section IV).

II. Mixed systems regarding remedies and sanctions

In competition and antitrust law, remedies and sanctions serve a purpose that is closely related to prohibitions and the economic reasons underlying

---

[2]See Section III.2.b(2).

[3]Originally, the AMA adopted a system modeling the U.S. system with criminal and civil enforcement. It also foresaw that the FTC should propose a consent order and, in case no agreement was reached, that the FTC should conduct an examination concluding with an administrative order. However, this system with a proposal, termed a JFTC recommendation (*kankoku*) decision, was abolished in 2005 and the JFTC began to issue cease-and-desist orders without consulting with the parties; instead, henceforth, they had to undergo a JFTC examination (*shinpan*) which was similar to the US ALJ procedure. In 2013, the examination system was abolished as well; currently, JFTC orders are subject to the review of the Tokyo district court.

these prohibitions. It does not matter whether these remedies and sanctions are of a civil, administrative, or criminal nature. In fact, all these types of remedies and sanctions are relevant in competition and antitrust cases. Thus, they are designed to protect (and potentially restore) competition. This goes beyond penalizing firms or individuals or preventing them from acting illegally in the future. The relation of remedies and sanctions to the substance of competition/antitrust law has to be kept in mind when looking at the legal consequences of violations, as they are set out in the following:

1. EU law

In EU law, the finding of a competition violation generally has the following consequences:

- The violating act is void (Article 101(2) TFEU; national law).
- The competent agencies may impose an administrative prohibition and/or fines as well as penalty payments.[4]
- Harmed private individuals are entitled to civil damages, which are then governed by national law.

The **fines** are imposed in **administrative procedures** by the European Commission or national administrative agencies. At EU level, they may amount to up to 10% of the worldwide total turnover per undertaking involved. The relevant turnover for the purpose of calculating the fine is usually based on the value of sales of the relevant product (i.e., the product affected by the violation)[5] in the EU in the preceding business year. The European Commission amends the resulting sum taking into account aggravating and mitigating circumstances and adds to this a deterrence amount (15–25%). Directive (EU) 2019/1 provides that fines under national law must have a maximum amount of at least 10% of worldwide turnover. The national rules typically provide for that sum, but the method

---

[4]Article 7, 23–24 Reg. 1/2003; European Commission, Guidelines on the method of setting fines imposed pursuant to Article 23(2)(a) of Regulation No. 1/2003, OJ C 210, 1 September 2006, p. 2. Regarding fines and penalty payments, the national law of Member States is partially harmonized under Reg. 1/2003 and Dir. 2019/1.

[5]This includes cartelized input products where only the final product is shipped into the EU; see European Commission, Decision of 8 December 2010, AT.39309 — *LCD*, §§380 ff.

for calculating the actual fine may diverge from the method used at EU level.

Whereas fines are imposed only on undertakings at EU level, Member States may also sanction the **individuals** involved, such as managers or officers.[6] Several Member States have made use of that competence.[7]

In cases of non-compliance, EU law provides for the imposition of **penalty payments** of up to 5% of the daily turnover. National law may diverge on the amount and the method of calculating penalty payments, and some jurisdictions even allow for coercive detention.

Sanctions at EU level are **not** meant to be **criminal**, which Article 23(5) Regulation 1/2003 also states expressly to clarify the limits of the EU competences. That said, the guarantees enshrined in the European Convention on Human Rights also apply to fines imposed under Regulation 1/2003.[8] Member States moreover are allowed to impose criminal sanctions if that contributes to the effective enforcement of Article 101 and Article 102 TFEU.[9] Several Member States have used that competence.[10]

On the other hand, national agencies may not put obstacles in the way of the implementation of Article 101 and Article 102 TFEU through a decision that there has been no violation of these provisions.[11]

In practice, as noted above (Ch. 4, Section IV), fines and criminal penalties are preferred as sanctions for horizontal collusion. In cases of other collaboration or unilateral behavior, the European Commission likewise imposes fines.[12] Member States sometimes do the same, but sometimes they simply prohibit the relevant conduct without imposing further sanctions (especially in novel or complex cases). However, the decision then often includes conduct obligations. In cases of unilateral abuses of

---

[6]See Article 23 and Recitals 64–65 of Dir. (EU) 2019/1.

[7]For example, Germany has done so in the procedural rules included in its Administrative Offense Act. See Section III.2.a(3) for the details.

[8]See Articles 6, 13 ECHR and European Court of Human Rights, Judgment of 14 February 2019, *SA-Capital Oy v. Finland* (Application No. 5556/10); ECJ, Judgment of 18 July 2013, Schindler Holding and others/Commission (C-501/11 P) ECLI:EU:C:2013:522, §§30 ff.

[9]Article 13(4) Dir. (EU) 2019/1.

[10]See Section III.2.a(3).

[11]ECJ, Judgment of 3 May 2011, *Tele2 Polska* (C-375/09, ECR 2011 p. I-3055) ECLI:EU:C:2011:270.

[12]European Commission, Decision of 17 December 2018, AT.40428 — *Guess*; Decision of 24 July 2018, AT.40182 — *Pioneer (vertical restraints)*.

dominance, the European Commission typically imposes fines and additional conduct obligations to terminate the abusive behavior. It does not impose measures to restore the damaged market structure though. The national agencies do the same.

The development of the sanctioning practice is **documented** particularly for cartels. At EU level, the cases listed in Figure 1 have been the 10 highest fines so far:

Year	Case name	Amount in €*
2016/2017	Trucks	3,807,022,000
2019/2021	Forex	1,413,274,000
2012	TV and computer monitor tubes	1,409,588,000
2013/2016/2021	Euro interest rates derivatives (EIRD)	1,308,172,000
2008	Carglass	1,185,500,000
2014	Automotive bearings	953,306,000
2021	Car emissions	875,189,000
2007	Elevators and escalators	832,422,250
2001	Vitamins	790,515,000
++2010/2017++	Airfreight (incl. re-adoption)	739,642,616

Figure 1.   Ten highest cartel fines per case (since 1969).

Note: *Amounts adjusted for changes following judgments of the Courts (General Court and Court of Justice) and/or amendment decisions.

Source: European Commission; current as of 30 March 2022.[13]

Note that the European Commission has only **adopted** 3–10 **decisions** per year since 2017.

The **table** only lists decisions adopted after the year 2000 although it includes the cartel enforcement practice by the European Commission since 1969. This is because there has been a trend toward ever-higher fines since a policy change around 1982.[14] That said, it should be noted that several investigations on the above list (and also others) were interrelated (e.g., TV, monitor tubes, other panel cartel investigations, EIRD/Forex/YIRD and car glass/automotive bearings). The vitamin cartel was the first EU cartel where very high fines were imposed.

Figure 2 shows the amounts **of fines** imposed per Commission term:

---

[13] See European Commission, Eleventh Report on Competition Policy, 1982, §42.

[14] See https://ec.europa.eu/competition-policy/document/download/b19175c3-c693-410b-b669-27d4360d359c_en?filename=cartels_cases_statistics.pdf.

Year	Amount in €*
1990–1994	537,491,550
1995–1999	292,838,000
2000–2004	3,458,421,100
2005–2009	9,355,867,500
2010–2014	7,917,218,674
2015–2019	8,274,222,000
++2020–2022++	2,222,928,000
total	**32,058,986,824**

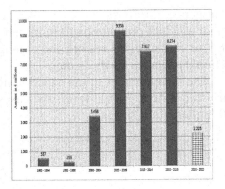

Figure 2.   Fines imposed (not adjusted for Court judgments) — Period 1990–2022.

Note: *Amounts imposed by the Commission (incl. corrections following amendment decisions) and not corrected for changes following judgments of the Courts (General Court and Court of Justice) and only considering cartel infringements under Article 101 TFEU.
Source: European Commission; current as of 29 November 2022.[15]

The fines must be put in relation to the **cases investigated**. In the last two European Commission terms before the year 2000, the European Commission decided 10 and 9 cartel cases, respectively.[16] The number of cartel cases increased sharply in 2000 from an average of 9 to 33 cases. That figure dropped back to below 30 in 2015, and fewer cartel cases are being investigated by national government as well, although the reasons for this are unclear.

Regarding **civil enforcement**, it is difficult to gain a practical overview of court actions and other civil remedies. This is because civil enforcement takes place exclusively at national level and has only been harmonized to a limited extent. The European Commission provides a collection of relevant documents on its website.[17] National court decisions, however, are not centrally collected on this website anymore.

2. U.S. law

In the U.S., antitrust rules are enforced mainly in civil or criminal court proceedings. Moreover, antitrust violations are treated as **crimes** and not merely as administrative offenses. The procedural competences of the

---

[15] See fn. 14 above.
[16] See Table 1.7 Cartel decisions adopted by the European Commission — Period 1990–2022 (fn. 14 above).
[17] See https://competition-policy.ec.europa.eu/antitrust/actions-damages_en.

DOJ and the FTC reflect these important characteristics of the U.S. system: Both the DOJ and the FTC may bring criminal or civil actions under the Sherman Act and the Clayton Act aside from private plaintiffs, e.g., companies harmed by a cartel. However, as noted, the FTC may also conduct its own administrative trial before an Administrative Law Judge under the FTC Act and may issue cease-and-desist orders.[18]

In addition, **U.S. States can act as private parties** under the federal rules. Of course, they may also enforce their own state antitrust laws *vis-à-vis* the companies and individuals participating in an infringement.

The development of **cartel enforcement** in the U.S. at federal level is set out in Figure 3.

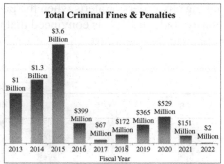 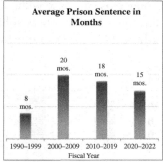

Figure 3.   Sanctions imposed in DOJ proceedings.

Source: DOJ Crim. Enforcement trends charts; current as of 29 June 2023.[19]

The sharp drop in criminal fines and penalties in 2015/2016 may be related to **policy changes** after Donald Trump became U.S. President in June 2015. President Joe Biden issued an Executive Order in July 2021 to promote more vigorous antitrust enforcement in certain markets.[20] It remains to be seen which effects this new policy shift will have in practice. In any event, the DOJ has filed 18–26 criminal cases per year since 2017 with 25 cases in 2021.

---

[18] See Section III.2.b(2) for details on the ALJ proceedings at the FTC.

[19] See https://www.justice.gov/atr/criminal-enforcement-fine-and-jail-charts.

[20] The White House, Executive Order on Promoting Competition in the American Economy and supporting Fact Sheet, 9 July 2021; accessible at https://www.whitehouse.gov/briefing-room/presidential-actions/2021/07/09/executive-order-on-promoting-competition-in-the-american-economy/; https://www.whitehouse.gov/briefing-room/statements-releases/2021/07/09/fact-sheet-executive-order-on-promoting-competition-in-the-american-economy/.

3. Japanese law

In Japan, the AMA is primarily enforced by the JFTC through its administrative procedure. The JFTC fundamentally aims to stop the violation by issuing a cease-and-desist order (Figure 4). With regard to specific types of infringements including private monopolization, unreasonable restraints of trade that affect price and output, and abuses of superior bargaining positions, the JFTC is obliged to issue the surcharge payment order for deterrence (see Figure 5). The level of administrative fines is low, although several AMA amendments have increased it. Japan introduced the commitment procedure in 2018, which is intensively used by the JFTC. The JFTC also uses non-binding informal measures such as warnings and alerts extensively. Furthermore, the JFTC may close the case without taking any orders or alerts when the parties take the corrective measures voluntarily, and the JFTC is convinced that they are sufficient to resolve competitive concerns (Figure 6).

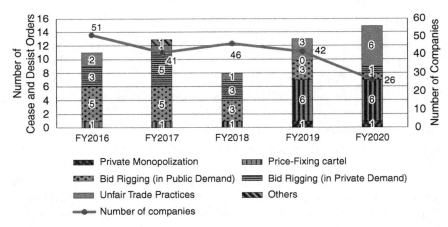

Figure 4.   Number of cases involving legal measures.[*]

Notes: *"Legal measures" refer to cease and desist orders, surcharge payment orders and approvals of the commitment plans. The case in which both a cease and desist order and a surcharge payment order were issued is counted as one legal measure.

The cases which fall into both private monopolization and unfair trade practice are categorized as "Private monopolization".

"Others" refer to cases of unjustly restricting the functions or activities of constituent companies by a trade association.

Source: JFTC, Annual Report on Competition Policy Developments in Japan 2020.[21]

---

[21]Annual Reports submitted to the OECD Competition Committee, https://www.jftc.go.jp/en/about_jftc/annual_reports/oecd_files/japan2020.pdf.

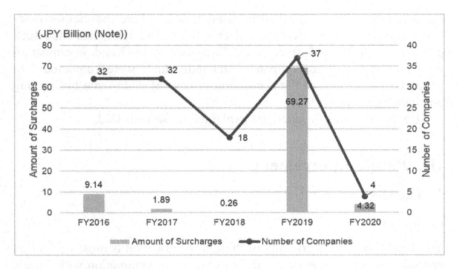

Figure 5.   Amount of surcharges fixed by the JFTC.

Note: Surcharges are rounded down to the nearest ten million yen.
Source: JFTC, Annual Report on Competition Policy Developments in Japan 2020.[22]

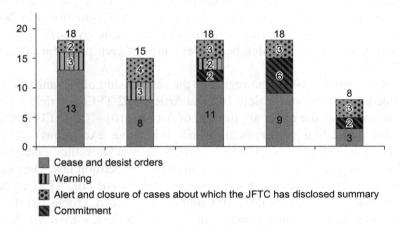

Figure 6.   Measures taken by the JFTC in FY 2017–2021.

A **criminal penalty** may be also imposed by the court but only when the JFTC files an accusation with the Public Prosecutors Office. The JFTC

---

[22]*Ibid.*

has a policy to file a criminal accusation only where the vicious practice has a grave impact on the citizen's life.[23] The JFTC has filed such
accusations in 24 cases since its establishment in 1947 and, in almost all
the cases, the accused companies and individuals were convicted.[24] In
practice, the JFTC files the accusation in case of wide-scale bid rigging
and hardcore cartels.

Private lawsuits in Japan are explained in **Section IV.3**.

III. Public enforcement

1. The law

(a) EU law

The Treaty on the Functioning of the European Union is mostly silent on
procedure. However, Article 103 TFEU (also in conjunction with Article
352 TFEU) empowers the EU legislature to **give effect to Articles 101–
102 TFEU**. On this basis, the EU Council and Parliament enacted
Regulation 1/2003, which provides the rules of the European Commission
procedure in investigations for infringements of Article 101 and Article
102 TFEU. **Implementing rules** can be found in Regulation 773/2004.
The enforcement of European Commission decisions *vis-à-vis* undertakings is governed by the Member States' rules of civil procedure (Article
299 TFEU).

Regulation 1/2003 also regulates the relationship of EU and national
proceedings to enforce Article 101 and Article 102 TFEU. Article 1 notably provides for the direct application of Articles 101–102 TFEU (removing the preceding requirement of administrative exceptions). Article
2 allocates the burden of proof. Article 3 regulates the relationship
between Article 101–102 TFEU and national competition law. The provision expressly requires the enforcement of Articles 101–102 TFEU, where
applicable, and prohibits decisions running counter to Article 101 TFEU
under national law. National abuse prohibitions may deviate from Article 102

---

[23] JFTC Policy on Criminal Accusation and Compulsory Investigation of Criminal Cases
Regarding Antimonopoly Violations, 7 October 2005, as last amended 23 October 2009.
[24] JFTC, Kokuhatsu Jiken Ichiran [List of accusation cases], https://www.jftc.go.jp/dk/
dk_qa_files/hansokuitiran.pdf. Note that, with regard to imprisonment, the courts always
give individuals suspended sentences.

TFEU if they are stricter. Also, merger control remains unaffected, and decisions under national law which predominantly pursues objectives different from those of Article 101 and Article 102 TFEU remain possible as well. Regulation 1/2003 was complemented with Directive (EU) 2019/1, which harmonizes the procedural law of Member States for the purposes of enforcing Article 101 and Article 102 TFEU through administrative intervention.

Moreover, the ECJ held that *the practical effect of the prohibition laid down in Article [101 TFEU] would be put at risk if it were not open to any individual to claim damages for loss caused to him by a contract or by conduct liable to restrict or distort competition.*[25] Therefore, the EU also passed **Directive 2014/104/EU** on certain rules governing actions for damages under national law for infringements of the competition law provisions of the Member States and of the European Union, which harmonizes the procedural law of Member States for the purposes of enforcing Article 101 and Article 102 TFEU in civil damage actions.

(b) U.S. law

In the U.S., the federal antitrust laws regulate not only the substance of the law but also the legal consequences of infringements as well as the competences of the relevant agencies for the purposes of enforcement. The **Sherman Act** includes the relevant rules in its §§4–6 (15 U.S.C. §§4–6), the **Clayton Act** in its §§4–5, 11 ff. (15 U.S.C. §§15–16, 21 ff.) and the **FTC Act** in its §§5, 7–10, 13–14, 19 ff. (15 U.S.C. §§45, 47–50, 53–54, 57b ff.). In cases handled by the FTC, the procedure for the Administrative Law Judge (see Section III.2.b(2)) is governed by 16 C.F.R. Part 3.

The procedure for the DOJ's antitrust actions before civil courts is laid down in the Antitrust Civil Process Act (15 U.S.C. §§1311 ff.). The DOJ may alternatively seek criminal penalties. In this case, the U.S. sentencing rules (18 U.S.C. §§3551 ff.) and the USSC Sentencing Guidelines apply.

Where **state laws** apply, these also govern the procedure before the State Attorney General and in state courts.

---

[25]ECJ, Judgment of 20 September 2001, *Courage and Crehan* (C-453/99, ECR 2001 p. I-6297) ECLI:EU:C:2001:465, §26; see also Judgment of 6 October 2021, *Sumal* (C-882/19) ECLI:EU:C:2021:800, §33.

(c) Japanese law

The AMA sets out the legal consequences of infringements as well as the **competences** of the relevant agencies for the purposes of enforcement. The most important provisions are AMA Articles 7, 7-2, 8-2, 20, 24, 25, 89 and 95. They provide administrative, civil and criminal sanctions. In case of a civil damage suit, Articles 90 and 709 of the Civil Code are also important. Several provisions apply to AMA investigations of agency procedure; other matters are governed by the Administrative Case Litigation Act, the Code of Civil Procedure and the Code of Criminal Procedure.

2. The procedure and decision competences

The imposition of remedies and sanctions follows an investigation into the relevant conduct, which is based on a suspicion of anticompetitive behavior. The procedure and, where existing, administrative decision competences of agencies in the relevant jurisdictions are examined in the following.

(a) EU law

The procedural law in the EU for competition enforcement is a complicated and confusing amalgamation of EU rules and national rules. The basic procedural provisions can be found in **Regulation 1/2003**.

Articles 4–6 of that regulation provide the European Commission with the competence to enforce Article 101 and Article 102 TFEU and also foresee minimum competences for national agencies and courts in that respect. Articles 11–15 regulate the cooperation between the European Commission and EU Member States. Article 16 bars Member State courts from deviating from European Commission decisions. In addition, Regulation 1/2003 includes rules for procedures and decisions at European Commission level, whereas the national enforcement is governed by other rules.

(1) European Commission procedure

Articles 17–22 of Regulation 1/2003 regulate the European Commission's **investigation powers** (*re* sector inquiry, requests for information, hearings, inspections). Articles 27–28 deal with the rights of the undertakings concerned and third parties (rights to be heard and of professional secrecy). These rights must be seen in conjunction with the fundamental right of private parties to be treated fairly in administrative proceedings.[26]

Implementing Regulation 773/2004 includes further rules addressing the conduct of proceedings. It is complemented by several notices and best-practice guidelines (*re* proceedings and evidence).[27] Article 2 of the Implementing Regulation deals with the initiation of proceedings, and Articles 3–4 empower the European Commission to take statements and its officials to ask oral questions during inspections. Article 5 ff. regulates the handling of complaints of third parties.[28] However, under a program governed by the EU leniency rules (Article 4a and Leniency Notice),[29] cartel members interested in obtaining immunity or leniency may themselves make a submission uncovering a cartel or providing new information on its workings (thereby, regularly, busting that cartel). The position of the undertakings concerned and third parties is further regulated by Article 10 ff., which includes additional rules on the right to be heard and the conduct of oral hearings, as well as Articles 15–16 regarding access to the European Commission's files.[30]

---

[26] Article 41 of the EU Charter of Fundamental Rights.

[27] See esp. European Commission, Commission notice on best practices for the conduct of proceedings concerning Articles 101 and 102 TFEU Text with EEA relevance, OJ C 308, 20 October 2011, p. 6; DG Competition Staff Working Paper, Best practices for the submission of economic evidence and data collection in cases concerning the application of Articles 101 and 102 TFEU and in merger cases, undated; available at https://ec.europa.eu/competition/antitrust/legislation/best_practices_submission_en.pdf.

[28] In that regard, see also European Commission, Commission Notice on the handling of complaints by the Commission under Articles 81 and 82 of the European Commission Treaty, OJ C 101 of 27 April 2004, p. 65.

[29] European Commission, Consolidated text: Commission Notice on Immunity from fines and reduction of fines in cartel cases, Document 02006XC1208(04)-20150805 (Leniency Notice).

[30] See also European Commission, Consolidated text: Commission Notice on the rules for access to the Commission file in cases pursuant to Articles 81 and 82 of the European Commission Treaty, Articles 53, 54 and 57 of the EEA Agreement and Council Regulation (EC) No. 139/2004 (2005/C 325/07), Document 02005XC1222(03)-20150806.

In addition, the European Commission published its internal **manual of procedures** in 2013 and revised versions in 2019 and 2023.[31] The manual can provide arguments to private parties to obtain equal treatment in European Commission procedures, but its legal relevance is even more limited than the relevance of the European Commission's notices and guidelines.

(2) The European Commission's decision competences

The European Commission may adopt decisions ordering the **termination** of an infringement (Article 7), take **interim measures** (Article 8), to accept **commitments** (Article 9) and **impose fines** and periodic **penalty payments** (Articles 23–24). The limitation periods are governed by Articles 25–26. The publication of decisions is regulated in Article 30. While the European Commission uses all its powers with regard to main proceedings, it shied away from taking interim measures for a long time because of the high standard of proof that the EU courts had required the European Commission to meet in that context.[32] It was almost 20 years after the last relevant judgment that the European Commission used that power again.[33]

Termination and commitment decisions may also include obligations to remedy the competition violation. The European Commission decides on the imposition unilaterally. However, in commitment decisions, it does so by accepting proposals of the undertakings concerned. Article 7 states expressly that both behavioral and structural obligations are possible. The obligations must be appropriate and necessary to terminate the infringement effectively. However, as noted above, the GC has interpreted this **proportionality** requirement very strictly. This has made the European Commission impose behavioral remedies in abuse cases concerning digital platforms which have been criticized for being ineffective.[34] In other foreclosure cases concerning network

---

[31] See https://competition-policy.ec.europa.eu/document/4dece098-82fb-4cdd-bd5c-1176 c52e4531_en.

[32] See ECJ, Order of 11 April 2002, *NDC Health/IMS* (C-481/01 P(R), ECR 2002 p. I-3401) ECLI:EU:C:2002:223.

[33] European Commission, Decision of 16 October 2019, AT.40608 — *Broadcom*.

[34] See ECJ, Judgment of 29 June 2010, *Commission/Alrosa* (C-441/07 P, ECR 2010 p. I-5949) ECLI:EU:C:2010:377, §39, and Ch. 4, Section IV, *re* the proportionality requirement. See again also the references in fn. 115 of Ch. 4.

industries, the European Commission had imposed structural remedies before.[35]

The decisions ordering termination regularly also impose fines at EU level, irrespective of whether the decision concerns a cartel, other collaborative conduct, or unilateral behavior.[36] The European Commission has published guidelines to explain the calculation of fines, and the availability of fine reductions in cartel cases for information helping to uncover the cartel (leniency notice) or to aid the European Commission in the investigation and to conclude the case after a shortened procedure and without appeal (settlement notice).[37] The decisions are published as non-confidential versions, which produces a "naming and shaming" effect.[38]

As noted in the previous paragraphs, European Commission proceedings may feature **cooperative elements**. In the case of horizontal cartels, cartel members may try to obtain (full) immunity or (partial) **leniency**. The European Commission may offer a **settlement** to cartel members to facilitate the investigation and its termination. Different from what the name suggests, however, the settlement is not negotiated (at least not officially), but the European Commission sets the conditions which the undertakings concerned may only accept or reject. Although settlements of some cartel members, but not all, are not very attractive to the European Commission, the European Commission has agreed to such "hybrid settlements" as well in the past. In cases of other collaboration and abuses, the European Commission does not use the tools of cartel proceedings (although it has developed a leniency policy for vertical cases).[39] It may agree to close the case against **commitments**, however.

---

[35] See European Commission, Decision of 4 May 2010, AT.39317 — *E. On gas foreclosure*; Decision of 26 November 2008, COMP/39.388 — *German Electricity Wholesale Market* and COMP/39.389 — *German Electricity Balancing Market*.

[36] Article 23 Reg. 1/2003.

[37] See European Commission, Guidelines on the method of setting fines imposed pursuant to Article 23(2)(a) of Regulation No. 1/2003, OJ C 210, 1 September 2006, p. 2 (with general application); Leniency Notice (fn. 29); Consolidated text: Commission Notice on the conduct of settlement procedures in view of the adoption of Decisions pursuant to Article 7 and Article 23 of Council Regulation (EC) No. 1/2003 in cartel cases, Document 02008XC0702(01)-20150805 (both specifically for cartels).

[38] This can be different in national law; which is the case, e.g., in Germany for cartels.

[39] See European Commission, Decision of 29 April 2019, AT.40049 — *Mastercard*, §118; Decision of 17 December 2018, AT.40428 — *Guess*, §199.

With regard to digital ecosystems, a new cooperative tool will be available with the (*ex ante*) **regulatory dialog** between the European Commission and designated gatekeepers, which will be used to specify some of their conduct obligations.[40]

The practice, however, has shown that European Commission proceedings with cooperative elements may give rise to certain problems. **Problem No. 1** is that the **balance of power** between the agency and the undertakings concerned **shifts over time**. At the beginning of the investigation, the undertakings concerned benefited from an information asymmetry toward the European Commission. For the European Commission, this makes starting an investigation without cooperation difficult. However, once the investigation has been initiated successfully, the European Commission can always use the threat to change into the regular termination and sanctioning procedure to exact cooperation from the undertakings. Furthermore, during the proceedings, the European Commission gradually obtains the information it needs and may use its pressure on the undertakings from then on to obtain (justified or unjustified) concessions.

In **commitment** investigations, a particular risk exists that the undertakings feel **forced to make concessions** even though the investigation does not have merit. This is because Article 9 Regulation 1/2003 only requires *concerns expressed to them by the Commission in its preliminary assessment* to open the door for commitment discussions. Thus, companies may be willing to make concessions simply to bring the investigation to an end. In settlements, the European Commission's emphasis that it does not "negotiate" may produce similar results.

Problem No. 2 is that only a **limited court review** is available **in settlement or commitment proceedings**. In these proceedings, the European Commission publishes only a short decision. Moreover, it requires the cooperating parties to effectively renounce their right to appeal (on substantive grounds). Both elements mean that the parties themselves obtain only limited information about the European Commission's findings and its legal assessment and the robustness of its case. In addition, no case precedent develops that might provide guidance to other market participants.

Problem No. 3 is that the **protection of third-party interests in commitment proceedings is weak**. The commitments proposed are

---

[40] Article 6 in conjunction with Article 7(2) DMA.

submitted to a market test to obtain the views of outside parties.[41] However, the results of that market test are not binding for the European Commission. What is more, there is a risk that the European Commission and the undertakings may use the cooperation to terminate the investigation effectively to the detriment of third parties. It was only recently that the ECJ clarified the right of third parties to lodge an appeal against such a decision.[42]

(3) Member State procedures and decisions

As stated before, the competition law procedure for enforcing Article 101 and Article 102 TFEU has been **harmonized** through Directive (EU) 2019/1. In the course of transposing the directive, the Member States amended their procedural rules usually also with effect for their national cartel and abuse prohibitions.

Directive (EU) 2019/1 contains general rules to ensure the compliance of national agencies and courts with fundamental rights, the independence and sufficient resources of national agencies.[43] It defines the investigation powers and decision competences that the agencies must have at the minimum.[44] It also includes detailed provisions regarding the national agencies fining competences and their power to grant leniency.[45] A number of its provisions concern the mutual assistance and cooperation of the Member State agencies with the European Commission and among each other.[46] In that context, the directive is supplemented by (older) guidelines on the **European Competition Network (ECN)**, which foresee, among others, that the European Commission *is particularly well placed* to take on cases if anticompetitive practices "have effects on

---

[41] Article 27(4) Reg. 1/2003.

[42] ECJ, Judgment of 9 December 2020, *Groupe Canal +/Commission* (C-132/19 P) ECLI:EU:C:2020:1007.

[43] Articles 3–5 Directive (EU) 2019/1. These requirements have not been implemented fully in national law so far. In Germany, for example, the FCO is still not completely independent as the Federal Ministry for the Economy may give "general instructions" to it "with regard to the issuance or non-issuance of decisions"; §52 of the Act Against Restraints on Competition.

[44] Articles 6–8 and Articles 10–12 Directive (EU) 2019/1, respectively.

[45] Article 13 ff. and Article 17 ff. Directive (EU) 2019/1, respectively.

[46] Article 24 ff. as well as Article 33 Directive (EU) 2019/1.

competition in more than three Member States".[47] Finally, the directive includes provisions on limitation periods and on matters related to national court proceedings, access to file and the admissibility of evidence.[48]

Despite the partial harmonization through Directive (EU) 2019/1, the **procedural rules** applicable in competition law cases **largely remain in the competence of the Member States**. Even before the directive was passed, the Member States had modeled many of their agencies' powers on the powers of the European Commission. That said, the national rules continue not to be in line completely with EU rules. For example, as noted before, several Member States foresee individual liability, including France, Germany and the Netherlands.[49] **Criminal sanctions** against individuals are available in some Member States as well, such as the Czech Republic, Greece and Romania, and play a major practical role in Ireland. In Austria and Germany, they are only available for bid rigging to the detriment of the state, given the high procedural safeguards in criminal courts and the risk of conflicts with the FCO's leniency program.[50]

Moreover, competition proceedings are regulated in **different codes** based on the legal traditions of the relevant Member States. For example, in Germany, it is necessary to distinguish between administrative (GWB and VwVfG) and administrative offense proceedings (GWB and OWiG). In any event, the German competition regulation is traditionally very agency-centric. This is also evidenced by the fact that Germany still does

---

[47]European Commission, Commission Notice on cooperation within the Network of Competition Authorities, OJ C 101, 27 April 2004, p. 43. On the ECN, see also https://ec.europa.eu/competition-policy/european-competition-network_en.

[48]Article 29 ff. Directive (EU) 2019/1.

[49]See, e.g., §§30, 130 of the German Law on Administrative Offenses (*Ordnungswidrigkeitengesetz — OWiG*).

[50]On the FCO's fining policy as well as the leniency and settlement programs, see FCO, Guidelines for the Setting of Fines in Cartel Administrative Offence Proceedings, Effective: 11 October 2021; Notice No. 14/2021 on General Administrative Principles relating to the Exercise of Discretionary Powers in the Conduct of the Procedure for and Application of the Leniency Regime in accordance with Sections 81h to 81n of the Act against Restraints of Competition (Guidelines on the Leniency Programme) of 23 August 2021; Information Leaflet on the Settlement procedure used by the Bundeskartellamt in fine proceedings, Effective: 1 February 2016; all available at https://www.bundeskartellamt.de/EN/Banoncartels/Further%20documents/Further%20Documents_node.html.

not provide for a market test of commitments imposed at the agency's discretion.

The adherence to the Member States' own traditions, however, also allows for some **flexibility** that clearly benefits competition law enforcement. For example, taking account of the difficulties with interim decisions at EU level, the German legislature recently lowered the intervention standard for interim measures, particularly to strengthen the enforcement in the digital platform economy.[51]

(b) U.S. law

In the U.S., the agencies conduct a preliminary investigation on their own but then take their cases to the courts to obtain a decision that is binding on the parties, at least in case of the U.S. DOJ. This section focuses on the administrative prong of investigation, which takes place outside the courts.[52] In this context, it is necessary to distinguish between the enforcement procedure of the DOJ and the FTC, respectively, and between enforcement at federal and state levels. This book focuses on the federal level and does not go into the details of state enforcement.

(1) DOJ enforcement

The DOJ pursues several objectives when seeking remedies. One is to achieve compensation for the harm the antitrust violation has inflicted on the federal government. Another one is deterrence, which the DOJ can achieve through criminal sanctions and treble damage claims. A third one is the restoration of competition through injunctive relief.[53]

The Sherman Act provides that violations of §1 and §2 are felonies punishable by imprisonment for up to 10 years and/or fines up to USD 1 million for individuals and USD 100 million for corporations, or up to

---

[51]§32a GWB.

[52]See Section III.4 regarding the role of the courts.

[53]See the reasoning of the Court of Appeals in *U.S. v. Microsoft*, 253 F.3d 34 (2001): *The Supreme Court has explained that a remedies decree in an antitrust case must seek to "unfetter a market from anticompetitive conduct", [...], to "terminate the illegal monopoly, deny to the defendant the fruits of its statutory violation, and ensure that there remain no practices likely to result in monopolization in the future".*

twice the gross gain or gross loss.[54] The DOJ may bring criminal or civil actions under the Sherman Act against both the relevant firms and individuals. It may bring civil actions also to recover damages suffered by the U.S. Government. The DOJ may moreover obtain civil injunctions and recover damages suffered by the U.S. Government under the Clayton Act.

Similar to the European Commission, the DOJ operates a leniency program, but differences between the programs exist.[55] In the DOJ leniency program, **only the first** qualifying entity may be granted leniency for a particular antitrust conspiracy, while others may get reductions through plea bargaining. The leniency applicant also has to admit to a criminal violation. A company cannot obtain leniency for a conspiracy under investigation, but it can still receive credit for substantial assistance for that conspiracy by reporting its involvement in a **separate** antitrust conspiracy ("Leniency Plus"). In contrast, if a company pleads guilty to an antitrust offense but **fails to report** an additional antitrust crime which otherwise comes to light, the company not only foregoes the potential credit from the DOJ's Leniency Plus policy, but the DOJ will generally seek a more severe punishment ("Penalty Plus").

(2) FTC enforcement

The FTC has similar powers to the DOJ in relation to civil injunction suits under the Clayton Act. However, the FTC may also conduct its own administrative trial before an Administrative Law Judge (ALJ) under the FTC Act and may issue cease-and-desist order and bring actions for civil penalties. The administrative trial before an ALJ is a peculiarity of the U.S. system.

In any case at hand, after carrying out an initial investigation, the FTC officials may negotiate a settlement. If the parties and FTC officials reach an agreement on the terms, the FTC votes whether it would accept a proposed consent order. Once accepted, the FTC issues the proposed complaints, the proposed consent order, and *analysis of proposed consent order to aid public comments* and invites comments. After the procedure, the proposed consent orders become final.

---

[54] 15 U.S.C. §§1–2, 18 U.S.C. §3571(d).

[55] On the DOJ leniency program, see DOJ, Antitrust Division Leniency Policy and Procedures, included in DOJ Justice Manual, Criminal Antitrust Enforcement, §7–3.300, as of 4 April 2022, and the additional information at https://www.justice.gov/atr/leniency-program.

However, if the FTC and the parties to the proceeding do not reach a settlement, the FTC must decide how to proceed further. It may decide that an administrative investigation is in the public interest.[56] In that case, the FTC may issue an administrative complaint and begin an in-depth examination. As noted above, the U.S. has an adversarial system. This is also true in cases of administrative enforcement before the ALJ, i.e., no agency investigation is conducted autonomously by the parties. Instead, the ALJ acts as an independent decision maker within the FTC.[57] When it has rendered an initial decision, both the FTC staff and the Respondent have the right to appeal that decision to the full Commission. The FTC may also instruct the ALJ to re-examine the case. In case there is neither appeal nor re-examination, the ALJ's initial decision becomes final and the FTC issues a cease-and-desist order. Only the Respondent may lodge a further appeal with any circuit court.[58] The ALJ may adopt cease-and-desist orders for termination and affirmative action. If the FTC seeks to obtain restitution or disgorgement, note that it may do so only (!) after having conducted an ALJ proceeding.[59] A violation of the FTC's order is punishable by a civil penalty.

Outside ALJ proceedings, the FTC, like the DOJ, enforces the rules in its competence area directly in court. Different from the DOJ, however, the FTC is responsible not only for competition but also for consumer and privacy protection. The FTC also publishes statistics on its competition enforcement practices, which include information on non-cartel cases.[60]

(3) The relationship of DOJ/FTC to other enforcers

In some instances, the DOJ or the FTC conducts investigations in matters where also other regulators are competent, or where the State Attorneys General may initiate proceedings under state antitrust rules.

---

[56] See §5(b) of the FTC Act (15 U.S.C. §45(b)).

[57] On the ALJ, see https://www.ftc.gov/about-ftc/bureaus-offices/office-administrative-law-judges. On the ALJ, see https://www.ftc.gov/about-ftc/bureaus-offices/office-administrative-law-judges.

[58] See Ohlhausen, Administrative litigation at the FTC: Effective tool for developing the law or rubber stamp? *Journal of Competition Law & Economics* 12 (4), 623, 635 (2016).

[59] *AMG Capital Management LLC .v. FTC*, 593 U.S. ___ (2021), S.Ct. No. 19–508. Argued 13 January 2021 — Decided 22 April 2021.

[60] See https://www.ftc.gov/competition-enforcement-database.

In matters of relevance for several public regulators, the DOJ/FTC typically charges themselves with the task of identifying the key issues at the interface of antitrust and regulation. They may comment in regulatory proceedings or even file an *amicus curiae* brief in court if this is in the public interest.[61] In the relationship to the states, it does not matter that, e.g., a cartel has a local nature. The DOJ also prosecutes local cartels if they may affect interstate commerce. In these instances, the State Attorneys General may bring cases in parallel but typically focus on securing monetary redress.[62]

(c) Japanese law

The JFTC can issue cease-and-desist orders for all kinds of violations under AMA Articles 7 (unreasonable restraint of trade and private monopolization), 8-2 (trade association's anticompetitive activities), 17-2 (merger transactions violating AMA) and 20 (unfair trade practice). Such orders are meant to stop activities contrary to the AMA and to ensure that such activities have been terminated. Although the JFTC has broad discretion in setting out a series of measures that the offender must take, it is inevitably limited to the extent necessary to stop violations or ensure their termination. Conventionally, the JFTC orders the offender to stop, or confirm that it has stopped, particular actions, inform its trading partners of the violation, and report the JFTC about the implementation. On the other hand, it does not order violators to set prices at a certain level or to pay damages to the aggrieved parties.

For serious offenses, the JFTC orders the violator to pay an administrative fine, called a surcharge (*kachokin*), under AMA Articles 7-2 (unreasonable restraint of trade that affects price or output), 7-9 (private monopolization that affects price or output), 8-3 (trade association activity resulting in substantial restriction of competition and affecting price or output), 20-2 (repeated concerted refusal to deal), 20-3 (repeated unjust discriminatory pricing), 20-4 (repeated unjust low price), 20-5 (repeated resale price maintenance) and 20-6 (continuous abuse of dominant

---

[61] Amicus curiae: interested party from outside proceedings (≠ intervenor).
[62] Baer, Public and private antitrust enforcement in the United States, 11 February 2014, https://www.justice.gov/atr/file/517756/download.

position). The money goes to the national treasury. The JFTC is obliged to issue a payment order when it issues cease-and-desist orders. The level of fine differs depending on the type of offense. Cartelists are ordered to pay 10% of their turnover and are also eligible for the limited leniency system, which offers full immunity to the first successful applicant and reduction of fines to subsequent applicants. It is worth noting that both criminal and administrative fines may be imposed on the enterprise that engages in a cartel. When the AMA was enacted in 1947, only criminal fines existed. Having realized such a sanctioning system, which was inevitably reliant on a rigid criminal prosecution procedure, the administrative fine was first introduced in 1977 in relation to certain types of unreasonable restraint of trade, expanded to cover private monopolization controlling practices in 2005, and again to cover private monopolization exclusionary practices as well as certain types of unfair trade practices in 2009.

The JFTC can also file a criminal accusation with the public prosecution office in case of unreasonable restraint of trade, private monopolization and trade associations' activities leading to substantial restriction of competition (AMA Article 74(1)). Along with the JFTC's cease-and-desist orders and private parties' actions for damages, a criminal sanctioning system has been always present since the enactment of the AMA in 1947. In practice, the JFTC files accusations in case of serious hard-core cartels and bid rigging.[63] Both individuals and corporations may be sanctioned criminally. In case of the former, up to 5 years imprisonment (possible to be suspended) and JPY 5 million (about EUR 35 thousand) criminal fine may be imposed, while the corporation can be charged up to JPY 500 million (about EUR 3.5 million) criminal fines (AMA Articles 89 and 95). A company may pay both an administrative fine and a criminal fine: in such case, the amount of the administrative fine is reduced by half.

The public prosecutor cannot bring the criminal case without the JFTC accusation (AMA Article 96), implying criminal penalties may be imposed only when the JFTC files an accusation. On the other hand, once the JFTC files accusations, the public prosecutor usually prosecutes; otherwise, the public prosecutor general must report inaction with reasons to the Prime Minister (AMA Article 74(3)).

---

[63] To encourage leniency application, the JFTC does not file an accusation in relation to the first leniency applicant.

In the past, the JFTC's order could be re-examined at the JFTC hearing procedure. In this procedure, the designated officer of the JFTC brought charges against the defendants in a quasi-judicial adversarial system. After the hearing, the JFTC examiner officer and the JFTC, who acted independently from the designated officer, issued a hearing decision. The Tokyo High Court had an exclusive jurisdiction over the JFTC hearing decision and, like in the U.S., the Tokyo High Court examined the case under the substantial evidence rule. The JFTC hearing system was abolished in 2013 and now appeal against the JFTC's order is made to the Tokyo District Court and then to the Tokyo High Court.

The JFTC has great discretion as to whether it commences and carries on an investigation. When the JFTC suspects an infringement but fails to substantiate it, the JFTC issues a warning or alert. Furthermore, it is not rare that the JFTC closes the case having accepted the measures voluntarily taken by defendants. In 2018, the commitment procedure was implemented under AMA Articles 48-2–48-9 and the JFTC began using it in exclusionary and abuse cases.

(d) **Comparison**

The three enforcement systems covered in this book vary considerably at the level of agency proceedings. Although the **EU** is composed of jurisdictions with heterogeneous administrative traditions, the system at EU level is clearly an inquisitorial system where the European Commission has on the one hand strong investigation and decision competences, which it may exercise at its discretion. These competences, on the other hand, come along with important duties to ensure fair proceedings and to respect the rights of the private parties to the proceedings (rights to be heard, professional secrecy). The same is generally true in the Member States. In practice, the competences and duties of the agencies can give rise to conflicts.

In contrast, the **U.S. antitrust enforcement system** is mainly adversarial. As a general matter, the agencies are supposed to develop a case that is tried in court, if necessary. Even where they may try a case internally, as the FTC in ALJ proceedings, the authority has to present a case to an impartial decision maker. For this reason, agencies may act more aggressively, whereas the balancing and duties are left to the courts.

The **Japanese** system combines features of both. While originally, the JFTC design strictly followed the model of the FTC, the original examination system (i.e., an equivalent of the ALJ) was abolished in 2013. Following this change, JFTC decisions are subject to immediate appeal to the Tokyo District Court. Note, however, that the JFTC handles most of its cases outside bid-rigging and other hardcore cartels informally, i.e., without a formal administrative decision.

3. The role of the courts in public enforcement

(a) EU law

In the EU, the courts are competent to hear **appeals** against the administrative decisions of the European Commission. The same holds for the courts in the Member States, with the exception of those Member States where agencies are not empowered to adopt decisions themselves but instead have to apply for a court order (e.g., Austria).

The decisions adopted by the European Commission can be appealed in questions of law and on the facts to the **General Court (GC)**. In questions of law, an additional appeal is available to the **European Court of Justice (ECJ)**.[64] The GC applies a **"manifest error" standard** for *complex economic appraisals* by the European Commission, i.e., the protection of the undertakings concerned is limited with respect to the substantive assessment of competition law infringements.[65]

The European courts recognize the need to protect the **rights of defense** of the parties to the proceeding. However, in questions relating to the substance of the law, the "principle of personal responsibility" applies for the whole undertaking concerned, which bars rights-related claims by legal entities forming part of the same undertaking.[66] It is only in procedural matters that legal persons belonging to an undertaking can assert

---

[64] Article 263 TFEU.

[65] See GC, Judgment of 21 April 2005, *Holcim (Deutschland)/Commission* (T-28/03, ECR 2005 p. II-1357) ECLI:EU:T:2005:139, §95.

[66] See ECJ, Judgment of 10 April 2014, *Commission/Siemens Österreich and others* and *Siemens Transmission & Distribution and others/Commission* (C-231/11 P, C-232/11 P and C-233/11 P) ECLI:EU:C:2014:256, §§44–47.

rights of defense of their own.[67] Moreover, EU law offers only limited protection against self-incrimination.[68]

The **national agency decisions** can be appealed under the national rules. In questions of substance, the national courts have to respect the principles of EU law and the decisions of the EU courts and the European Commission in the same cases.[69] The ECJ's holdings on questions of EU law are binding on Member State courts as well. Questions relating to the **interpretation of EU law** can be brought before the ECJ via a Member State's court request for a preliminary ruling.[70] In procedural matters, the national courts may apply national law, which may offer a farther-reaching protection to the legal addressees of an investigation.

The protection against **double jeopardy** ("*ne bis in idem*") is limited in the EU because, for the principle to apply, the facts of the two cases must be the same, the offender the same and the legal interest protected the same.[71] However, EU law pursues objectives different from national law, meaning that competition law sanctions do not violate the principle if one is imposed for failure to comply with Article 101 or Article 102 TFEU and the other one for failure to comply with national law.[72] Moreover, the principle does not preclude a second sanction for violation of EU competition law in another Member State, provided that the latter decision is not based on a finding of an anticompetitive object or effect in the territory of the first Member State.[73] It does not preclude such a sanction either if the second sanction is imposed after a final decision against the company in respect of the same facts for failure to comply with a

---

[67] See, e.g., ECJ Judgment of 18 October 1989, *Orkem/Commission* (374/87, ECR 1989 p. 3283) ECLI:EU:C:1989:387.

[68] ECJ Judgment of 12 January 2017, *Timab Industries and CFPR/Commission* (C-411/15 P, Publié au Recueil numérique) ECLI:EU:C:2017:11, §86.

[69] Articles 264, 280 TFEU, Article 16 Reg. 1/2003.

[70] Article 267 TFEU; Recommendations to national courts and tribunals in relation to the initiation of preliminary ruling proceedings, OJ C 380, 8 November 2019, p. 1.

[71] See previously ECJ, Judgment of 14 February 2012, *Toshiba Corporation e.a.* (C-17/10) ECLI:EU:C:2012:72, §97.

[72] ECJ, Judgment of 13 February 1969, *Walt Wilhelm and others / Bundeskartellamt* (14/68, ECR 1969 p. 1) ECLI:EU:C:1969:4, §§9, 11.

[73] ECJ, Judgment of 22 March 2022, *Nordzucker and others* (C-151/20) ECLI:EU:C:2022: 203, §§26 ff.

sector-specific regulation.[74] The imposition of sanctions under national law may be subject to a stricter standard under the national double jeopardy rules!

(b) U.S. law

In the U.S., the courts hear civil and criminal actions brought by the agencies for enforcement purposes. Thus, unlike in the EU, the U.S. courts are not limited to hearing cases only after an agency decision on appeal. At **federal level**, where the DOJ or the FTC is seeking a judgment or order in court, the case is first tried before the D.C. District Court (judging the facts and the law) and can then be appealed (in law) to the D.C. Court of Appeals as well as the U.S. Supreme Court. The Supreme Court, however, reviews cases only on a discretionary basis. Thus, not every antitrust case is reviewed by the Supreme Court upon appeal. The FTC's Commission decisions in ALJ proceedings may be appealed in state circuit courts.

Where cases are settled, no appeal takes place. This entails a risk that the settlement power is being abused. Therefore, when the DOJ seeks a consent decree in civil antitrust cases, federal courts have to review the proposed decree under the Antitrust Procedures and Penalties Act (Tunney Act) before adopting it to ensure that the remedy proposed in the consent is in the public interest.[75] The FTC is empowered to issue consent orders on its own. Instead of a court review in the public interest, the FTC publishes its proposed consent orders for public comments.[76]

At **state level**, the state courts are competent to hear the cases brought under the state antitrust law by the State Attorneys General. Their decisions can be appealed to the state courts of appeal and the state supreme courts.

Since the U.S. is a common law system, **final court decisions set precedents** that are binding not only on the parties to the relevant proceeding but also on the same court and on lower courts deciding on the same questions in later cases (principle of *stare decisis*). They may only

---

[74]ECJ, Judgment of 22 March 2022, *bpost* (C-117/20) ECLI:EU:C:2022:202, §§47, 50, 58.
[75]Pub.L. 93–528, 88 Stat. 1708, enacted 21 December 1974, encoded in: 15 U.S.C. §16. See, e.g., OECD, Commitment Decisions in Antitrust Cases, Note by the United States, 15–17 June 2016, §§6–12 with further details.
[76]OECD, Commitment Decisions in Antitrust Cases, Note by the United States, 15–17 June 2016, §§13–14.

be overruled by higher courts or the same court if it is found that the principles underpinning the previous decision were erroneous in law or have been overtaken by new legislation or developments.[77] Decisions from courts of equivalent authority in the legal system or courts of other circuits may be persuasive authority but not binding precedent.

The **"double jeopardy" clause** (5th amendment) of the U.S. Constitution is applicable in antitrust proceedings. The double jeopardy clause "protects against three distinct abuses: a second prosecution for the same offense after acquittal; a second prosecution for the same offense after conviction; and multiple punishments for the same offense".[78] However, the clause is interpreted narrowly nowadays. It protects only against the imposition of multiple punishments for the same offense which the legislature intended to be criminal (i.e., not civil law fines).[79] Nevertheless, the clause underlines the proposition that levying multiple fines for the same conduct is a harm that other constitutional protections may address (e.g., the "excessive fines" or the "due process" clause in the 8th and 5th amendments, respectively). Moreover, double jeopardy can still play a role with respect to the imposition of multiple government fines if the fines in their entirety amount to a criminal penalty.

(c) Japanese law

When the JFTC examination system existed, a special appeal was available under the AMA. The Tokyo High Court had exclusive jurisdiction to hear this appeal at first instance, and the substantial evidence rule was applied (see Section III.2.c). Since the abolishment of such procedure, the decision of the JFTC is examined in accordance with the general rules provided in the **Administrative Case Litigation Act** unless the AMA includes special provisions. The JFTC's decision is first examined by the Tokyo District Court, then by the Tokyo High Court and lastly by the Supreme Court.

Double jeopardy does not apply if administrative fines are followed by civil or criminal sanctions. The reason is that the subsequent sanctions are imposed in a different procedure and pursue different objectives.

---

[77] A higher court may also order a lower court to modify its judgment on remand.

[78] *United States v. Halper*, 490 U.S. 435, 440 (1989).

[79] *United States v. Hudson*, 522 U.S. 93, 99 (1997).

However, sanctions must be proportionate in total, which may prevent excessive sanctions.

4. The political debate concerning the effectiveness of remedies and sanctions

The effectiveness of remedies and sanctions in competition and antitrust cases is an issue of **ongoing debate**. This is because egregious violations continue to occur. However, the effect on competition is frequently difficult to ascertain as other factors may produce overlapping effects on the markets.

As regards **cartels**, especially the **EU system** with company fines has been criticized repeatedly as being unsuitable to prevent violations. This was because company management may benefit personally from cartel violations, whereas the fines are paid by the company (and, hence, its shareholders). The responsibility of individuals is not taken into account at all at EU level and at national level only to a limited extent, while the protection of individuals in proceedings allowing for individual sanctions at national level tends to be high. However, the effectiveness of the cartel sanctions systems cannot be verified easily.[80] That said, other characteristics of the enforcement systems (especially the possibility of immunity applications, risk of private damage claims, potentially also accountability and transparency obligations under corporate law) certainly have produced some effects. This indicates that the systems are indeed apt to improve both management compliance and the competitive situation.[81] The question then narrows down to whether cartel remedies and sanctions make a significant contribution to the development.

Regarding **non-cartel** horizontal or vertical **collaboration** violating the competition rules, the effect of remedies and sanctions is even more unclear. However, some market developments indicate that agency interference may produce both beneficial and harmful effects in the market or at least not the desired effects. For example, the agency-administered

---

[80] See OECD, Fighting Hard Core Cartels: Harm, Effective Sanctions and Leniency Programmes, 2002, p. 3, noting *that sanctions currently imposed are often too light when set against the gains to the cartel.*

[81] An indication of that kind is most notably that there has been a drop in both immunity applications and cartel investigations in recent years.

allocation of broadcasting rights for football games has proved largely ineffective in protecting consumer interests.[82]

In cases of **unilateral behavior**, as noted, market participants complain that the imposed remedies are ineffective particularly when it comes to violations in the platform industry in the EU. In the U.S., there has been very limited enforcement of the anti-monopolization rules for a long time, so remedies are rarely imposed as well.

IV. Private enforcement

As a matter of principle, private parties can use most civil law instruments to assert their rights *vis-à-vis* other market participants that violate the competition rules. Although private parties can notably bring injunctive suits in all jurisdictions covered in this book, we focus on private damage suits.

1. EU law

The Treaty on the Functioning of the European Union includes limited provisions on the legal effects of violations for civil enforcement purposes. Most importantly, Article 101(2) TFEU provides that agreements restricting competition without justification are **void automatically**. Article 102 TFEU does not include any such express provision. However, the legislatures of the EU Member States have to ensure the **effective and non-discriminatory enforcement** of the provision and consequently provide that abusive unilateral actions do not have legal effects under national law.

In spite of the limited provisions at the level of EU Treaties, the general rule is that **private enforcement is meant to complement public enforcement**.[83] The European Commission supports this idea by stressing expressly in its cartel and abuse press releases that it is possible to claim damages for established infringements before national courts.[84] The ECJ has bolstered the role of private enforcement in a number of important

---

[82] Monopolies Commission, Biennial Report XXIII, 2020, §§471 ff.

[83] ECJ, Judgment of 20 September 2001, *Courage and Crehan* (C-453/99, ECR 2001 p. I-6297) ECLI:EU:C:2001:465, §§26–27.

[84] In this context, see also European Commission, Commission Notice on the co-operation between the Commission and the courts of the EU Member States in the application of Articles 81 and 82 EC, OJ C 101, 27 April 2004, p. 54.

judgments. For example, it has confirmed that national courts may not deviate from the European Commission's findings in private damage actions.[85] Moreover, it has held that it is necessary to balance the effectiveness of agency proceedings and right to damages in the light of the individual circumstances where a claimant requests access to leniency documents.[86]

The ECJ has also derived important elements of a cartel damage claim directly from Article **101 TFEU**. Thus, it has held that private damages may be claimed from the "undertaking" in terms of EU competition law.[87] Moreover, it has held that the claim may be brought against a subsidiary of the fined entity, which is not referred to in the relevant decision, where those entities *together constitute a single economic unit.*[88] This is not hindered by a statement in a recital of the EU Directive on damage actions, which provides that national rules on *imputability, adequacy or culpability* continue to apply alongside the directive.[89]

Furthermore, based on Article 101 TFEU, the ECJ has required national courts to find a causal connection between the relevant conduct and harm to the claimant.[90] It has also ruled on the recoverable damages, which must include the actual loss, losses of profit and interest to ensure the effectiveness of Article 101 TFEU in civil actions.[91] Moreover, damages may also consist of indirect effects, such as an increased need for subsidies.[92] Finally, they may also arise for claimants that did not buy

[85]ECJ, Judgment of 6 November 2012, *Otis and others* (C-199/11) ECLI:EU:C:2012:684, §§50–51 referring to Article 16 Reg. 1/2003.
[86]ECJ, Judgment of 14 June 2011, *Pfleiderer* (C-360/09, ECR 2011 p. I-5161) ECLI:EU:C:2011:389, §§30–32.
[87]ECJ, Judgment of 14 March 2019, *Skanska Industrial Solutions and others* (C-724/17) ECLI:EU:C:2019:204, §47.
[88]ECJ, Judgment of 6 October 2021, *Sumal* (C-882/19) ECLI:EU:C:2021:800.
[89]Recital 11 of Dir. 2014/104/EU.
[90]ECJ, Judgment of 13 July 2006, *Manfredi* (C-295/04 to C-298/04, ECR 2006 p. I-6619) ECLI:EU:C:2006:461, §61.
[91]ECJ, Judgment of 6 June 2013, *Donau Chemie and others* (C-536/11) ECLI:EU:C:2013:366, §24.
[92]ECJ, Judgment of 12 December 2019, *Otis and others* (C-435/18) ECLI:EU:C:2019:1069, §§31–32.

from a cartel member but from a third party that had adapted its prices to an elevated cartel price level (so-called umbrella price effect).[93]

Directive 2014/104/EU on actions for damages for EU competition law infringements, which is mentioned above,[94] combines aspects of substantive law (regarding a claimant's entitlement to damages) and procedural aspects. It provides for a right to full compensation that respects the EU principles of effectiveness and equivalence.[95] It also includes detailed provisions on the disclosure of evidence.[96] It is unclear whether the broad exclusion of access to **leniency**/settlement materials in this context is in line with the ECJ's jurisprudence cited above.[97] Other provisions regulate that national agency decisions have a binding effect in other Member States and deal with limitation periods.[98] An important aspect regulated in the directive is the scope and allocation of liability, i.e., the issues of joint and several liabilities of cartel members, the avoidance of overcompensation and the availability of a passing-on defense, and the rights of indirect purchasers.[99] Importantly, one provision in this context establishes a presumption of damages (but not the amount).[100] The final provisions of the directive deal with consensual dispute resolution.[101]

---

[93] ECJ, Judgment of 5 June 2014, *Kone and others* (C-557/12) ECLI:EU:C:2014:1317, §§30–34.

[94] Directive 2014/104/EU on certain rules governing actions for damages under national law for infringements of the competition law provisions of the Member States and of the European Union, OJ L 349 of 5 December 2014, p. 1.

[95] Articles 3–4 Dir. 2014/104/EU.

[96] Articles 5–8 Dir. 2014/104/EU. See also European Commission, Communication on the protection of confidential information by national courts in proceedings for the private enforcement of EU competition law, OJ C 242, 22 July 2020, p. 1.

[97] See fn. 86.

[98] Articles 9 and 10 Dir. 2014/104/EU.

[99] Article 11 ff. Dir. 2014/104/EU. See also European Commission, Communication from the Commission — Guidelines for national courts on how to estimate the share of overcharge which was passed on to the indirect purchaser, OJ C 267, 9 August 2019, p. 4.

[100] Article 17 Dir. 2014/104/EU. See also European Commission, Communication from the Commission on quantifying harm in actions for damages based on breaches of Article 101 or 102 of the Treaty on the Functioning of the European Union, OJ C 167, 13 June 2013, p. 19; Commission Staff Working Document, Practical Guide quantifying harm in actions for damages based on breaches of Article 101 or 102 of the Treaty on the Functioning of the European Union, SWD(2013) 205, 11 June 2013.

[101] Articles 18–19 Dir. 2014/104/EU.

A problem arising in the context of private damage claims is that **damages** for competition law infringements are **frequently dispersed** among many market participants. This is the case in particular where resellers pass on their damages to the consumers (e.g., through elevated prices). **Representative actions** or mechanisms for **collective redress** are alternative solutions to this problem. In that regard, the landscape in Europe has remained fairly heterogeneous. Directive 2020/1828 introduced representative actions for consumers but not for cartel damages.[102] There is only a European Commission Recommendation for introducing collective redress mechanisms in national laws.[103] In Member States such as Germany, the rules on representative actions have proved to be mostly ineffective.[104] One reason is that qualified associations (i.e., consumer associations) miss relevant information. Moreover, they have limited incentives to bring actions because they are not allowed to retain any portion of the damages for themselves. Model declaratory actions were introduced in the context of the German diesel scandal — the effect remains to be seen.[105] Other European countries, notably the UK, have introduced collective redress mechanisms.[106] In relation to collective redress, a policy choice has to be made between an opt-in or opt-out system (depending on whether the members of any class of claimants are automatically covered by a court holding or not).

2. U.S. law

The U.S. federal litigation system is attractive for damage actions given the possibility of **treble damages and class actions**. The class-action system is established and operates as an opt-out system. According to the

---

[102] Directive (EU) 2020/1828 of the European Parliament and of the Council of 25 November 2020 on representative actions for the protection of the collective interests of consumers and repealing Directive 2009/22/European Commission, OJ L 409, 4 December 2020, p. 1.

[103] European Commission, Commission Recommendation of 11 June 2013 on common principles for injunctive and compensatory collective redress mechanisms in the Member States concerning violations of rights granted under Union Law, OJ L 201, 26 July 2013, pp. 60–65.

[104] §34a GWB.

[105] §§606 ff. of the Civil Proced. Code.

[106] §47B of Competition Act 1998.

American Antitrust Institute, the **cumulative total recovered** for victims in antitrust class actions was more than USD 19 billion in the period 2013–2018.[107]

In the following, we provide an overview of some key aspects regarding the procedure **(Subsection a)** and the condition under which plaintiffs may be entitled to damages **(Subsection b)**. We also set out some key aspects of the relationship between U.S. private actions and public enforcement by the FTC and the DOJ **(Subsection c)**.

(a) Procedure

Plaintiffs have to decide whether they want to file their action in a federal court or in a state court. For a class action to be allowed in a **federal court**, plaintiffs need to show (i) numerosity, (ii) commonality of a question of law or of fact, (iii) typicality of the claims and defenses available to all class members, and (iv) adequacy of the representative parties.[108] In federal courts, §4 of the Clayton Act allows injured persons to sue and collect treble damages and costs. Moreover, §16 of the Clayton Act provides for injunctive relief. **State antitrust** laws can only be enforced in state courts.

Defendants have to pay close attention particularly to the question of whether the action establishes a **sufficient nexus** between the defendant and the forum. In actions brought under federal law, the defendant must regularly be an inhabitant or transacting business in the district in order for there to be sufficient "minimum contacts" to the forum.[109] In cases involving foreign conduct, the Foreign Trade Antitrust Improvements Act (FTAIA) specifically requires a "direct, substantial and reasonably foreseeable" effect on U.S. domestic or import commerce in order for a federal court to have jurisdiction.[110]

To handle private antitrust actions efficiently, courts may **consolidate** several cases dealing with parallel issues. Thus, parallel federal actions against common defendants may be consolidated in one court for reasons

---

[107] The American Antitrust Institute, The State of Antitrust Enforcement and Competition Policy in the U.S., 14 April 2020; available at https://www.antitrustinstitute.org/wp-content/uploads/2020/04/AAI_StateofAntitrust2019_FINAL3.pdf.

[108] Federal Rule of Civil Procedure 23(a).

[109] §12 of the Clayton Act.

[110] 15 U.S.C. §6a.

of judicial economy. Indirect purchaser actions brought in a state court can moreover be consolidated with federal direct purchaser actions.

(b) Substance (i.e., entitlement to damages)

Under §4 of the Clayton Act, the plaintiff must show, by preponderance of the evidence, that a **causal connection** exists between the violation and that plaintiff's injury (similar to EU law). Where injury has been proved to a reasonable degree of certainty, a jury may make a just and **reasonable estimate** of the damage (similar to the power of courts in EU national law, e.g., German law).[111]

    U.S. federal law does not allow for a passing-on defense, which is a consequence of the deterrent nature of antitrust damages (different from EU law).[112] Moreover, **indirect claims are generally barred** by federal antitrust laws (different from EU law).[113] Some 20–30 U.S. states have enacted "*Illinois Brick* repealer" statutes to allow indirect claims.[114] This became controversial under the Trump administration. However, under the Biden administration, a bill introduced in the U.S. Senate has proposed to overturn the Supreme Court jurisprudence establishing the aforementioned rules altogether.[115]

    Finally, a plaintiff has a **duty to mitigate damages** under U.S. law (similar to EU national law, e.g., German law).[116]

(c) Relationship to DOJ/FTC enforcement

Under §5(a) Clayton Act, **collateral estoppel** continues to apply to judgments from prior DOJ actions but not prior FTC actions under

---

[111] §§286, 287 of the German Civil Proc. Code.

[112] *Hanover Shoe, Inc. v. United Shoe Machinery Corp.*, 392 U.S. 481 (1968).

[113] See *Illinois Brick Co. v. Illinois*, 431 U.S. 720 (1977).

[114] On Illinois Brick repealers, see https://www.faegredrinker.com/en/insights/publications/2018/1/bringing-back-indirect-purchasers-doj-considers-seeking-reversal-of-illinois-brick#:~:text=Almost%2030%20states%E2%80%94familiarly%20known%20as%20%E2%80%9C%20Illinois%20Brick,purchasers%20to%20recover%20antitrust%20damages%20alongside%20direct%20purchasers.

[115] S.2039 — Tougher Enforcement Against Monopolists (TEAM) Act.

[116] §254 of the German Civil Code.

§5 FTC Act.[117] Nevertheless, courts may admit evidence from previous DOJ civil or criminal proceedings and rely on previous judgments.[118] Apart from that, the DOJ and the FTC may not only act themselves as plaintiffs in federal court, but they may also file *amicus curiae* briefs in state court proceedings.[119]

An issue of significant practical relevance arises if a **leniency applicant** is **subject to private damage claims**. Exposure to such claims might deter cartel members from making leniency applications and, thus, defeat the purpose of the leniency system. Therefore, in the EU, evidence provided by leniency applicants in agency proceedings under Article 101 TFEU is generally inadmissible in civil court pursuant to the EU Damage Claims Directive.[120] Under the Antitrust Criminal Penalty Enhancement and Reform Act (**ACPERA**), a company accepted into the DOJ leniency program may limit its exposure in civil damages litigation to its *pro rata* share of the total damages before trebling, provided that the company cooperates with the plaintiffs in the damages action.

3. Japanese law

Private parties may initiate **suits for damages** (both as follow-on under AMA Articles 25 and 26 or on a standalone basis under Article 709 of the Civil Code (tort)), request **injunctive orders** (AMA Article 24), as well as bring actions to **nullify contractual terms** (Article 90, Civil Code).

AMA Article 25 explicitly allows private parties to sue an **offender** for damages. The offender is made liable even if he/she did not act negligently (AMA Article 26). An AMA Article 25 damage suit, however, is only possible after the JFTC's order against the offender becomes final

---

[117] §5(a) Clayton Act (15 U.S.C. §16(a)). In common law, collateral estoppel prevents a person from litigating the same issue a second time.

[118] Cf. Article 16 Reg. 1/2003, Article 9 Dir. 2014/104/EU on the binding effect of EU agency decisions.

[119] According to the American Antitrust Institute, FTC filings fell off during the Trump administration. DOJ filings increased but often with positions detrimental to consumers; see the document referenced in fn. 107.

[120] See Section IV.1, with reference to ECJ case law with which the directive may not be in line completely.

(AMA Article 26), meaning that this is possible only **as a follow-on suit**. Different from the situation in the EU, JFTC orders are not binding for the courts. But rarely will the courts disregard a prior infringement finding by the JFTC. The scope of the finding may be limited, though, because the JFTC commonly refers to only a few aggrieved parties on a unanimous basis in its decisions expressly but not necessarily all parties affected by unlawful actions.

Separately, private parties can bring the damage claim under Article 709 of the Civil Code as **torts**. A preceding JFTC action is not necessary for this. The plaintiff must establish that the defendant's conduct was willful or at least negligent.

In both AMA Article 25 and tort cases, the plaintiff must establish the fact that the defendant **caused the damage to the plaintiff, causation between the defendant's violation and damage**, as well as the **amount of damage**, which is not an easy task. In relation to the amount of damage, however, Article 248 of the Code of Civil Procedure empowers judges to determine the amount of damages when proving that amount is exceedingly difficult. This rule often applies in the AMA cases to ease the plaintiff's burden.

Private lawsuits have never been used vigorously in competition cases in Japan. Neither double nor treble damages are available in Japan. There is no class action system either. Japanese civil procedure rule generally does not have a U.S.-style extensive discovery system and, thus, it is very difficult for plaintiffs to collect relevant evidence to prove that the defendant committed the AMA violation to begin with. These inhibit aggrieved parties to bring the AMA case to the court.

4. Comparison

While all three covered jurisdictions consider private actions to play a role for competition protection, they do so to a **varying degree**. In the **U.S.**, the private damages regime features major differences to the systems in continental Europe, which make bringing damage actions more **attractive** there. Most importantly, the U.S. system allows for class actions, i.e., it is an opt-out system. This increases the likelihood that plaintiffs represent a sufficient share of the market such that lodging the action makes economic sense and to overcome causation issues. Further, the law allows for contingency fees, meaning that bringing an action is also attractive for the plaintiff's lawyers. Next, the parties may ask for a jury trial and for pre-trial discovery. Plaintiffs can obtain treble damages as a policy means to deter wrongful conduct.[121]

The private damage regimes in the **EU** are only **partially harmonized** and continue to be governed by the law of the Member States. This makes it difficult to make general statements. It is certainly true that ECJ case law and the Damage Claims Directive have facilitated private actions by bolstering the rights of both direct and indirect claimants to full compensation (which is available to indirect claimants in the U.S. only to a limited extent). Just like in the U.S., a number of auxiliary means (presumptions and fair estimate) are available for plaintiffs where calculating damages is difficult. However, the rules on disclosure of evidence, and notably the strict limitations for the disclosure of leniency or settlement materials, put up obstacles that do not exist in U.S. courts, where unlimited discovery is available. Although indications exist that private damage actions and the threat of such actions have had a substantial impact on competition enforcement in general in recent years (e.g., the number of immunity/leniency applications has dropped substantially), they probably remain less relevant than in the U.S.

In **Japan**, private damages have played only a **minor role** so far. Different from the EU, plaintiffs in follow-on actions cannot rely on the binding effect of an infringement finding in agency decisions. Different from the U.S., no punitive damages or class actions are available. However, no legislative plans exist to ease the positions of plaintiffs further at this stage.

Good to know: What are the options for firms harmed by an international cartel?

When a company becomes aware (e.g., through an enforcement agency's press release) that it has been harmed by a cartel, it can contact cartel members to reach a private settlement, it can enter into civil arbitration (if its contracts with cartel members contain an arbitration clause), it can file a civil court action, or it can assign or cede its claims to a third party,

---

[121] §4 Clayton Act allows injured persons to sue and collect treble damages and costs in federal courts.

(Continued)

e.g., a firm specialized in pursuing antitrust damage claims (representative action).

In its decision on which route to pursue, the company will regularly weigh up the expected outcome (i.e., its chances of success), the time and cost associated with each route, its negotiation power and the risk of disrupting future business relations, and the statute of limitations (given that cartels are usually secret and investigations are long, which means that the statute of limitations frequently lapses before a claim is made).[122]

The time and cost are particularly relevant factors. For example, considering the situation in Europe, for a settlement out of court, it makes sense to calculate 1–2 months of preparation; 4–5 months to conduct settlement discussions, conclude a confidentiality agreement, and obtain economic opinions; 1–2 months to hand over the economic opinion to the opponent; and 4–5 months for the second round of settlement discussions. Court litigation may make sense particularly if the action can be based on an agency decision ("follow-on action"). That does not mean, however, that litigation is likely to be swift and easy for the plaintiff company: It is not only necessary to calculate again 1–2 months of preparation and potentially 4–5 months to conduct settlement discussions, but then also at least 2–3 years litigation (1st instance), one or several months as an appeals period, at least 1 year for an appeal in law and facts or just in law, and potentially another appeals period and another year for the second appeal itself.

If the company decides to go to court, it will have to choose the right forum. This decision depends not only on the legal rules on jurisdiction (especially the rules on necessary nexus)[123] but also on potential advantages/disadvantages of individual jurisdictions, the familiarity of the client

(Continued)

---

[122]However, negotiations may suspend the run of the statute of limitations temporarily; see, e.g., §203 of the German Civil Code.

[123]In EU law, check venue of company seat (Article 4(1) Reg. 1215/2012); contractually agreed venue (Article 7(1) Reg. 1215/2012); venue of tortious conduct/effect (Article 7(2) Reg. 1215/2012); venue of "close connection" (Article 8 Reg. 1215/2012). In U.S. law, it is necessary to establish personal jurisdiction (general/specific), subject-matter jurisdiction (limited under FTAIA for foreign claims: "direct, substantial, and foreseeable effect") and

---

(Continued)

(or its counsel) with the jurisdiction and the expertise of courts; the available evidence and possibilities to obtain evidence[124]; the expected duration and costs of court proceedings[125]; and the amount of damages that may be obtained in that forum (e.g., compensatory or punitive damages).

---

venue (less of an issue). Restrictions apply on class actions: *Direct v. Imburgia*, 136 S. Ct. 463; *Spokeo v. Robins*, 136 S. Ct. 1540.

[124] In the EU, consider access to agency file + binding effect of agency decisions; in the U.S., consider the availability of discovery.

[125] Advantageous in Germany, the Netherlands and several other EU civil law jurisdictions, whereas the duration in Italy is long. However, the long existing risk of an abuse of slow proceedings ("Italian torpedo") was mitigated because the law now foresees the primary competence of courts designated by agreement; see Article 31(2)–(3) and Recital 22 of Reg. 1215/2012. In comparison with civil law jurisdictions, a longer duration is generally to be expected in common law jurisdictions.

Chapter 7

Mergers

I. The law

1. EU law

In EU law, merger control is governed by Regulation 139/2004 — the EU Merger Control Regulation, in particular the following provisions:

Article 1. Scope

1. *Without prejudice to Article 4(5) and Article 22, this Regulation shall apply to all concentrations with a Community dimension as defined in this Article.*
2. *A concentration has a Community dimension where:*
    (a) *the combined aggregate worldwide turnover of all the undertakings concerned is more than EUR 5000 million; and*
    (b) *the aggregate Community-wide turnover of each of at least two of the undertakings concerned is more than EUR 250 million, unless each of the undertakings concerned achieves more than two-thirds of its aggregate Community-wide turnover within one and the same Member State.*
3. *A concentration that does not meet the thresholds laid down in paragraph 2 has a Community dimension where:*
    (a) *the combined aggregate worldwide turnover of all the undertakings concerned is more than EUR 2500 million;*

(b) in each of at least three Member States, the combined aggregate turnover of all the undertakings concerned is more than EUR 100 million;

(c) in each of at least three Member States included for the purpose of point (b), the aggregate turnover of each of at least two of the undertakings concerned is more than EUR 25 million; and

(d) the aggregate Community-wide turnover of each of at least two of the undertakings concerned is more than EUR 100 million, unless each of the undertakings concerned achieves more than two-thirds of its aggregate Community-wide turnover within one and the same Member State. [...]

Article 2. Appraisal of concentrations

1. Concentrations within the scope of this Regulation shall be appraised in accordance with the objectives of this Regulation and the following provisions with a view to establishing whether or not they are compatible with the common market.

In making this appraisal, the Commission shall take into account:

(a) the need to maintain and develop effective competition within the common market in view of, among other things, the structure of all the markets concerned and the actual or potential competition from undertakings located either within or outwith the Community;

(b) the market position of the undertakings concerned and their economic and financial power, the alternatives available to suppliers and users, their access to supplies or markets, any legal or other barriers to entry, supply and demand trends for the relevant goods and services, the interests of the intermediate and ultimate consumers, and the development of technical and economic progress provided that it is to consumers' advantage and does not form an obstacle to competition.

2. A concentration which would not significantly impede effective competition in the common market or in a substantial part of it, in particular as a result of the creation or strengthening of a dominant position, shall be declared compatible with the common market.

3. A concentration which would significantly impede effective competition, in the common market or in a substantial part of it, in particular as a result of the creation or strengthening of a dominant position, shall be declared incompatible with the common market.

4. *To the extent that the creation of a joint venture constituting a concentration pursuant to Article 3 has as its object or effect the coordination of the competitive behaviour of undertakings that remain independent, such coordination shall be appraised in accordance with the criteria of Article 81(1) and (3) of the Treaty, with a view to establishing whether or not the operation is compatible with the common market.*

5. *In making this appraisal, the Commission shall take into account in particular: [...]*

Article 3. Definition of concentration

"1. A concentration shall be deemed to arise where a change of control on a lasting basis results from:
   (a) the merger of two or more previously independent undertakings or parts of undertakings, or
   (b) the acquisition, by one or more persons already controlling at least one undertaking, or by one or more undertakings, whether by purchase of securities or assets, by contract or by any other means, of direct or indirect control of the whole or parts of one or more other undertakings.

2. *Control shall be constituted by rights, contracts or any other means which, either separately or in combination and having regard to the considerations of fact or law involved, confer the possibility of exercising decisive influence on an undertaking, in particular by:*
   (a) ownership or the right to use all or part of the assets of an undertaking;
   (b) rights or contracts which confer decisive influence on the composition, voting or decisions of the organs of an undertaking.

3. *Control is acquired by persons or undertakings which:*
   (a) are holders of the rights or entitled to rights under the contracts concerned; or
   (b) while not being holders of such rights or entitled to rights under such contracts, have the power to exercise the rights deriving therefrom.

4. *The creation of a joint venture performing on a lasting basis all the functions of an autonomous economic entity shall constitute a concentration within the meaning of paragraph 1(b).*

5. *A concentration shall not be deemed to arise where: [...]"*

Article 4. Prior notification of concentrations and pre-notification referral at the request of the notifying parties

1. *Concentrations with a Community dimension defined in this Regulation shall be notified to the Commission prior to their implementation and following the conclusion of the agreement, the announcement of the public bid, or the acquisition of a controlling interest.*

   Notification may also be made where the undertakings concerned demonstrate to the Commission a good faith intention to conclude an agreement or, in the case of a public bid, where they have publicly announced an intention to make such a bid, provided that the intended agreement or bid would result in a concentration with a Community dimension. [...]

2. *A concentration which consists of a merger within the meaning of Article 3(1)(a) or in the acquisition of joint control within the meaning of Article 3(1)(b) shall be notified jointly by the parties to the merger or by those acquiring joint control as the case may be. In all other cases, the notification shall be effected by the person or undertaking acquiring control of the whole or parts of one or more undertakings.*

To make the notification, the parties to the transaction have to complete forms provided in Annexes to the Implementing Regulation 2023/914, i.e.:

- Form CO for all concentrations,
- Short Form CO for concentrations unlikely to raise competition concerns,
- Form RS for referral requests, and
- Form RM for commitments

2. U.S. law

In U.S. law, existing merger control was transformed by the Hart-Scott-Rodino Act, which amended the Clayton Act in 1976 and created the system with pre-merger filings that exists today. The most important provisions are as follows:

§7 (15 U.S.C. §18)

No person engaged in commerce or in any activity affecting commerce shall acquire, directly or indirectly, the whole or any part of the stock or other share capital and no person subject to the jurisdiction of the Federal Trade Commission shall acquire the whole or any part of the assets of another person engaged also in commerce or in any activity affecting commerce, where in any line of commerce or in any activity affecting commerce in any section of the country, the effect of such acquisition may be substantially to lessen competition, or to tend to create a monopoly.

No person shall acquire, directly or indirectly, the whole or any part of the stock or other share capital and no person subject to the jurisdiction of the Federal Trade Commission shall acquire the whole or any part of the assets of one or more persons engaged in commerce or in any activity affecting commerce, where in any line of commerce or in any activity affecting commerce in any section of the country, the effect of such acquisition, of such stocks or assets, or of the use of such stock by the voting or granting of proxies or otherwise, may be substantially to lessen competition, or to tend to create a monopoly.

This section shall not apply to persons purchasing such stock solely for investment and not using the same by voting or otherwise to bring about, or in attempting to bring about, the substantial lessening of competition. Nor shall anything contained in this section prevent a corporation engaged in commerce or in any activity affecting commerce from causing the formation of subsidiary corporations for the actual carrying on of their immediate lawful business, or the natural and legitimate branches or extensions thereof, or from owning and holding all or a part of the stock of such subsidiary corporations, when the effect of such formation is not to substantially lessen competition.

[...]

§7A (15 U.S.C. §18a)

(a) Filing
Except as exempted pursuant to subsection (c), no person shall acquire, directly or indirectly, any voting securities or assets of any other person, unless both persons (or in the case of a tender offer, the acquiring person) file notification pursuant to rules under subsection (d)(1) and the waiting period described in subsection (b)(1) has expired, if —

(1) the acquiring person, or the person whose voting securities or assets are being acquired, is engaged in commerce or in any activity affecting commerce; and

(2) as a result of such acquisition, the acquiring person would hold an aggregate total amount of the voting securities and assets of the acquired person —

(A) in excess of $200,000,000 (as adjusted and published for each fiscal year beginning after September 30, 2004, in the same manner as provided in section 19(a)(5) of this title to reflect the percentage change in the gross national product for such fiscal year compared to the gross national product for the year ending September 30, 2003); or

(B)

    (i) in excess of $50,000,000 (as so adjusted and published) but not in excess of $200,000,000 (as so adjusted and published); and

    (ii)

        (I) any voting securities or assets of a person engaged in manufacturing which has annual net sales or total assets of $10,000,000 (as so adjusted and published) or more are being acquired by any person which has total assets or annual net sales of $100,000,000 (as so adjusted and published) or more;

        (II) any voting securities or assets of a person not engaged in manufacturing which has total assets of $10,000,000 (as so adjusted and published) or more are being acquired by any person which has total assets or annual net sales of $100,000,000 (as so adjusted and published) or more; or

        (III) any voting securities or assets of a person with annual net sales or total assets of $100,000,000 (as so adjusted and published) or more are being acquired by any person with total assets or annual net sales of $10,000,000 (as so adjusted and published) or more.

In the case of a tender offer, the person whose voting securities are sought to be acquired by a person required to file notification under this subsection shall file notification pursuant to rules under subsection (d).

(b) Waiting period; publication; voting securities

    (1) The waiting period required under subsection (a) shall —

        (A) begin on the date of the receipt by the Federal Trade Commission and the Assistant Attorney General in charge of the Antitrust Division of the Department of Justice

(*hereinafter referred to in this section as the "Assistant Attorney General"*) *of* —

    (i) *the completed notification required under subsection (a), or*

    (ii) *if such notification is not completed, the notification to the extent completed and a statement of the reasons for such noncompliance, from both persons, or, in the case of a tender offer, the acquiring person; and*

  (B) *end on the thirtieth day after the date of such receipt (or in the case of a cash tender offer, the fifteenth day), or on such later date as may be set under subsection (e)(2) or (g)(2).*

(2) *The Federal Trade Commission and the Assistant Attorney General may, in individual cases, terminate the waiting period specified in paragraph (1) and allow any person to proceed with any acquisition subject to this section, and promptly shall cause to be published in the Federal Register a notice that neither intends to take any action within such period with respect to such acquisition.*

(3) *As used in this section* —

  (A) *The term "voting securities" means any securities which at present or upon conversion entitle the owner or holder thereof to vote for the election of directors of the issuer or, with respect to unincorporated issuers, persons exercising similar functions.*

  (B) *The amount or percentage of voting securities or assets of a person which are acquired or held by another person shall be determined by aggregating the amount or percentage of such voting securities or assets held or acquired by such other person and each affiliate thereof.*

(c) *Exempt transactions*
  [...]

(e) *Additional information; waiting period extensions*
  (1)

  (A) *The Federal Trade Commission or the Assistant Attorney General may, prior to the expiration of the 30-day waiting period (or in the case of a cash tender offer, the 15-day waiting period) specified in subsection (b)(1) of this section, require the submission of additional information or documentary material relevant to the proposed acquisition, from a*

> *person required to file notification with respect to such acquisition under subsection (a) of this section prior to the expiration of the waiting period specified in subsection (b)(1) of this section, or from any officer, director, partner, agent, or employee of such person.*
>
> *(B) [...]"*

Additional procedural rules can be found in the HSR Rules (16 CFR Parts 801–803) and the HSR Statements of Basis and Purpose (86 FR 7870 *et al.*), among others.[1]

3. Japanese law

In Japan, mergers are regulated by the AMA. The most important provisions in the present context are as follows:

Article 9

(1)   No company may be established that would cause an excessive concentration of economic power due to share holding (including equity interest; the same applies hereinafter) in other companies in Japan.

(2)   No company (including a foreign company; the same applies hereinafter) may become a company that causes an excessive concentration of economic power in Japan by acquiring or holding shares in other companies in Japan.

(3)   The term 'excessive concentration of economic power' in the preceding two paragraphs means that the overall business scale of a company, its subsidiary companies, and other domestic companies whose business activities it controls through shareholding, is extremely large across a considerable number of business fields; that a company, its subsidiary companies, and other domestic companies it controls have a great amount of power to influence other enterprises through transactions with their funds; or that a company, its subsidiary companies, and other domestic companies it controls occupy influential positions in a considerable number of interrelated fields of business; and that any of these factors have a large effect on the national economy and impede fair and free competition from moving forward.

---

[1] See also: https://www.ftc.gov/enforcement/premerger-notification-program/hsr-resources.

Article 10

(1)   No company may acquire or hold shares of any other companies if its acquisition or holding of shares substantially restrains competition in any particular field of trade, nor may any company use unfair trade practices to acquire or hold shares in another company.
[...]

Article 13

(1)   An officer or an employee (meaning, in this Article, a person other than an officer engaged in the business of a company on a regular basis) of a company may not hold a position as an officer of another company at the same time, if the person's doing so substantially restrains competition in any particular field of trade.
[...]

Article 15

(1)   No company may effect a merger if any of the following items applies:
  (i)   if the merger substantially restrains competition in a particular field of trade
  (ii)   if unfair trade practices are employed in the course of the merger.
  [...]

Article 15–2

(1)   No company may effect a joint incorporation-type company split (meaning an incorporation-type company split that a company effects jointly with another company; the same applies hereinafter) or an absorption-type split if any of the following items applies:
  (i)   if the joint incorporation-type company split or absorption-type split substantially restrains competition in a particular field of trade
  (ii)   if unfair trade practices have been employed in the course of the joint incorporation-type company split or absorption-type split
  [...]

Article 15–3

(1)   No company may engage in a joint share transfer (meaning a share transfer carried out by a company jointly with another company; the same applies hereinafter) if it falls under either of the following items:

   (i)   if the joint share transfer substantially restrains competition in a particular field of trade
   (ii)   if unfair trade practices have been employed in the course of the share transfer
   [...]

Article 16

(1)   No company may engage in any of the following acts if its doing so substantially restrains competition in any particular field of trade, nor may it engage in any of the following acts through unfair trade practices:

   (i)   accepting assignment of the whole or a substantial part of the business of another company
   (ii)   accepting assignment of the whole or a substantial part of the fixed assets used for the business of another company
   (iii)   taking on a lease of the whole or a substantial part of the business of another company
   (iv)   undertaking the management of the whole or a substantial part of the business of another company
   (iv)   entering into a contract which provides for a joint profit and loss account for business with another company
   [...]

Article 17

No person may engage in any act, irrespective of the name given to that act, that evades the prohibitions and restrictions provided for in the provisions of Articles 9 to 16 inclusive.

In addition, the AMA includes detailed provisions on notification thresholds and the requirement of notification prior to consummation in Articles 10(2), 15(2), 15-2(2), 15-3(2) and 16(2). These are not listed here for the sake of brevity, but the main points concerning the notification requirements are set out in the following text.

II. What is merger control?

Merger control is **mainly administrative control** (although private parties and, in the U.S., the DOJ can bring civil actions against mergers under tort law). As structure-related control, it was frequently introduced only some time after the prohibitions of anticompetitive conduct. In the **EU**, merger control was introduced in 1990, whereas Articles 101–102 TFEU go back to provisions in the Treaty on the European Economic Community of 1957. In Germany, merger control was included in amendment of 1974 to the Competition Act (*Gesetz gegen Wettbewerbsbeschränkungen* — GWB), which dates back to 1957. In the **U.S.**, the Clayton Act of 1914 followed upon the Sherman Act of 1890.

In contrast, in **Japan**, structure-related control was the very first step in introducing any law and measures to maintain a competitive market. Prior to enactment of the AMA, the series of legislation enabled the Holding Company Liquidation Commission (HCLC) (dissolved 1951) to break up large conglomerates called *zaibatsu*, which used to have exceptionally significant economic power (aggregated economic power) and political influence throughout Japan, and companies with extensive market power in particular markets.[2] In parallel, the AMA was enacted in 1947 and, after break-ups and other measures to restore competition, the AMA was expected to maintain such a free and competitive market structure and, thus, the merger control carried top priority during its early years of AMA history. Over time, concern about the re-emergence of mighty conglomerates like *zaibatsu* has become less and the merger regulation has become generally less stringent in Japan, except for digital platforms presenting new competitive issues.

The situation, however, was **different in several jurisdictions** which modeled competition law on U.S. or EU law. For instance, merger control was likewise part of China's Anti-Monopoly Law of 2008 and the Korean Monopoly Regulation and Fair Trade Act 1981 from the start.

The **objective** of merger control is generally to prevent market power that is not acquired by business acumen (internal growth) but by simple acquisition, especially of competitors (external growth). Once substantial market power has been achieved, it may lead to anticompetitive high prices, reductions of output or a downgrade of quality. However,

---

[2]See Wakui, Antimonopoly Law: Competition Law and Policy in Japan, 2nd ed., 2018, 6 ff. for details.

dissolving a merger transaction after its implementation is regularly both ineffective and inefficient. Thus, merger control is usually fashioned as an *ex ante* instrument that seeks to prevent potential anticompetitive integration (and potential subsequent anticompetitive conducts). Regarding its geographic reach, merger control tends to kick in whenever a merger or takeover (concentration) has a territorial effect in the relevant jurisdiction. This implies that merger or takeover operations require a so-called multi-jurisdictional (self-)assessment by the relevant firms in order to find out whether the operation must be submitted to the competent agencies. The authorities have provided guidance templates to facilitate these self-assessments.[3]

The **workload** of the agencies has increased over time, reflecting the trend toward increased global business cooperation. Although notification thresholds differ across jurisdictions, a parallel upward trend can be observed in several jurisdictions. For instance, in 2011–2018, the number of merger filings in the **EU** rose from approximately 300 to roughly 410. The number of filings in Member States rose substantially as well. This upward trend was particularly noticeable in Germany, where that number rose from approximately 1,100 to approximately 1,400. Given the high number of notifiable transactions, the German legislature has meanwhile raised the domestic turnover threshold for the second party from EUR 5 to EUR 10 million.[4] In the **U.S.**, the number of filings with the FTC/DOJ rose from 1,450 (2011) to 2,111 (2018).[5]

Most mergers do not go through detailed assessment (called, e.g., a phase II or second request) or are blocked. In the **EU**, only one to two transactions are blocked per year. In Germany, only one to three cases were blocked between 2011 and 2018. In the **U.S.**, only 3% went through second request from 2011 through 2018, and 35–40 transactions were challenged. Meanwhile, the JFTC in **Japan** employs a softer approach based on communication and voluntary initiative. For instance, although the JFTC has carried out detailed analysis in at least ten cases in FY 2021, no transaction was officially blocked. Eight applications were withdrawn during the review.

---

[3] See, e.g., on the ICN website: https://www.internationalcompetitionnetwork.org/working-groups/merger/templates/.

[4] §35 GWB as amended by 10th Amendment to the Competition Act.

[5] DOJ & FTC, Annual Reports to Congress Pursuant to the Hart-Scott-Rodino Antitrust Improvements Act of 1976 (2020) https://www.ftc.gov/system/files/documents/reports/hart-scott-rodino-annual-report-fiscal-year-2020/fy2020_-_hsr_annual_report_-_final.pdf.

III. Formal aspects of merger control

1. Notification

(a) General aspects

Transactions subject to merger control must be filed with the competent authority. In the **EU**, a so-called "one-stop shop" system applies: Although the EU has a two-tiered system of competition enforcement, the European Commission is competent only for concentrations with an "EU dimension," whereas the agencies in the Member States retain the competence to review transactions that meet national control thresholds but not EU thresholds. Therefore, transactions may have to be notified in parallel, e.g., to the German Federal Cartel Office, the French Autorité de la concurrence, the Austrian Bundeswettbewerbsbehörde (BWB), the Italian Autorità Garante della Concorrenza e del Mercato (AGCM), the Polish Urząd Ochrony Konkurencji i Konsumentów (UOKiK), the Spanish Comisión Nacional de los Mercados y la Competencia (CNMC) and/or the Swedish Konkurrensverket.

That said, since concentrations may turn out to be better handled at EU or at national level, **referrals** are possible as well. Referrals require a request of the notifying parties or the Member States affected.[6] To complicate things further, the European Commission has exclusive jurisdiction within the **European Economic Area (EEA)**, meaning that it can also decide on mergers with an EU dimension affecting Iceland, Liechtenstein or Norway.

Moreover, European transactions may have to be notified also to the Competition and Markets Authority (CMA) in the UK, the Wettbewerbskommission (WEKO) in Switzerland and other European authorities **outside the EU**.

In the **U.S.**, in comparison, merger control is relatively straightforward because the **Federal Trade Commission (FTC)** is the only competent authority to assess the competition aspects of the relevant transactions in an administrative procedure for the U.S. However, the **DOJ** is empowered

---

[6]Articles 4, 9 and 22 Reg. 139/2004; see also European Commission, Commission Notice on Case Referral in respect of concentrations, OJ C 56, 5 March 2005, p. 2; Communication from the Commission Guidance on the application of the referral mechanism set out in Article 22 of the Merger Regulation to certain categories of cases, OJ C 113, 31 March 2021, p. 1.

to challenge transactions raising competition concerns in court. Therefore, the parties to the transaction are obliged to also inform the DOJ (using the same form as for the FTC filing). In any event, following the notification by the parties, only one agency reviews the proposed transaction. The U.S. agencies have a clearance process to allocate responsibility for review to either the FTC or the DOJ. The allocation is generally made based on each agency's expertise.[7] Moreover, just like in the EU, sector regulators may be competent to assess other aspects of those transactions.

In jurisdictions that have neither a federal structure nor an EU-like supranational institution, the merger notification is rather simple in comparison. In **Japan**, the notification must be filed with the Japan Fair Trade Commission (JFTC). Similarly, the State Administration for Market Regulation (SAMR) is authorized to review merger transactions in China, the Korean Fair Trade Commission (KFTC) in Korea, etc.

Notification is **mostly mandatory** (exception is the UK), but some agencies may also prosecute mergers substantially lessening competition *ex post* even if they are not notifiable (e.g., JFTC and U.S. DOJ). The U.S. is an outlier in that the DOJ can challenge merger transactions even after clearance.

(b) Merger notification

Whether a transaction needs to be notified depends on two elements. The first is whether the parties to the transaction and/or the transaction meet the relevant notification thresholds. The second is whether the transaction meets the definition of a notifiable transaction.

(1) EU law

In the **EU**, the **notification thresholds** to be met by the parties to the transaction are set out in Articles 1 and 5 Regulation 139/2004. Thus, a turnover threshold applies, which indicates the EU dimension of the transaction.[8] **Member States** may go further. In Germany, for example,

---

[7] FTC/DOJ, ICN Merger Notification and Procedures Template — Merger Working Group United States of America, 1 February 2021, p. 5.

[8] See also European Commission, Commission Consolidated Jurisdictional Notice under Council Regulation (EC) No. 139/2004 on the control of concentrations between undertakings, OJ C 95, 16 April 2008, p. 1, §124 ff.

the transaction value may trigger merger control as well.[9] In Portugal and Spain, the market shares of the parties to the transaction are likewise relevant.[10] Moreover, the DMA and German law also require notification of all acquisitions by large companies for informational purposes.[11]

The transactions to be notified at **EU** level must constitute a "**concentration**". Concentrations are defined in Article 3 Regulation 139/2004 as a horizontal merger of two firms (practically irrelevant), the **acquisition of control** over another company or the acquisition of joint control over a full-function joint venture (JV).[12] The acquisition of control is the most common form of concentration in practice. Control in this context is a "decisive influence" over the strategic business decisions of the other company (≠ day-to-day management).[13] Negative control, i.e., blocking rights, is considered sufficient. Furthermore, certain financial acquisitions are excepted from the definition of a concentration in Article 3(5) Regulation 139/2004, but these exceptions are not very relevant in practice.[14] **Member States** may again go further. For instance, Germany defines concentrations as acquisitions of all or a substantial part of assets, control (like in the EU), certain shareholdings (25% and 50%) or a competitively significant interest (similar to materiality test in the UK).[15]

The merger notification, **in practice**, requires the notifying parties to complete the forms provided in Annexes to the **Implementing Regulation 802/2004**, i.e., the **Form CO** for all concentrations, the **Short Form CO** for concentrations unlikely to raise competition concerns, the **Form RS** for a referral request, and Form RM for commitments.[16] Due to

---

[9]FCO/BWB, Guidance on Transaction Value Thresholds for Mandatory Pre-merger Notification, Effective: 20 August 2018.
[10]§35 GWB.
[11]Article 12 DMA; §39a GWB.
[12]Article 3(1) in conjunction with (2); Article 3(4) Reg. 139/2004.
[13]See European Commission, Consolidated Jurisdictional Notice (fn. 8), §54.
[14]See GC, Judgment of 18 May 2022, *Canon/Commission* (T-609/19) ECLI:EU:T:2022:299 on a "warehousing" structure. Note that certain acquisitions in a two-year time period are viewed together for purposes of calculating the turnover, which is relevant particularly for staggered takeovers, including financial investment transactions (Article 5(2) Reg. 139/2004).
[15]§37(1) GWB.
[16]Commission Implementing Regulation (EU) 2023/914 of 20 April 2023 implementing Council Regulation (EC) No. 139/2004 on the control of concentrations between undertakings and repealing Commission Regulation (EC) No. 802/2004, OJ L 119, 5 May 2023, p. 22.

tight deadlines, however, the European Commission typically only accepts notifications as complete after so-called informal pre-merger discussions.[17] These pre-merger discussions are ambivalent. On the one hand, they may be used by the European Commission to circumvent the tight deadlines of EU merger control and to amass market knowledge based on company submissions ($\approx$ market investigation). On the other hand, they may also be to the parties' benefit, for example, by raising red flags that allow the parties to abandon concentrations at an early stage that are unlikely to succeed.

(2) U.S. law

Notification in the U.S. is rather straightforward as compared with the requirements in the EU. The parties to the transaction are required to complete and submit a **Notification and Report Form** to the FTC and DOJ.[18] The required information is less extensive than in the EU.

The **notification thresholds** relate to both the parties to the transaction and the transaction itself. The thresholds have been adjusted annually since 2005.[19] The original threshold for the so-called "size of transaction" test was USD 200 million. However, if the transaction is valued in excess of USD 50 million, but at the same time is USD 200 million (as adjusted) or less, the notification is likewise mandatory under the "size of person" test if the parties to the transaction meet certain size requirements. Exemptions may apply.[20]

---

[17] See European Commission, DG Competition Best Practices on the conduct of European Commission merger proceedings, 20 January 2004, §§5 ff.; available at: https://ec.europa.eu/competition-policy/system/files/2021-03/proceedings.pdf. This policy has also developed before the German FCO in complex cases.

[18] See: https://www.ftc.gov/system/files/attachments/form-instructions/hsr_form_instructions_9-25-19.pdf. This is based on 15 USC 18a(d) and set out with the consent of the DOJ.

[19] See 86 FR 7870 with the Revised Thresholds for 2021.

[20] For details, see FTC Premerger Notification Office, Introductory Guide II: To File or Not to File, When You Must File a Premerger Notification Report Form, Revised: September 2008; available at: https://www.ftc.gov/sites/default/files/attachments/premerger-introductory-guides/guide2.pdf.

It should be noted, though, that the FTC and DOJ **may pursue concentrations "substantially lessening competition"** within the meaning of §7 of the Clayton Act **even if they do not meet the notification thresholds.**[21] This allows the U.S. agencies to intervene, e.g., when a transaction would harm competition in platform markets where the parties do not meet the thresholds.[22] However, given the risk to legal certainty and the practical difficulties of divestiture, such interventions are not frequent.

A **notifiable concentration** exists in cases of an acquisition of voting securities, assets or non-corporate interests. In the latter case, a change of control is sufficient.[23] Similar to the situation in the EU, certain financial transactions concerning voting securities are exempt from the filing requirement.[24]

(3) Japanese law

Japanese law distinguishes mergers and other types of transactions resulting in **business combinations**. Depending on the type, Articles 10(2), 15(2), 15-2(2), 15-3(2) and 16(2) oblige the parties to notify the JFTC of the merger and other transactions to combine companies in advance where the size of companies exceeds certain criteria. Generally, the relevant **notification criteria** are that the transaction will combine a company whose total amount of domestic sales of the company exceeds JPY 20 billion and a company whose total amount of domestic sales of a company exceeds JPY 5 billion, although the total amount of domestic sales criteria is set lower, at JPY 10 billion and JPY 3 billion, in case of acquisition of business and absorption-type company split.

The AMA allows only for the prohibition of transfers **creating a business combination**, which may cause a **substantial restriction of competition**. A business **combination** requires that the parties to the transaction cease to operate their businesses independently from each other. If there is no such combination relationship, the transfer cannot create any AMA concerns. The **notification thresholds are set in**

---

[21] https://www.oecd.org/officialdocuments/publicdisplaydocumentpdf/?cote=DAF/COMP/WP3/WD(2014)23&docLanguage=En.

[22] *United States v. Bazaarvoice, Inc.*, Case No. 13-cv-00133-WHO.

[23] See §801.1(b) of the HSR Rules.

[24] See §802.9 of HSR Rules.

accordance with this principle. For example, in the case of stock acquisition, notification is mandatory where the acquiring company group becomes a sole leading shareholder by (i) acquiring more than 50% of voting stock or (ii) acquiring more than 20% of voting stock to become the largest voting shareholder. In relation to business transfers, no notification is necessary unless the transferred business potentially constitutes a business entity operatable on its own and has substantial value to transferring party, as otherwise there would be no combination of business entities.

The JFTC may review and challenge mergers which do not meet the notification thresholds. Parties whose transfer does not meet the notification criteria can consult with the JFTC as to the compatibility with the AMA in advance. When consulted, the JFTC would review the case in the same manner as the notified merger.

2. Review procedure

(a) EU law

In the EU, the review of the notified transaction typically takes place in a **one- or two-phase procedure** that is subject to time limits. At EU level, Article 10 Regulation 139/2004 provides for a Phase I of 25 (extended to 35) working days and a Phase II of 90 (extended to 120) working days with a consensual further extension of up to 20 working days. In both phases, the European Commission may conclude the investigation with a decision (Articles 6 and 8 Regulation 139/2004). The decision may consist of unconditional or conditional clearance (the latter if the parties proposed suitable remedies). In Phase II, the Commission may also prohibit the transaction. At EU level, a simplified review procedure is available in case of Short Form notifications and other notifications not raising competition concerns.[25]

During the review procedure, the parties are **prohibited from implementing** (consummating) **the transaction**. In cases of certain financial transactions, they may request a derogation, which is, however, granted rarely (Article 7 Reg. 139/2004). The European Commission may impose

---

[25]See European Commission, Commission Notice on a simplified procedure for treatment of certain concentrations under Council Regulation (EC) No. 139/2004, OJ C 366, 14 December 2013, p. 5.

fines for so-called gun-jumping if it finds out that the parties have started implementing the transaction before clearance or if they have exchanged strategic information in violation of Article 101 TFEU.[26]

The European Commission **publishes** both filings and decisions.[27] Additional information on important cases is provided in the European Commission's annual Competition Reports. No filing fees apply at EU level.

In the **Member States**, the review procedure may diverge. In Germany, for example, the first review phase lasts one month and the second phase generally five months.[28] Moreover, information on filings is only published temporarily in an online list (with limited information), and the FCO only publishes its decisions in the second phase. Filing fees apply.

(b) U.S. law

The FTC/DOJ procedure likewise consists of **one or two phases**, subject to time limits. In contrast to the procedure in the EU, however, no timetable exists for an express approval of the transaction. Rather, the parties are generally required only to observe an initial waiting period of 30 days (15 days in case of cash tender offers/bankruptcy filings). This initial waiting period may be extended by another 30 days in case of a "**Second Request**", which allows the agencies to examine the transaction more closely. In contrast to that, the parties may also request an early termination of the waiting period in order to implement the transaction. In cases giving rise to concerns, the acquirer may elect to "pull and refile". If the acquirer does so, within 2 business days, the initial waiting period of the original filing may be extended, allowing the parties to complete the transaction faster than if the whole procedure started anew. No simplified procedure is available in the U.S.

---

[26] See ECJ, Judgment of 31 May 2018, *Ernst & Young* (C-633/16) ECLI:EU:C:2018:371, §§46 ff. on the distinction between both offenses.

[27] *Re* the practical aspects, see EU, Guidance on the preparation of public versions of Commission Decisions adopted under the Merger Regulation, undated; available at: https://ec.europa.eu/competition/mergers/legislation/guidance_on_preparation_of_public_versions_mergers_26052015.pdf.

[28] §40 GWB.

If the responsible agency finds that a transaction raises **significant antitrust concerns**, it must go to court to obtain an injunction in order to prevent the merger from occurring. In turn, the parties may offer **remedies** to prevent such court action and to reach a settlement with the FTC/DOJ.[29] Unlike the situation in the EU, the agencies' decision not to take action does not bar future actions by the U.S. agencies.[30]

The agencies do not publish filings, but they **publish** grants of an early termination. Filing fees apply based on the size of the transaction.

(c) Japanese law

The JFTC conducts a **preliminary review** of the planned merger within 30 days of receipt of filings. During the period, parties may **not initiate the merger**. The waiting period may be shortened when requested and the JFTC considers that there is no AMA concern.

When the JFTC considers a detailed assessment necessary, it **requests additional information and documents**. This examination period must be completed within 90 days from receipt of filing. Within this period, the JFTC is authorized to notify the parties to the transaction that it will not take action or to issue a notice of hearing opportunities if there are competition concerns.

When the JFTC considers that the notified merger is likely to **substantially restrict competition** in any relevant market, it may issue a **cease-and-desist order** (AMA Article 17-2). The JFTC must begin this procedure leading to such an order by issuing the hearing notice to the parties concerned during the examination period.

Conventionally, the parties will try to avoid such an outcome by **committing to implement remedies** or by simply dropping the planned transaction. When the parties commit to implement remedies, either structural or behavioral, these remedies are indicated in the merger notification in which the parties describe not only what and how the parties will merge but also what measures the parties will take to address any competitive

---

[29] See FTC, Statement of the Federal Trade Commission's Bureau of Competition on Negotiating Merger Remedies, January 2012; available at: https://www.ftc.gov/advice-guidance/competition-guidance/negotiating-merger-remedies. DOJ, Merger Remedial Manual (2020) https://www.justice.gov/atr/page/file/1312416/download.
[30] 15 U.S.C. §18a(i)(1).

concerns. Failing to take action accordingly creates the possibility for one year that the JFTC issues a cease-and-desist order based on AMA Article 17-2.

The summary of the merger filing is **published** when it moves to the second stage or when the JFTC chooses to disclose it as a reference for future cases. In practice, the party customarily withdraws the notification before moving to the second stage and re-submitting a notification, triggering the first-stage examination.

IV. Substantive assessment

1. General aspects

The substantive test for merger control has become gradually aligned in the EU and the U.S. It is U.S. law that developed the test that basically set the standard also for the EU. The test used in the U.S. is whether the transaction substantially lessens competition **(SLC test)**.[31] A similar test is also used in **Japan**, where it has to be assessed whether the transaction is likely to *substantially restrict competition*. In the EU, the test for the European Commission is whether the transaction "substantially impedes effective competition, in particular as a result of the creation or strengthening of a dominant position" **(SIEC test)**.[32] This test is again similar but may diverge particularly when it comes to the risks of horizontal collusion (see Section 2.a in this chapter). Please note that the U.S. agencies are currently reviewing their interpretation of the SLC test (see Section 3(b)).

2. Horizontal mergers

Across the EU, the U.S. and Japan, the substantial assessment of concentrations between competitors (i.e., at horizontal level) is **similar**. In practice, concentrations between (full or partial) competitors are the scenario that is most common in merger control.

---

[31]§7 Clayton Act (15 U.S.C. §18). The UK nowadays uses the SLC test as well; UK Enterprise Act 2002. This test was preceded by a "public interest" test, which, however, did not prove very effective.
[32]Article 2(2)-(3) Reg. 139/2004.

(a) EU law

In the EU, the European Commission's **Horizontal Merger Guidelines** provide extensive guidance on how to assess horizontal mergers.[33] Note that the Guidelines themselves speak of "mergers" in this context (following the common parlance); yet, what is meant is not "mergers" within the meaning of Article 3(1)(a) Regulation 139/2004 but all sorts of "concentrations".

According to the Guidelines, the assessment starts with the **delineation of the relevant markets** affected by the transaction, i.e., the markets where the parties to the transaction engage in overlapping business activities (horizontal overlap).[34]

The next step is the **competitive assessment** to find out whether the transaction significantly impedes effective competition (SIEC). To this end, it is common to start with the calculation of combined market shares and concentration levels post-merger. The Herfindahl–Hirschman Index (HHI) may be used to identify the cases that merit an in-depth assessment. The HHI is calculated by summing the squares of the individual market shares of all the participants. An HHI < 1,000 indicates that the relevant market is unconcentrated and an HHI > 2,000 that the market is highly concentrated.

Where the market shares and the HHI militate in favor of a closer assessment, this assessment starts with an analysis of the effects that the transaction will have on competition in the relevant market. The effects may be of two types:

1. **Non-coordinated effects** include the loss of competition between the parties to the transaction. However, such effects may also arise if the merged firm can unilaterally impede or eliminate competition. The likelihood of non-coordinated effects is assessed depending on the

---

[33] European Commission, Guidelines on the assessment of horizontal mergers under the Council Regulation on the control of concentrations between undertakings, OJ C 31, 5 February 2004, p. 5.

[34] See European Commission, Commission notice on the definition of the Relevant Market for the purposes of Community competition law, OJ C 372, 9 December 1997, p. 5. The notice is currently under review; see here: https://ec.europa.eu/info/law/better-regulation/have-your-say/initiatives/12325-EU-competition-law-market-definition-notice-evaluation-_en.

combined market shares, the closeness of competition between merging firms, the switching options for customers, the likelihood of competitors to step in with supplies, the erection of entry barriers and the potential removal of a competitive force through the acquisition.

2. **Coordinated effects** may arise if the merged firm coordinates its behavior explicitly or implicitly (tacit collusion) with remaining competitors. Coordinated effects require an assessment of (i) terms to reach coordination and (ii) its sustainability (mechanisms for monitoring deviations/deterrent mechanisms and reactions of outsiders).

Once the interplay of the merged firm and its actual competitors in the relevant market has been assessed, the likelihood that **buyer power** could act **as a countervailing factor** as well as **market entry by potential competitors** is evaluated.

After that, **efficiencies** may be assessed although these have not led to a clearance of transactions yet where these transactions were found to otherwise significantly impede effective competition.[35] Finally, the so-called **failing-firm defense** may allow parties to argue that the transaction will not cause any harm to competition that would not arise absent the transaction because the failing firm would have to leave the market anyway in the near future, no less anticompetitive alternative to the transaction is available and the assets of the failing firm would inevitably exit the market.

Good to know: What is peculiar about the SIEC test in the EU?

In the EU, the current SIEC test for merger control was adopted in 2004.[36] In spite of many similarities to the U.S. test, the two tests are not the same. This is, in part, due to historical reasons. The preceding Merger Regulation, Regulation 4064/89, had the two elements "SIEC" and

(Continued)

---

[35]See European Commission, Decision of 27 March 2017, M.7932 — *Dow/DuPont*, §§3236 ff., 3239 ff., 3265 ff. and Annex 4; Decision of 21 March 2018, M.8084 — *Bayer/Monsanto*, §§98 ff., 1043 ff.

[36]Article 2(2)-(3) Reg. 139/2004.

(Continued)

"dominance" in the opposite order.[37] Under that Regulation, it was argued that the dominance criterion did capture most cases that would involve a "substantial lessening of competition". However, it remained unclear whether merger control in the EU covered also tacit collusion in oligopoly situations. The new SIEC test under Regulation 139/2004 is meant and understood to cover such tacit collusion. That being said, it is still unclear to what extent the SIEC test also applies below the level of dominance. In any event, it should be cautioned against using the SLC and the SIEC tests as proxies in borderline cases.[38]

(b) U.S. law

The assessment under the **U.S. Horizontal Merger Guidelines** again starts with the definition of the relevant markets and an assessment of market shares and concentration levels based on the HHI. Regarding the market definition, the Guidelines place more weight on the possibility of suppliers to price-discriminate than the EU guidelines. In the assessment of concentration levels, an HHI < 1,000 indicates that the relevant market is unconcentrated, whereas an HHI > 1,800, i.e., stricter than in the EU, indicates that the market is highly concentrated.

Where the HHI figures suggest the need for a closer assessment, it must be analyzed whether adverse competitive effects are to be expected post-merger.

1.   Regarding **unilateral effects**, the guidelines consider the same effects relevant as the EU guidelines, but they distinguish between a setting where firms in the market are distinguished by product differentiation

---

[37] Council Regulation (EEC) No. 4064/89 of 21 December 1989 on the control of concentrations between undertakings, OJ L 395, 30 December 1989, p. 1; Corrigenda — Whole text republished in: OJ L 257/90, p. 13.

[38] See European Commission, DG Competition Staff Working Paper, Best Practices for the submission of economic evidence and data collection in cases concerning the application of Articles 101 and 102 TFEU and in merger cases, undated (March 2021); available at: https://eur-lex.europa.eu/legal-content/EN/ALL/?uri=CELEX:52011SC1216.

and a setting where firms distinguish themselves primarily by their capacities.

2. Regarding **coordinated effects**, it must be assessed whether the market conditions are "conducive" to *[1] reaching terms of coordination that are profitable to the firms involved and [2] an ability to detect and punish deviations that would undermine the coordinated interaction.*

Once the competitive situation in the relevant market has been established, the guidelines foresee an **entry analysis** with regard to **potential competitors**. Relevant criteria in this context are the "timeliness, likelihood, and sufficiency" of entry.

Finally, also the U.S. Horizontal Merger Guidelines foresee an assessment of **efficiencies** brought about by the merger. They also allow for a **failing-firm defense**. In the U.S., even a "flailing-firm defense" has been discussed in cases where the acquired target company is weak financially or at least not as strong a competitor as it was in the past.[39] However, the discussion of "flailing firms" is not reflected in the guidelines, unlike the established failing-firm defense.[40]

(c) Japanese law

There used to be an active **discussion** as to whether the merger regulations under the AMA address the coordinated effects. The Tokyo High Court once indicated that substantial restraint of trade occurs when other market participants would become unable to freely decide trading conditions including price, output and quality and carry on their business activities independently and profitably.[41] In line with such understandings, the JFTC examined whether rivals would be able to carry on their business activities independently after the *Fuji/Yawata* merger and cleared it concluding that they would.[42] This was seen as problematic as such a view can ignore the coordinated effects. In other words, such a view may indicate that the merger is lawful as long as a competitor exists in the market

---

[39] OECD, Policy Roundtables, Failing Firm Defence (1995), OCDE/GD(96)23, 1996, pp. 7, 21–22.
[40] DOJ/FTC, Horizontal Merger Guidelines, 19 August 2010, pt. 11.
[41] Tokyo High Court, 19 September 1951, 4-XIV Koto Saibansho Minji Hanrei-shu 497 (*Toho-Subaru*).
[42] JFTC Consent Decision, 30 October 1969, 16 Shinketsu-shu 46 (*Fuji/Yawata*).

even where such a competitor is unlikely to compete against the merging parties vigorously and instead would choose to be engaged in collusive behavior. Since then, the theory and JFTC's decisional practices have evolved, and it is now clear that **both unilateral effects and coordinated effects may cause an AMA concern**.

Currently, it is understood that the **unilateral effects** are assessed in light of the merging parties' share and position in the market, the competitors' capacity to increase output, the disparity between merging parties and competitors, product differentiation, competitive constraints posed by new entries imports, neighboring products and customers as well as pro-competitive effects. Similar to the U.S. failing-firm defense, where there are special circumstances that would create the market power without merger because one of the merging parties is about to exit, or the size of the market has become too small for more than one company to survive in the market, the merger is viewed lawful.[43]

On the other hand, in relation to **coordinated effects**, the key questions are whether the market will become more prone to collusion. Thus, the number of competitors, price and product differentiation (or similarities), transparency of the market and other factors that would facilitate coordination are assessed. As in case of unilateral effects, the competitive constraints, procompetitive effects, financial state of merging parties and size of the market may also be taken into account.[44]

3. Non-horizontal mergers

Non-horizontal mergers may be vertical or conglomerate. **Vertical** mergers take place between companies active at different levels of the supply chain. This type is the least frequent type of merger. **Conglomerate** mergers are notified more often. They are the most demanding when it comes to formulating a theory of harm.

(a) EU law

In the EU, the European Commission published its **Non-horizontal Merger Guidelines** for the assessment of vertical and conglomerate

---

[43] JFTC, Guidelines to Application of the Antimonopoly Act Concerning Review of Business Combination (last amended 17 December 2019).
[44] *Ibid.*

mergers.[45] The competitive assessment is technically similar to one of the horizontal transactions. However, regarding non-coordinated effects, extensive guidance is provided regarding both input and customer **foreclosure** particularly in **vertical** settings. In both cases, foreclosure requires a finding of the ability and incentive to foreclose and of a competitive impact of the foreclosure. The guidelines note that also other non-coordinated effects may have to be considered, arising out of, e.g., the access to strategic information. The analysis of coordinated effects runs in parallel to that in case of horizontal concentrations.

Regarding **conglomerate** settings, the guidelines note that particularly foreclosure risks are of concern as non-coordinated effects. However, overall, the guidelines mostly refer back to the relevant passages on vertical mergers.

In both vertical and conglomerate settings, it is necessary to balance the prospective anticompetitive effects against **efficiencies**, which are considered more likely here than for horizontal mergers.

(b) U.S. law

In the U.S., the FTC and the DOJ jointly published new **Vertical Merger Guidelines** in 2020.[46] In 2021, however, the FTC withdrew the guidelines again, and instead published new draft guidelines (on horizontal/non-horizontal mergers) for comment in summer 2023.[47] The new Vertical Merger Guidelines were meant to replace the Non-Horizontal Merger Guidelines of 1984, which were outdated and not applied anymore in recent years anyway.[48] The new guidelines did **not** address **conglomerate** mergers specifically, although they included a conglomerate hypothetical example (Example 7).

---

[45] European Commission, Guidelines on the assessment of non-horizontal mergers under the Council Regulation on the control of concentrations between undertakings, OJ C 265 of 18 October 2008.

[46] DOJ/FTC, Vertical Merger Guidelines, 30 June 2020.

[47] FTC, press release of 15 September 2021; DOJ, statement of the same day, see: https://www.justice.gov/opa/pr/justice-department-issues-statement-vertical-merger-guidelines.

[48] DOJ, Non-Horizontal Merger Guidelines, 14 June 1984; available at: https://www.justice.gov/atr/page/file/1175141/download?splash=1. Further, see Draft FTC-DOJ Merger Guidelines for Public Comment, Matter No. P859910, 19 July 2023; available at: https://www.ftc.gov/system/files/ftc_gov/pdf/p859910draftmergerguidelines2023.pdf.

The new Vertical Merger Guidelines required **evidence of adverse competitive effects before a more detailed assessment** would be warranted. If such evidence existed, they foresaw a market definition and the calculation of market shares and concentration levels. Different from the Horizontal Merger Guidelines (but similar to the EU Guidelines), they then foresaw an **analysis of** the prospective **unilateral effects** of the transaction. Regarding **coordinated effects**, the guidelines required an assessment of the parties' ability to reach tacit agreements with the remaining competitors in the relevant market, to detect deviations and to punish cheating behavior.

This methodological approach would be consistent with agency practice. However, the FTC withdrew the guidelines because they *include[d] unsound economic theories that are unsupported by the law or market realities* (emphasis added). The FTC's reservations concerned particularly the treatment of efficiencies. It remains to be seen whether the FTC and the DOJ will update their merger guidance another time.

(c) Japanese law

The **JFTC merger guidelines** cover not only **horizontal** mergers but also **vertical and conglomerate mergers**. The concerns for these types of mergers include **foreclosure** by inhibiting access to input or customers (vertical mergers) or bundling products (conglomerate mergers). The JFTC assesses whether the merger will enhance the merging parties' capacity and incentive to engage in foreclosure by looking at the merging parties' market share, (in)existence of alternative trading partners, competitive constraints, such as a new entry and strong bargaining position of customers, and profitability of the products.[49]

Other theories of harm that the JFTC regularly assesses relate to competitive sensitive information. The merging parties may start using the information to gain a competitive advantage over their rivals. Alternatively, the shared information may facilitate the coordinated behaviors among the participants in the relevant markets. Such a possibility is considered in light of various factors including competitive

---

[49] JFTC, Guidelines to Application of the Antimonopoly Act Concerning Review of Business Combination (last amended 17 December 2019).

constraints. In all cases, procompetitive effects, financial status (failing company situation) and size of the market may be also considered.[50]

4. Comparison

According to the relevant guidelines, the assessment of merger transactions in the EU and the U.S. is overall **similar, with differences in nuances**. A comparison of the actual practice is also difficult. Divergent decisions may come about simply because the territorial reach of the merger control rules is limited to the relevant jurisdictions. Hence, differences in the market situation may lead to different assessment outcomes.

That being said, in individual cases in the past, there may have been **indications that EU merger control was more aggressive** (or interventionist) than U.S. merger control. Notably, in *GE/Honeywell*, the European Commission blocked a transaction that the DOJ had approved before. In its analysis of the case, the European Commission examined several theories of harm in relation to unilateral effects. The DOJ had admitted only one of these theories and had dismissed it. The DOJ found that GE's and Honeywell's product ranges were mostly complementary and did not find a risk of bundling that forecloses rivals from the market without any legitimate business purpose.[51]

Repeatedly, the European Commission has been concerned with **unilateral actions** by a dominant firm (exercise of dominant power) as such, whereas the U.S. agencies would be more likely to intervene if there had been a risk of collusion between competitors.[52] In Japan, both unilateral and coordinated effects would be considered beside one another, but either type of effect could justify a prohibition in the same way.

In any event, note that all relevant jurisdictions have undergone **changes in their enforcement approaches** since the *GE/Honeywell* merger, in the U.S. in particular since the appointment of a new FTC chair. The merger authorities cooperate more closely with each other. In addition, the EU Merger Regulation was recast in 2004. Thus, it is currently unclear whether the differences set out above are still relevant.

---

[50] *Ibid.*

[51] Rivers, General Electric/Honeywell merger: European Commission antitrust decision strikes a sour note, 9 ILSA Journal of international & Comparative Law 525, 529 (2003).

[52] See Ruffner, The Failed GE/Honeywell Merger: The Return of Portfolio — Effects Theory? 52 DePaul Law Review 1285, 1300 (2003).

Good to know: Merger control in EU Member States

The SIEC test was adopted also by many EU Member States after the entry into force of the current Merger Regulation (Reg. 139/2004). Nevertheless, the rules for the substantive assessment of merger transactions in the EU Member States can still diverge significantly from the assessment at EU level. In Germany, for instance, §36(1) GWB provides that only effects countervailing an SIEC on the relevant market are relevant, not effects on third markets.[53] Moreover, the provision rules out a prohibition of concentrations on *de-minimis* markets and restricts the possibility of prohibitions in press markets to allow the press to merge to better cope with competitive pressures on digital markets.[54] In addition, special "combination" and "multi-parent clauses" as well as a "holding clause" contain special definitions of the relevant undertakings for the purpose of merger control (an aspect that is handled in the European Commission's Consolidated Jurisdictional Notice at EU level).[55] In view of the broad definition of concentrations in §37(1) GWB, §37(2) moreover limits merger control where an existing combination is "not considerably" strengthened. Finally, German law allows for a ministerial authorization of blocked mergers in view of the advantages for economy as a whole or overriding public interest (§42 GWB).

---

5. Application of conduct-related rules

The existence of merger control is no legal obstacle to the application of the general rules to the relevant transactions, i.e., of Articles 101–102 TFEU in the EU or §1 and §2 Sherman Act in the U.S. According to the ECJ, however, Article 101 TFEU applies only to the conduct of undertakings that are — and remain — independent but not to transactions that

---

[53] §36(1)(2) No. 1 GWB. Thus, efficiencies accruing to merging undertakings only are not sufficient to potentially justify the transaction.
[54] §36(1)(2) Nos. 2–3 GWB. Note that, at the same time, turnover thresholds are tightened for press and broadcasting mergers for constitutional reasons (i.e., the interest in free speech). Note also that private broadcasting mergers are subject to additional control by the Media Concentration Commission for constitutional reasons.
[55] §36(2) and (3) GWB.

remove that independence. Article 102 TFEU requires a dominant position and, thus, does not apply to transactions that, if anything, only allow an undertaking concerned to acquire such a position. In any event, Articles 101–102 TFEU are not relevant for the assessment of the structure-related aspects of EU merger control in practice.[56]

On the other hand, Article 2(4) Regulation 139/2004 provides that the prospective relations between joint venture parents post-merger must be assessed under Article 101 TFEU in the context of the merger review procedure. Moreover, ancillary restraints (e.g., between joint venture parents and the joint venture) are excepted from Article 101(1) TFEU only if they are directly related and necessary to the relevant transaction.[57]

In **Japan**, the use of an acquisition to create a monopoly not meeting the notification thresholds could still violate the merger control rules under Chapter 4 of the AMA or be considered to constitute private monopolization.

V. Transnational open issues

The globalization and digitalization of market activities over the past decades have brought about new challenges to merger control. The basic assumption underlying the merger control rules is that one company's acquisitions of a controlling stake in another company may give rise to concerns if the transaction strengthens the position of the relevant companies in relevant markets. However, it has become apparent that examining individual stakeholdings or on individual relevant markets may be insufficient where multiple markets or stakeholdings are interconnected. In the following section, we discuss the challenges associated with platform dominance (Section 1) and indirect horizontal links (Section 2).

1. Platform dominance

It is stated above that economic platforms act as intermediaries between different groups of platform users, though not necessarily between

---

[56] In EU secondary law, see also Article 21(1) and Recital 7 of Reg. 139/2004; Article 3(3) Reg. 1/2003.

[57] See European Commission, Commission Notice on restrictions directly related and necessary to concentrations, OJ C 56, 5 March 2005, p. 2.

relevant markets.[58] This applies notably to online platforms but also to other platforms (e.g., farmers' markets, media outlets serving viewers/ readers and ad customers in parallel).[59] Platforms require an analysis going beyond the individual platform sides. For example, services on one platform side may be financed by another side (e.g., ad customers). In that case, the business model of the platform operator and its competitive reactions can be understood only if all platform sides are viewed together.

The fact that platforms intermediate between different user groups means that platforms can help overcome market failure. For example, when private individuals have a room or a free seat in their car to share, but advertising this room or car seat would require too much effort, platform operators such as Airbnb or Uber may step in to connect them with other individuals seeking those amenities. Thus, the intermediary services of platforms may even contribute to the emergence of additional markets.

However, the intermediary activities of platforms also mean that platforms become increasingly attractive depending on how many users they have. Thus, concentration tendencies may arise depending on network effects and other factors.[60] Concentration tendencies are not a problem as long as users are free to multi-home or switch to other service providers and as long as the position of the platform operator remains contestable by other service providers. Otherwise, market power may develop beyond concentration, for example, due to the platform operator's exclusive access to data.

The agency's approach to finding market power is still evolving. The European Commission appears to keep to its traditional approach for now. That is to say, the European Commission examines individual product markets, regardless of whether the relevant companies active in those markets are non-platform or platform companies. In platform cases, it takes network effects into account in view of each market that it has defined beforehand.[61] However, in its analysis, the European Commission does not proceed directly from the intermediary function of platform

---

[58] See Chapter 5, Section I.1.

[59] For an example where this has come up in practice, see *Oyama Agri Co-op*, JFTC, Cease and Desist Order, 10 December 2009, 56-II Shnketsu-shu 79 (Konohana Garten).

[60] See Chapter 5, Section I.1.

[61] European Commission, Decision of 3 October 2014, M.7217 — *Facebook/WhatsApp*; Decision of 17 December 2020, M.9660 — *Google/Fitbit*.

operators. Thus, the European Commission's approach comes along with a risk that platform-inherent concentration tendencies are being underestimated.

The German FCO, in contrast, has moved away from the traditional approach and takes a consolidated view of all platform sides where the following three conditions are met:

1. The product consists in connecting user groups.
2. The product requires users connected to each other to be connected also to the platform.
3. Also, the users view the product to require user connection.[62]

In the U.S., the Supreme Court's holding in *Ohio v. Amex* (16–1454), concerning a transaction platform, likewise points in the direction of assessing the platform as a whole. It remains to be seen how the holding will influence agency practice in the U.S.

In Japan, although the JFTC examines individual product markets, it takes network effects into account.

In some cases, platforms also give rise to issues that are difficult to handle even if the markets are defined in a way allowing for an appropriate assessment of the competitive position of the relevant platform. One information-related issue concerns product markets: It is controversial currently whether large platform operators engage in so-called **killing** (or killer) **acquisitions**, using exclusive data to identify and buy start-ups on future markets. In fact, the U.S. Congress report calling for reform of the U.S. antitrust rules in 2020 included examples of such practices.[63] Moreover, the FTC conducted its own survey of past Big Tech acquisitions.[64] The FTC found that Big Tech companies have indeed acquired many firms, but it did not make an assessment of whether the acquisitions

---

[62]See FCO, Decision of 22 October 2015, B6-57/15 — *Parship/Elitepartner*, §§71 ff., 129 ff.; Decision of 23 November 2017, B6-35/17 — *CTS/Eventim*, §§63 ff.

[63]Nadler *et al.*, Investigation of Competition in Digital Markets, Majority Staff Report, U.S. House of Representatives, 2020, e.g., pp. 261–267 (on Amazon's suppression of competition); accessible: https://democrats-judiciary.house.gov/uploadedfiles/competition_in_digital_markets.pdf.

[64]FTC, press release of 11 February 2020, and report dated 15 September 2021. The investigation covered 616 transactions, with the transaction value in the clear majority of cases (65%) ranging from USD 1 million to USD 25 million.

were anticompetitive. However, given the information advantages of Big Tech companies, it cannot be ruled out that these firms buy up start-ups that might otherwise become a competitive threat to their business in the future.

Another issue related to the notification thresholds are **geographic markets**. In several instances, platform operators have been able to monopolize regional markets or nascent start-up markets through acquisitions because no company involved had a turnover large enough to meet the turnover thresholds. In Europe, e.g., the markets for coach services and food delivery were monopolized in that way. As noted above, the JFTC clarified that the merger not satisfying notification criteria may be prohibited wherever it is likely to substantially restrict competition.

2. Indirect horizontal links ("common" and "cross" ownership)

Indirect horizontal links are an issue that has been discussed increasingly in recent years. However, the issue is perceived differently in the West and the East, and also the applicable rules differ.

(a) Situation in the U.S. and Europe

(1) The issue

In the U.S. and Europe, indirect horizontal links have given rise to discussion because large **financial investors**, mostly asset managers offering ETF funds, are investing in parallel in many companies reflecting the indexes that they reproduce or map with their funds. In some industry sectors, virtually all major suppliers are indirectly connected horizontally via the non-controlling shareholdings of those financial investors. Figure 1 shows the situation in the European/German road fuel markets.

In this situation, the **financial investors are typically rather passive**: If their funds require certain investments to reflect the composition of an index, they cannot acquire or sell shares because of their interests in particular companies. That said, the investors can still voice their satisfaction or dissatisfaction with company management, e.g., in meetings with management, in shareholder assemblies or through the media. In any event, researchers have observed a **dampening of competition** in various

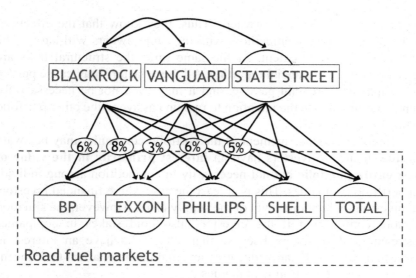

Figure 1.   Indirect horizontal links in German road fuel market.

Source: Monopolies Commission, Biennial Report XXII, Competition 2018, 2018, §421; illustration by John Weche.

industry areas where indirect horizontal links exist.[65] The reasons for this have not been identified conclusively yet.

Taking the economic principles recognized in the merger control guidelines as a basis, some researchers have argued that the financial investments produce anticompetitive **unilateral effects** on the relevant markets. This might be the case because the portfolio companies are aware that competitive advances may have negative effects on

---

[65]Newham, M./Seldeslachts, J./Banal-Estanol, A., Common Ownership and Market Entry: Evidence from the Pharmaceutical Industry, DIW Discussion Paper No. 1738, May 2018; Azar, J./Schmalz, M./Tecu, I., Reply to: "Common Ownership Does Not Have Anticompetitive Effects in the Airline Industry", SSRN Working Paper, 24 April 2018; Azar, J./Schmalz, M.C./Tecu, I., Anti-Competitive Effects of Common Ownership, Ross School of Business Working Paper No. 1235, April 2015; divergent: Dennis, P./Gerardi, K./ Schenone, C., Common Ownership Does Not Have Anticompetitive Effects in the Airline Industry, SSRN Working Paper, 5 February 2018. See also Monopolies Commission, Biennial Report XXI, Competition 2016, 2016, §§668 ff.; Biennial Report XXII, Competition 2018, 2018, §§413 ff. English excerpts from the Biennial Report XXII are available here: https://www.monopolkommission.de/images/HG22/Main_Report_XXII_ Common_Ownership.pdf.

competitors with the same owners. Thus, they know that the effects of their own actions on competitors with the same owners will have to be internalized to some extent. At the same time, the structural links are transparent due to financial reporting. All these factors may cause portfolio companies to remain passive, and it may even not be necessary for them to communicate the intention to remain passive to the other portfolio companies.

Moreover, the management of the portfolio companies may be aware that the financial investors have an **interest primarily in the value of their entire portfolio** but not necessarily in competition among individual portfolio companies. This is at least the case where financial investors are investing only at one level of the supply chain. However, the situation is more complicated if the investors also hold stakes in companies upstream or downstream because then, they also have an interest in upstream and downstream value creation, and this may affect their incentives *vis-à-vis* the portfolio companies.

Finally, it is difficult to say how the **fiduciary duties** of shareholders, members of management and of the supervisory board play out in the individual case: Their fiduciary duties require both financial investors and the representatives of portfolio companies to act in the interest of individual companies. Usually, this means that companies will be pushed to compete. However, where indirect horizontal links produce a market structure susceptible to collusion, then fiduciary duties may actually reinforce the trend not to compete.

In addition, researchers have also pointed to possible **coordinated effects** at both investor and portfolio levels. At portfolio level, the indirect horizontal links improve market transparency because portfolio companies may profit from the in-depth market knowledge of professional diversified investors. In addition, at both levels, the expectations of competitor behavior could play an important role (this may also be seen as a unilateral effect).

(2) The rules

If indirect horizontal links contribute to a **lessening of competition** at portfolio level and potentially also to **coordinated effects** at investor level, the problem is that the existing competition rules are ill-suited to deal with the problems.

As a starting point, indirect horizontal links are a structural issue, which means that one could try to handle the problems using merger control instruments. However, **merger control does not capture the relevant scenarios**: Regarding the market effects, the theories of harm mentioned above are not based on individual structural links but on their cumulative effects. This certainly does not exclude applying those theories of harm when individual stock acquisitions make the market tip. However, when this particular situation is about to arise is an open question beforehand. It is also unclear how much in advance authorities need to look in their prospective analysis in order to correctly identify the developments that may be relevant under the theories of harm mentioned above.

In addition, the individual **structural links are typically too weak** (e.g., shareholdings < 10%) to confer control (*decisive influence*).[66] It is also an open question whether several investors exercise "joint control" in the given scenarios because joint control, at least in the EU, requires a *common understanding [of] commercial policy* of the target. A shared profit interest of the financial investors would not be enough.

Further, horizontal coordination at the level of either investors or portfolio undertakings is **not sufficient to trigger notification requirements** under the merger rules. Horizontal coordination may certainly be caught by Articles 101 and 102 TFEU. But this would be dealing with mere symptoms because it is less the coordination that is the problem and more the structural links providing the incentives to coordinate.

For these reasons, the application of competition and antitrust rules in the given scenarios is viewed increasingly skeptically. That being said, capital markets and corporate policy measures may be implemented to increase the **transparency obligations** for institutional investors further. This would allow one to uncover and better understand the nature and the extent of the problems.[67] Additional measures could then follow later on.

---

[66]Note that German merger control reaches farther because a "competitively significant interest" is sufficient to trigger notification requirements (§37(1) No. 4GWB); see Section III.1.b in this chapter. However, the "competitively significant interest" has not been applied to indirect horizontal links as discussed in this section yet.

[67]See, e.g., Article 3g Dir. 2017/828/EU and §134b of the German Stock Corporations Act *(Aktiengesetz — AktG)*.

(b) Situation in Japan

In Japan, *keiretsu* are characterized by minority shareholdings, which establish indirect horizontal links between subsidiaries operating in multiple relevant markets. These corporate structures are not perceived to give rise to the passivity problems discussed in the U.S. and the EU. However, it has been observed that financial investors holding shares in firms with complementary business activities may try to use the groups to **secure themselves a monopoly** in the markets of their portfolio companies. This strategy would be similar to the one pursued by a private equity investor in the EU case of *CVC/Lenzing*.[68]

Acquisitions of 20% of shares or important assets trigger a merger notification obligation in Japan. This could, theoretically, become relevant also in cases giving rise to common ownership concerns. Moreover, note that Japan has special rules on **excessive concentration of economic power** (Article 9(1) AMA). This rule is intended to prevent the re-emergence of *zaibatsu*, large-scale financial conglomerates, and companies with influential positions allowing them to control leading companies in a considerable number of interrelated major business fields.[69]

VI. Remedies

If a concentration is to be blocked for competitive reasons, the parties may offer remedies/commitments in order to obtain clearance (EU) or to avoid an injunction (U.S./Japan). In these cases, in the **EU**, the **clearance will be conditioned** upon the implementation of remedies in line with what the parties to the transaction have offered. In the **U.S. and Japan**, a similar result may be achieved where the competition authorities settle through a **consent decree (DOJ) or a consent order (FTC)**, or where the **JFTC** notifies the parties that it intends **not to implement any measures** based on the notified remedies. The remedies can, in principle, be structural or behavioral. However, the agencies generally show a strong preference for structural remedies inasmuch as behavioral remedies usually cannot guarantee that the harm to the market structure brought about by

---

[68] See European Commission, Decision of 17 October 2001, M.2187 — CVC/Lenzing.
[69] See Wakui, Antimonopoly Law, 2nd ed., 2019, pp. 135–136 for details.

the transaction will be neutralized. In Germany, the Competition Act even excludes behavioral remedies as a matter of principle.[70]

A number of agencies competent for merger control have issued **guidelines** to clarify which remedies they will accept.[71] Thus, e.g., the European Commission considers divestitures or other structural remedies to be acceptable. **Divestiture is the preferred remedy** and generally requires the transfer of a viable, standalone business to another company, potentially with a non-reacquisition clause. The other company may be considered to be a suitable buyer if it is independent of and unconnected to parties to the transaction, has sufficient resources and does not engage in activities creating a risk of new competition problems. If obstacles exist, the parties to the transaction may only implement the transaction after the European Commission has accepted the **buyer up-front** (prior to clearance). The European Commission may alternatively require them to even enter into a binding agreement already during the European Commission merger procedure (**"fix-it-first"**) to obtain clearance. The carve-out of non-viable business units is acceptable only in exceptional cases. Moreover, the divestiture of licenses, brands, etc. is usually acceptable only in addition to a business divestiture. If the preferred divestiture option does not succeed, the parties will be required to make an alternative commitment involving **"crown jewels"** (i.e., assets of a particular strategic value).

Other structural remedies deemed acceptable by the European Commission involve, e.g., the granting of access to a key infrastructure or to input products on non-discriminatory terms, if such access allows third parties to build up a viable competitive position in the market.

---

[70] §40(3)(2) GWB.

[71] See, e.g., European Commission, Commission notice on remedies acceptable under Council Regulation (EC) No. 139/2004 and under Commission Regulation (EC) No. 802/2004, OJ C 267, 22 October 2008, p. 1; Explanatory note — Best Practice Guidelines: The Commission's Model Texts for Divestiture Commitments and the Trustee Mandate under the European Commission Merger Regulation, 5 December 2013; available at: https://ec.europa.eu/competition-policy/system/files/2021-03/best_practice_commitments_trustee_en.pdf.

Chapter 8

State Measures

It is not only private actors that can interfere with competition. States can do the same and even more effectively. The purpose of State interference can be to **regulate markets for other reasons than to protect competition**, such as to remedy market failure (e.g., in the network industries or the financial industry), to protect individual rights (e.g., free speech) or for both of these aspects (e.g., in health insurance). Moreover, the State may **pursue objectives** that are not or only indirectly related to the economy, e.g., cultural or sustainability objectives. In all these cases, when States interfere with functioning markets, a compromise must be found between the protection of competition and the relevant other objectives.

The **approaches** of the competition jurisdictions covered in this book to State interference with the markets **differ considerably**. Moreover, the relevant scenarios are very diverse. Therefore, this chapter only describes some important concepts.

I. EU law: Measures by the EU *v.* measures by Member States

1. The law

Article 106 TFEU

1. *In the case of public undertakings and undertakings to which Member States grant special or exclusive rights, Member States shall neither enact nor maintain in force any measure contrary to the rules*

contained in the Treaties, in particular to those rules provided for in Article 18 and Articles 101 to 109.

2.   Undertakings entrusted with the operation of services of general economic interest or having the character of a revenue-producing monopoly shall be subject to the rules contained in the Treaties, in particular to the rules on competition, in so far as the application of such rules does not obstruct the performance, in law or in fact, of the particular tasks assigned to them. The development of trade must not be affected to such an extent as would be contrary to the interests of the Union.

3.   The Commission shall ensure the application of the provisions of this Article and shall, where necessary, address appropriate directives or decisions to Member States.

Article 107 TFEU

1.   Save as otherwise provided in the Treaties, any aid granted by a Member State or through State resources in any form whatsoever which distorts or threatens to distort competition by favouring certain undertakings or the production of certain goods shall, in so far as it affects trade between Member States, be incompatible with the internal market.

2.   The following shall be compatible with the internal market:
   (a)   aid having a social character, granted to individual consumers, provided that such aid is granted without discrimination related to the origin of the products concerned;
   (b)   aid to make good the damage caused by natural disasters or exceptional occurrences;
   (c)   aid granted to the economy of certain areas of the Federal Republic of Germany affected by the division of Germany, in so far as such aid is required in order to compensate for the economic disadvantages caused by that division. Five years after the entry into force of the Treaty of Lisbon, the Council, acting on a proposal from the Commission, may adopt a decision repealing this point.

3.   The following may be considered to be compatible with the internal market:
   (a)   aid to promote the economic development of areas where the standard of living is abnormally low or where there is serious underemployment, and of the regions referred to in Article 349, in view of their structural, economic and social situation;

(b) *aid to promote the execution of an important project of common European interest or to remedy a serious disturbance in the economy of a Member State;*

(c) *aid to facilitate the development of certain economic activities or of certain economic areas, where such aid does not adversely affect trading conditions to an extent contrary to the common interest;*

(d) *aid to promote culture and heritage conservation where such aid does not affect trading conditions and competition in the Union to an extent that is contrary to the common interest;*

(e) *such other categories of aid as may be specified by decision of the Council on a proposal from the Commission.*

2. General notes

The **European Treaties** not only regulate competition among companies, but they include also differentiated rules for state interference with markets. This is because also state measures can harm the development of the EU's internal market.

Notably, to make sure that private market participants are not hindered in their cross-border activities in the EU, Articles 34 ff. TFEU protect fundamental **market freedoms *vis-à-vis* the Member States**.[1] These freedoms apply whenever Member States use sovereign measures to restrict the free movement of goods, persons, services and capital. Moreover, they apply in parallel to Articles 101 ff. TFEU in conjunction with the **loyalty principle** of Article 4(3) TEU, where Member States resort to sovereign measures (e.g., statutes) that impose a conduct on companies that would have to be considered anticompetitive if the companies were free to decide on that conduct themselves.[2] In such case, the sovereign measure may itself be regarded unlawful if the interference with the market is not justified by overriding reasons of public policy.

In cases where sovereign measures leave the market participants **leeway to act**, the Member States generally do not violate the loyalty

---

[1] These freedoms also apply *vis-à-vis* the EU, but they are practically relevant mostly in relation to the Member States.

[2] Example: Statutes requiring publishers to fix a resale price for books and requiring book sellers to adhere to that resale price. See also ECJ, Judgment of 21 September 1988, *Van Eycke/ASPA* (267/86, ECR 1988 p. 4769), ECLI:EU:C:1988:427, regarding Member State-induced cartels.

principle **by imposing regulation in the public interest** of companies. However, to the extent that the market participants are not bound by regulation, they are able to engage in independent behavior. This means that also regulated companies are regarded as **"undertakings"** for the purposes of Articles 101 and 102 TFEU and held accountable under these provisions.[3] This is true irrespective of whether the regulated companies are wholly private owned or controlled by the state. Moreover, Articles 101 and 102 TFEU apply even where a state regulator has granted regulatory permission with regard to the company behavior.[4]

In addition to these general observations and rules, the EU Treaties include two sets of competition-related provisions that go beyond Articles 101 and 102 TFEU and merit a closer look. One is Article 106 TFEU, which deals with **State-Owned Enterprises** (SOEs) and companies entrusted with the provision of services of general interest (Section 3). The other is Article 107 ff. TFEU, which deals with Member State measures of **economic aid** to the benefit of individual undertakings or production sectors (Section 4). In both cases, the Member States and not the relevant companies are the legal addressees of the Treaty provisions.

3. SOEs and companies entrusted with services of general economic interest

Article 106 TFEU contains two provisions that can apply separately from each other. Therefore, it makes sense to deal with them in two separate text sections. Whereas **Article 106(1) TFEU** leads a shadowy existence in practice, **Article 106(2) TFEU** has been invoked in numerous cases where companies were charged with a violation of Article 101 or Article 102 TFEU. In these instances, the companies claimed that they were exempt from the competition rules under Article 106(2) TFEU.

(a) SOEs

Article 106(1) TFEU deals with all measures that Member States take in relation to public undertakings and undertakings to which they grant

---

[3] See ECJ, Judgment of 14 October 2010, *Deutsche Telekom/Commission* (C-280/08 P, ECR 2010 p. I-9555) ECLI:EU:C:2010:603, §§80 ff., 157 ff.

[4] ECJ, Judgment of 17 February 2011, *TeliaSonera Sverige* (C-52/09, ECR 2011 p. I-527) ECLI:EU:C:2011:83; Judgment of 14 October 2010, *Deutsche Telekom/Commission* (C-280/08 P, ECR 2010 p. I-9555) ECLI:EU:C:2010:603.

special or exclusive rights. In practice, the provision is applied mostly in relation to public infrastructure operators (e.g., port operators or vertically integrated railroad companies), development banks and similar market players.

In the relevant cases, Member States are prohibited from taking **measures contrary to any provision in the Treaties**. This includes, but is not limited to, Articles 101 and 102 TFEU. The objective is to ensure the *"equality of opportunity between the individual economic operators"*.[5] Thus, a measure that may fall foul of Article 106(1) TFEU may be any measure that creates unequal conditions of competition between undertakings, thereby affecting the "structure of the market".[6]

This is relevant **particularly** when the undertaking in question enjoys a **dominant position**. The fact alone that a Member State has created an undertaking in a dominant position does not violate Article 106(1) TFEU. However, according to the case law of the European Court of Justice, a Member State violates Article 106(1) in conjunction with Article 102 TFEU if the Member State creates a situation in which (i) *the undertaking [...] merely by exercising the preferential rights conferred upon it, is led to abuse its dominant position* or (ii) *those rights are liable to create a situation in which that undertaking is led to commit such abuses.*[7] This could e.g., be the case where a Member State obliges an SOE controlling an essential infrastructure to favor the subsidiaries using the infrastructure, and at the same time neutralizes incentives for the SOE to provide services to other users.

(b) Services of general economic interest

Article 106(2) TFEU limits the scope of application of the European competition rules when undertakings are entrusted with the provision of services in the general economic interest. The provision must be seen in the **context with other Treaty provisions** dealing with such services

---

[5] ECJ, Judgment of 17 July 2014, *Commission / DEI* (C-553/12 P) ECLI:EU:C:2014:2083, §§43–44.
[6] *Ibid.*, para. 46.
[7] *Ibid.*, §41.

(in general, but also, notably, *vis-à-vis* public broadcasting).[8] It mainly **defines the Member State competences** to pursue public policy goals via entrusted undertakings in relation to the EU's competition competences.

The provision limits the application of the EU competition rules where the **following conditions** are met: (i) an undertaking (ii) provides services of general economic interest, (iii) after having been entrusted with that task by a public authority. Moreover, (iv) an exception to the competition rules must be necessary because otherwise the fulfillment of the assigned special task would be endangered.[9] Finally, (v) the granted exception may not have effects on trade in the internal market that are contrary to the Union interest.

Out of these requirements, the fourth one is particularly controversial. This holds particularly for the **burden of proof**, which, according to the ECJ, lies with the Member States.[10] Moreover, the ECJ has developed special rules to apply it in the context of bundled services, and in relation to the compensation for the provision of services.[11]

In any event, since Article 106(2) TFEU provides for an **exception** from the competition provisions of the EU Treaties, the provision is to be **construed narrowly**.[12] Otherwise, it would allow the Member States to circumvent the competition rules by simply claiming that they consider an exemption to be necessary.

4. State aid/subsidies

The internal market in the EU is not only at risk of being fragmented through State measures that are imposed with sovereign force.

---

[8]Article 14 TFEU, Protocols 26, 29 to the Treaties.

[9]ECJ, Judgment of 19 May 1993, *Corbeau* (C-320/91, ECR 1993 p. I-2533), ECLI:EU:C:1993:198, §16.

[10]ECJ, Judgment of 13 May 2003, *Commission/Spain* (C-463/00, ECR 2003 p. I-4581) ECLI:EU:C:2003:272, §82; different: GC, Judgment of 12 February 2008, *BUPA and others/Commission* (T-289/03, ECR 2008 p. II-81) ECLI:EU:T:2008:29, §§220–221, 266.

[11]See ECJ, Judgment of 19 May 1993, *Corbeau* (C-320/91, ECR 1993 p. I-2533), ECLI:EU:C:1993:198, §§17, 19; Judgment of 21 September 1999, *Albany* (C-67/96, ECR 1999 p. I-5751) ECLI:EU:C:1999:430, §§119–120, and Judgment of 24 July 2003, *Altmark Trans and Regierungspräsidium Magdeburg* (C-280/00, ECR 2003 p. I-7747) ECLI:EU:C:2003:415, §§87–93 respectively.

[12]ECJ, Judgment of 23 October 1997, *Commission/France* (C-159/94, ECR 1997 p. I-5815) ECLI:EU:C:1997:501, §53.

Its development can also be harmed through State measures that benefit individual companies economically but not others. EU law traditionally includes rules to deal with economic aid granted by the EU Member States **(Subsection a)**. Given the increasing importance of third-country investors in the EU, EU legislature recently decided to submit economic aid granted by third countries to a similar review regime in the future **(Subsection b)**.[13] However, at least regarding the already existing State aid law, it is necessary to distinguish the rules and their application as the enforcement is far less stringent than one might think **(Subsection c)**.

(a) EU Member State aid

Articles 107 ff. TFEU are intended to protect the EU internal market against **fragmentation and distortions** caused by economic support measures which the Member States use to selectively favor certain undertakings or the production of certain goods and which distort competition. State aid control is *ex ante* **control**, requiring Member States to file a notification with the European Commission, which then decides whether the measures indeed amount to state aid and whether it is compatible with the EU single market.[14]

However, a State aid notification must only be filed if the relevant measure meets certain criteria set out in Article 107(1) TFEU. In particular, the measure must **provide an economic benefit** and in that regard go beyond an investment that a market investor would make who expects a return on the investment (so-called market investor test).[15] Moreover, the measure must **favor selected undertakings or the production of selected goods**. Thus, policy measures of general application do not trigger State aid control (e.g., benefits under the corporate or tax rules for all companies). It does not matter that those general measures may fragment the internal market as well. However, even tax measures can meet the selectivity criterion if these measures benefit selected

---

[13]Council, Meeting no. 3913 and press release of 28 November 2022; EU Parliament, Decision of 10 November 2022, 1st reading, T9-0379/2022.

[14]See Article 108(3) TFEU on the notification requirement.

[15]See European Commission, Commission Notice on the notion of State aid as referred to in Article 107(1) of the Treaty on the Functioning of the European Union, OJ C 262 of 9 July 2016, p. 1 (Notice on the notion of State aid), §§73 ff.

companies.[16] Further, also indirect advantages may constitute State aid, e.g., when the measure is a State guarantee provided to a bank and if the bank then grants a loan to a company.[17] Lastly, the advantage must generally be granted **out of state resources**, i.e., out of funds directly or indirectly controlled by the relevant Member State (and not by anyone else).[18] However, under these conditions, even a measure such as a public statement by a minister may constitute State aid.[19]

When a financial measure is deemed to constitute State aid, it can generally be presumed to also **distort competition** under Article 107(1) TFEU.[20] For other measures, the distortion must be established in the individual case. In addition, the aid must affect trade in the internal market.[21] However, even if the relevant measure meets these conditions, it may still be found to be compatible with the internal market. Articles 107(2) and (3) TFEU set out criteria under which measures meeting the conditions of Article 107(1) TFEU can be justified. The criteria for justification have been specified in more detail in a **General Block Exemption Regulation** and numerous guidelines for measures of a specific type (State guarantees, fiscal aid and export credit insurance), other aid measures not limited to individual sectors ("horizontal aid") or measures adopted to support undertakings in individual sectors.[22]

While the European Commission is reviewing State aid measures, the Member States are not allowed to grant the aid **(implementation suspension)**. If the European Commission finds a State aid measure not to be

---

[16]GC, Judgment of 8 June 2022, *United Kingdom/Commission* (T-363/19 and T-456/19) ECLI:EU:T:2022:349, §§69 ff.; Judgment of 15 July 2020, *Ireland/Commission* (T-778/16) ECLI:EU:T:2020:338 (appeal pending: C-465/20).

[17]See ECJ, Judgment of 8 December 2011, *Residex Capital IV* (C-275/10, ECR 2011 p. I-13043) ECLI:EU:C:2011:814 on this issue: case-by-case assessment *re* the beneficiary necessary.

[18]ECJ, Judgment of 28 March 2019, *Germany/Commission* (C-405/16 P) ECLI:EU:C:2019:268, §§57 ff.

[19]ECJ, Judgment of 19 March 2013, *Bouygues and Bouygues Télécom/Commission and others* (C-399/10 P and C-401/10 P) ECLI:EU:C:2013:175, §§100 ff.; however, see also Judgment of 30 November 2016, *Commission/France and Orange* (C-486/15 P) ECLI:EU:C:2016:912, §§142–143.

[20]European Commission, Commission Notice on the notion of State aid (fn. 15), §187.

[21]See European Commission, Commission Notice on the notion of State aid (fn. 15), §§190 ff.

[22]See: https://ec.europa.eu/competition-policy/state-aid/legislation_en.

compatible with the EU single market, any aid already granted has to be repaid to the relevant Member State. National principles to protect legitimate expectations on the side of the recipient cannot be invoked to negate the repayment obligation.

(b) Third-country subsidy rules

The globalization of world trade has given rise to business connections that had not existed before. These include business connections between countries with very diverse economic systems. Notably, companies from the EU have started to expand their business in **China** significantly and EU Member States have opened their markets to Chinese investors. However, China is a "Socialist Market Economy with Chinese Characteristics", i.e., it pursues a hybrid economic model that contains both state-economy and market-economy elements.[23] In addition, state measures to boost the home economy have become popular also in countries with systems closer to the EU system in the current economic downturn, for example, in the **U.S.**[24]

Traditionally, it is the task of **anti-dumping and anti-subsidy instruments** (at EU level) to protect European companies against third-country measures favoring third-country rivals and the task of **foreign direct-investment rules** (chiefly at Member State level) to protect the interests of EU Member States by safeguarding infrastructures and businesses that are critical for national security. These instruments are recognized globally, and particularly the anti-dumping and anti-subsidy instruments have been shaped in accordance with World Trade Organization (WTO) principles. However, they are based on reciprocity concepts. Thus, especially when anti-dumping instruments are used, the protection of European undertakings in terms of European industrial policy is in the foreground and not the protection of competition in the EU internal market. Thus, anti-dumping measures dampen price competition from foreign suppliers. However, neither anti-dumping nor anti-subsidy instruments fully neutralize the competitive advantages that foreign competitors have if they benefit from third-country state support. Moreover, pursuant to the **WTO agreements**, EU anti-dumping and anti-subsidy rules cover only goods but not subsidized company takeovers or services.

---

[23] See Monopolies Commission, Biennial Report XXIII, Competition 2020, 1st ed. 2020, §§559 ff.
[24] See notably H.R.5376 — Inflation Reduction Act of 2022.

The EU, therefore, perceives a **gap** in the protection of the internal market. This gap exists essentially because Member State support to selected undertakings and production sectors is subject to EU State aid control, whereas comparable third-country measures are not. Thus, the European Commission proposed a regulation regarding third-country subsidies, which was enacted as **Regulation (EU) 2022/2065** in December 2022 and is meant to protect the level playing field in the EU internal market.[25] The regulation sets out when the EU assumes the existence of a foreign subsidy potentially distorting the EU internal market.[26] In its general rules, it also provides for a balancing of the distortive effects and any associated benefits that may be relevant to the EU interest.[27] The regulation includes three sub-instruments to deal with third-country subsidies *ex officio* and in the context of company takeovers and procurement proceedings (where the subsidy is being passed on to the company seller or the contracting State).[28] In the latter cases, the subsidy has to be notified if it meets certain thresholds. The regulation also includes various procedural provisions that are intended to make the new instruments effective and to align them with existing rules (especially merger control and procurement rules).[29]

It is still **unclear** whether the new instrument is **compatible with the WTO rules**. In any event, it is high on the political agenda, together with additional instruments to strengthen the traditional trade rules (especially an "International Procurement Instrument" to ensure reciprocity in procurement standards).[30] The new regulation on third-country subsidies applies from 12 July 2023, its notification requirements from 12 October 2023.[31]

---

[25] Regulation (EU) 2022/2560 of the European Parliament and of the Council of 14 December 2022 on foreign subsidies distorting the internal market, OJ L 330 of 23 December 2022, p. 1.

[26] Articles 1–5.

[27] Article 6.

[28] Article 9 ff., 19 ff., 27 ff.

[29] See Article 7-8, 34 ff. in addition to the procedural rules concerning the individual instruments.

[30] See Regulation (EU) 2022/1031 of the European Parliament and of the Council of 23 June 2022 on the access of third-country goods and services to the Union's public procurement and concession markets and goods and services to the public procurement and concession markets and procedures supporting negotiations on access of Union economic operators, goods and services to the public procurement markets of third countries, OJ L 173 of 30 June 2022, p. 1.

[31] Articles 54(2), (4).

(c) **Differences between the State aid rules and their applications**

EU State aid law is **in theory stringent** and allows the control of all distortions brought about by Member State measures providing economic advantages to selected economic entities or production sectors and distorting competition in the internal market. In practice, however, it is increasingly regarded as toothless. This is for several reasons:

- State aid law only addresses Member State actions distorting competition but **not EU actions**. EU interventions in the market are mostly subject only to very general limitations set out in the Treaties or in the frameworks providing for particular measures. Thus, EU measures can be used rather easily to circumvent State aid law.
- The EU has created so-called **temporary frameworks** to allow for flexibility in the application of State aid law regarding crisis measures. These temporary frameworks were created for financial crisis aid and COVID-related aid so far.[32] Since the start of the financial crisis in 2008, they have been softened more and more and may also have contributed to the significant softening of EU interventions against State aid in general.
- The **exceptions** provided for in Articles 107(2) and (3) TFEU have traditionally been interpreted very broadly to account for Member State "discretion" in the shaping of their economic policies. In times of crisis, this generous approach has been broadened more and more.

Nevertheless, State aid law remains necessary. The **EU Member States follow divergent traditions**. In several Member States, economic policy is still much less competition-friendly and more industrial-policy oriented (protectionist) than, e.g., in the U.S. This gives rise to continuing threats of fragmentation of the internal market. In other Member States, outright state corruption and a lack of rule enforcement (e.g., when it comes to tax equality principles or to anti-money laundering rules)

---

[32] See European Commission, State Aid Temporary Rules established in response to the economic and financial crisis, listed here: https://ec.europa.eu/competition-policy/sectors/financial-services/legislation_en; Communication from the Commission Temporary Framework for State aid measures to support the economy in the current COVID-19 outbreak 2020/C 91 I/01, OJ C 91I, 20 March 2020, p. 1.

contribute to competition distortions and hinder the development of the internal market.

II. U.S. law

In the U.S., the law does not contain specific rules to further the development of the competition in the market and to protect it against governmental interference. However, a question to be answered also in U.S. law is what the **relationship** is **between regulation and the antitrust rules**. Furthermore, the relationship between the **federal antitrust law and the states** presents complicated issues where each of the 50 U.S. states holds sovereign power. Thus, a distinction must be made between, on the one hand, the relationship between federal antitrust law and federal regulation and, on the other hand, the relationship between federal antitrust law and the action of states.

1. Antitrust law and federal regulation

Federal antitrust law and federal regulation are of the **same legal rank**. Thus, antitrust law does not trump federal regulation nor does federal regulation limit the application of the antitrust rules. However, federal antitrust law can help ensure that regulation achieves its objectives, make markets perform more competitively and step in where the regulatory oversight over private conduct is insufficient.[33]

The relationship between antitrust law and federal regulation is clear if **regulation expressly exempts** matters from the antitrust rules or expressly submits them to additional antitrust review. Where no express provisions exist, the question must be answered whether it is justified to assume an **implied exemption**. The basic position toward implied exemption is as follows: *Repeal is to be regarded as implied only if necessary to make [regulation] work, and, even then, only to the minimum extent necessary.*[34] The Supreme Court also stated the following: *Implied antitrust immunity is not favored, and can be justified only by a convincing showing of clear repugnancy between the antitrust laws and the*

---

[33] Hovenkamp, Federal Antitrust Policy, 6th ed., 2020, p. 899.
[34] *Silver v. New York Stock Exchange*, 373 U.S. 341, 357 (1963).

regulatory system.[35] Indeed, the Supreme Court has held that the securities law implicitly precludes the application of the antitrust laws at last as a practical matter due to the risk that the two regimes *would produce conflicting [...] standards of conduct.*[36] An open question to date is whether it is sufficient that regulation foresees an exemption or whether there also has to be effective regulatory oversight.[37] Moreover, note that courts are allowed to stay an action while a federal regulatory agency makes its initial determinations ("primary jurisdiction").[38] This, however, is only a procedural rule and does not constitute a genuine antitrust exemption.

Assuming that antitrust law is generally applicable in regulated industries, another issue is **to what extent** the relevant company may be held **liable for its conduct** if that conduct takes place within an environment governed by regulation and not only by market forces. Thus, it is conceivable that regulation gives the regulated companies an exclusive right to deal with consumers and that the regulation also includes rules on prices. However, even where rates are fixed by regulation, the relevant company retains incentives to increase its market share as long as regulation leaves a margin to that company, and these remaining incentives may still give rise to anticompetitive behavior ($\rightarrow$ risk of monopolization). Nevertheless, U.S. antitrust law is more deferent to regulation than EU law.[39] That is, according to the Supreme Court, rates approved by an agency cannot be subjected to a private claim for treble damages.[40]

2. The state action doctrine

As noted earlier, U.S. **federal antitrust law** is meant to **govern interstate commerce** based on U.S. Constitution Article 1, Section 8, Cl. 3. The States retain the power to regulate commerce and economic activities **within each state** and to enact their **own antitrust laws**. Although most states have enacted laws similar to the federal antitrust law, the state

---

[35] *United States v. NASD, Inc.*, 422 U.S. 694, 719 (1975).
[36] *Credit Suisse Securities (USA) LLC v. Billing*, 551 U.S. 264 (2007).
[37] Hovenkamp, Federal Antitrust Policy, 6th ed., 2020, p. 905.
[38] *Far East Conference v. United States*, 342 U.S. 570, 574–575 (1952).
[39] See Section I.2 in this chapter.
[40] *Keogh v. Chicago & Northwestern Rwy*, 260 U.S. 156 (1922).

laws are not necessarily preempted even if they differ from federal antitrust law. State laws that tighten antitrust liability are regularly permitted. This was the basis on which several states allowed indirect purchaser claims through *"Illinois Brick* repealer" statutes. In contrast, the federal rules preempt state statutes which mandate conduct that constitutes a *per se* violation. Where the state statute in question mandates conduct that is subject to the rule of reason, it is not preempted. The relationship between federal and state antitrust laws is assessed in light of provisions of the U.S. Constitution and several constitutional principles including the Supremacy Clause (U.S. Constitution Article 6, Cl. 2).

Outside the federal-state antitrust matter, a different set of issues arises where the **state acts as sovereign**, which the *Sherman Act did not undertake to prohibit.*[41] Private parties are also immunized when they merely perform the state's regulatory function. Under the state action doctrine, a non-state entity's action is immunized from the antitrust prohibitions provided that (i) a *clearly articulated* state regulatory policy authorizes the relevant conduct and (ii) the authorized conduct is subject to active supervision.[42] Authorization must come directly or indirectly from the state. Hence, municipal action or authorization may benefit from the state action doctrine only if the municipality itself has been authorized by the state.[43] This authorization must be express.[44] As a rule, the authority authorizing the conduct is considered the supervisor. In any event, supervision must be independent of the regulated conduct. It must also be effective to ensure that the regulated companies — provided that regulation leaves them some independence to act at all — act in accordance with state policy.[45]

III. Japanese law

The AMA is **only applicable to the enterprise and not to the action of government** unless the government operates business activities within the

[41] *Parker v. Brown*, 317 U.S. 341, 352 (1943).
[42] *Cal. Liquor Dealers v. Midcal Aluminum, Inc.*, 445 U.S. 97 (1980); *Parker v. Brown*, 317 U.S. 341 (1943).
[43] *Community Communications v. City of Boulder*, 455 U.S. 40 (1982).
[44] *Southern Motor Carriers Rate Conference, Inc., et al. v. United States*, 471 U.S. 48 (1985).
[45] *N.C. State Bd. of Dental Exam'rs v. FTC*, 574 U.S. 494 (2015).

meaning of AMA Article 2(1). There are laws, regulations and other governmental activities that restrict competition. Where such laws and regulations exist, or are expected to be implemented, the JFTC tries to coordinate and discuss the matter with responsible ministers and regulators, without guarantee of success. Occasionally over-restrictive legal rules and regulations, which are not reasonably necessary to achieve the stated aim, are struck down by the court as a breach of the Constitution of Japan guaranteeing freedom of occupation and business. This is the only formal way to remedy the government's anticompetitive regulation and legislation. No enterprise is liable under the AMA for actions in compliance with legislation or regulation in general.

Where there is no clear legal ground for the government's actions, the situation is more complicated. This is particularly relevant to **administrative guidance that is not based on clearly articulated laws**. The Supreme Court stated that such advice may be deemed legitimate where it is necessary and constitutes an appropriate means to achieve certain goals, unless such advice is incompatible with the goal of the AMA, namely protecting the interests of the general consumer and democratic, wholesome growth of national economy. The Court went on to rule that enterprises are **not liable** for their actions where they merely aim to cooperate with the government's initiative and comply with legitimate advice.[46]

Meanwhile, where a government official **aids or causes an enterprise to engage in AMA violations** in breach of its general duty to comply with law, the aided enterprise cannot be **immunized**. There is also special legislation prohibiting them from being involved in bid rigging,[47] under which the JFTC may request the relevant minister or governor of the local government to take action to eliminate such involvement. Once such a request is made, the minister or the governor must also bring a civil suit against the official to recover damages caused by their gross negligence and implement disciplinary actions. The criminal liability may be imposed upon the relevant governmental officials under the special law.[48]

---

[46] Supreme Court, 24 February 1984, 38-IV Keishu 1287 (Oil Cartel [Criminal]).

[47] Act on Elimination and Prevention of Involvement in Bid Rigging, etc. and Punishments for Acts by Employees that Harm Fairness of Bidding, etc., Act No. 101 of 2002, last amended by Act No. 68 of 2022.

[48] *Ibid.*, Article 8.

IV. Comparison

In all three jurisdictions covered in this book, the courts recognize certain **limitations to applying antitrust and competition rules to state measures**. The EU Treaties include a number of express provisions that deal with EU Member State interference with the market. They all acknowledge that **governmental action must be distinguished from market behavior** and that government action only regulates market behavior (although this does not exclude the possibility that the state may also act as a market participant in other situations).

The jurisdictions diverge, however, on the **relationship between regulation and competition law**. While all three jurisdictions exempt regulated conduct from liability under their competition laws, the authorities and courts are the ones who determine which rules apply in the individual case. The factors militating in favor of an exemption can be general interests distinct from the interest in free and undistorted competition (e.g., affordable healthcare; see Article 106(2) TFEU) or the fact that regulation imposes standards of conduct that conflict with the conduct obligations under the antitrust and competition rules (see U.S. law). In all covered jurisdictions, it is necessary to balance the relevant conflicting interests and the interest of protecting competition.

The **EU** and the **U.S.** include **additional rules** to account for the fact that these jurisdictions comprise a union or federal layer and a Member State or State layer. In that regard, U.S. law is relatively straightforward in regulating conflicts between federal and state antitrust law in a way that ensures uniform regulation of interstate commerce and is rather deferent to U.S. States on other matters. However, given the broad application of the U.S. interstate commerce clause, the scope for sovereign state regulation is limited. In the EU, the Treaties include particular subjective rights and market freedoms and particular control mechanisms for subsidies and other favoring mechanisms threatening to undermine and fragment the EU internal market. These additional rules appear legally pervasive but have a limited impact in practice. In contrast, Article 106 TFEU, in conjunction with the general competition rules (Articles 101 and 102 TFEU), enjoys a broad scope of application and restrains the possibilities of Member States from interfering with competition. The European "effect on trade" requirement works similar to the interstate commerce clause in the U.S.

The new EU tools to subject **foreign subsidies** to some sort of competition control finally lead to new questions: Although it is accepted in all jurisdictions that antitrust and competition rules may apply if there is a territorial effect in the relevant jurisdiction, it has also long been a common understanding that trade relations with third countries, as such, are outside the ambit of domestic competition rules and are governed by international trade rules. The new EU legislation is shifting the boundary of competition law, and it remains to be seen whether the new EU standard for third-country subsidy control will be accepted in other jurisdictions.

* * *

Selected Literatures

Books

John Duns/Arlen Duke/Brendan Sweeney, *Comparative Competition Law*, 2017, 528 pages, Edward Elgar Publishing Ltd., ISBN: 9781788111201.

Roger J. Van den Bergh, *Comparative Competition Law and Economics*, 2017, 545 pages, Edward Elgar Publishing, ISBN-10: 1786438321, ISBN-13: 978-1786438324.

Maher M. Dabbah, *International and Comparative Competition Law*, June 2012 (online)/2010 (print), Cambridge University Press, Online ISBN: 9780511777745.

Einar Elhauge/Damien Geradin, *Global Competition Law and Economics*, 2nd edition, 2011, 1324 pages, Bloomsbury Publishing Plc, ISBN-10: 1849460442, ISBN-13: 9781849460446.

Ariel Ezrachi, *Competition and Antitrust Law: A Very Short Introduction*, 2021, 160 pages, Oxford University Press, Online ISBN: 9780191892493, Print ISBN: 9780198860303.

Ariel Ezrachi, *Research Handbook on International Competition Law*, 2012, 616 pages, Edward Elgar, ISBN: 9780857934796.

David J. Gerber, *Competition Law and Antitrust*, 2020, 208 pages, Oxford University Press, ISBN: 9780198727477.

Barry J. Rodger, *Landmark Cases in Competition Law: Around the World in Fourteen Stories*, 377 pages, Wolters Kluwer, 2013, ISBN: 9789041138439.

Masako Wakui, *Antimonopoly Law: Competition Law and Policy in Japan*, 2nd edition, 20 October 2018; accessible at: https://ssrn.com/abstract=3270141.

Databases

Columbia University: Comparative Competition Law.org, https://comparative competitionlaw.org/data/.

Kluwer Competition Law, https://www.wolterskluwer.com/en/solutions/kluwer competitionlaw/research.

Lexology: Getting the Deal Through (GTDT), https://www.lexology.com/gtdt.

Global Competition & Antitrust, https://globalcompetitionreview.com/insight/ guides.

Practical Law Global Antitrust, https://content.next.westlaw.com/practical-law/ global/antitrust-competition?transitionType=Default&contextData=(sc.Defa ult)&navId=165B7979AB8FCBBAC3954128B3CFA431&tabName= Topics#.

Competition Law International, https://www.ibanet.org/Publications/ Competition_Law_International.

The Legal 500: Competition Litigation, https://www.legal500.com/guides/guide/ competition-litigation/.

Index

Printed in the United States
by Baker & Taylor Publisher Services